TRIUMPHANT
DEMOCRACY

TRIUMPHANT DEMOCRACY

🙂 To my favourite American,
I hope you feel as at home
here as my favourite Scotsmen
Did in America.

Scott

ANDREW CARNEGIE

COSIMO CLASSICS

NEW YORK

Triumphant Democracy

© 2005 Cosimo, Inc.

All rights reserved. No part of this book may be used or reproduced in any manner whatsoever without prior written permission except in the case of brief quotations embodied in critical articles or reviews. For information, address:

Cosimo, P.O. Box 416
Old Chelsea Station
New York, NY 10113-0416

or visit our website at:
www.cosimobooks.com

Triumphant Democracy originally published by Doubleday Doran & Co. in 1886.

Library of Congress Cataloging-in-Publication Data
A catalog record for this book is available from the Library of Congress

Cover design by www.wiselephant.com

ISBN: 1-59605-561-8

TO THE

BELOVED REPUBLIC

UNDER WHOSE EQUAL LAWS I AM

MADE THE PEER OF ANY MAN, ALTHOUGH DENIED

POLITICAL EQUALITY BY MY NATIVE LAND,

I DEDICATE THIS BOOK

WITH AN INTENSITY OF GRATITUDE

AND ADMIRATION WHICH THE NATIVE-BORN CITIZEN

CAN NEITHER FEEL NOR UNDERSTAND

Andrew Carnegie

Preface

BORN *a subject of the Monarchy, adopted a citizen of the Republic, how could it be otherwise than that I should love both lands and long to do whatever in me lay to bring their people to a like affection for each other! The lamentable ignorance concerning the new land which I have found even in the highest political circles of the old first suggested to me how delightful the task would be to endeavor to show something of what the Republic really is, and thus remove, at least in part, the misconceptions which still linger in the minds of many good people of Britain. I believed, also, that my attempt would give to Americans a better idea of the great work their country had done and is still doing in the world. Probably few Americans will read this book without being astonished at some of the facts elicited. During its progress I have been deeply interested in it, and it may truly be regarded as a labor of love—the tribute of a very dutiful and grateful adopted son to the country which has removed the stigma of inferiority which his native land saw proper to impress upon him at birth, and has made him, in the estimation of its great laws as well as in his own estima-*

*tion (much the more important consideration), the peer
of any human being who draws the breath of life, be he
pope, kaiser, priest or king—henceforth the subject of no
man, but a free man, a citizen!*

*It is to the people, the plain, common folk, the De-
mocracy of Britain, that I seek to show the progress,
prosperity, and happiness of their child, the Republic,
that they may still more deeply love it and learn that the
government of the people through the republican form
and not the government of a class through the monarchical form is the surest foundation of individual growth
and of national greatness.*

*To the whole body of Americans I have been anxious
to give a juster estimate than prevails in some quarters
of the political and social advantages which they so
abundantly possess over the people of the older and less
advanced lands, that they may be still prouder and even
more devoted if possible to their institutions than they
are; and I have, also, been no less anxious that the influence of every page of this book might be to incline the
American to regard with reverence and affection the
great parent people from whom he has sprung, from
whose sacrifices in the cause of civil and religious liberty
he has reaped so rich a harvest, and to whom he owes a
debt of gratitude which can never be adequately repaid.*

The work once decided upon, I naturally obtained all

preceding books bearing upon the subject. As the pile of reference books, census reports, and statistical works lay around upon tables and shelves, the question suggested itself, "Shall these dry bones live?" I hope, therefore, indulgent readers, that you will not be warranted in accusing me of giving too much solid information. I have tried to coat the wholesome medicine of facts in the sweetest and purest sugar of fancy at my command. Pray you, open your mouths and swallow it in small doses, and like the sugar even if you detest the pill. One word, however, to the critical statistician, and let this be very clearly understood: although designedly written in as light a style as I am master of, mark me, no liberties have been taken with facts, figures, or calculations. Every statement has been carefully verified and re-verified; every calculation has been gone over and over again. My readers may safely rely upon the correctness of every quantitative statement made. Considered as a book of reference, what is herein stated is under-stated rather than over-stated.

I acknowledge with great pleasure the almost indispensable aid received in the preparation of this work from my clever secretary, Mr. Bridge. I am also indebted to Mr. John D. Champlin, Jr., for many valuable suggestions and for careful supervision as it went through the press.

The books and documents and official reports con-

sulted have been legion; I cannot, therefore, undertake to mention them, but I have received more data from that marvellous work—"Scribner's Statistical Atlas"— than from any other source or, indeed, from any several sources combined.

And now, if I have succeeded in giving my countrymen on either or both sides of the Atlantic even a small amount of information about the Republic of my love, or brought them nearer together in the bonds of genial affection, or hastened by one hour the day in which my native land shall stand forth with my adopted land under the only noble political creed—that which proclaims the equality of the citizen—I shall have received an ample reward.

THE AUTHOR.

Contents

TRIUMPHANT DEMOCRACY

Chapter I

THE REPUBLIC

"Methinks I see in my mind a noble and puissant nation rousing herself like a strong man after sleep, and shaking her invincible locks; methinks I see her as an eagle mewing her mighty youth, and kindling her undazzled eyes at the full mid-day beam; purging and unscaling her long-abused sight at the fountain itself of heavenly radiance; while the whole noise of timorous and flocking birds, with those also that love the twilight, flutter about, amazed at what she means."—MILTON.

THE old nations of the earth creep on at a snail's pace; the Republic thunders past with the rush of the express. The United States, the growth of a single century, has already reached the foremost rank among nations, and is destined soon to out-distance all others in the race. In population, in wealth, in annual savings, and in public credit; in freedom from debt, in agriculture, and in manufactures, America already leads the civilized world.

France, with her fertile plains and sunny skies, requires a hundred and sixty years to grow two Frenchmen where one grew before. Great Britain, whose rate of increase is greater than that of any other European nation, takes seventy years to double her population. The Republic has repeatedly doubled hers in twenty-five years.

In 1831, Great Britain and Ireland contained twenty-four millions of people, and fifty years later (1881) thirty-four millions. France increased, during the same period, from thirty-two and a half to thirty-seven and a half millions. The Republic bounded from thirteen to fifty millions. England gained ten, France five, the United States thirty-seven millions! Thus the Republic, in one half-century, added to her numbers as many as the present total population of France, and more than the present population of the United Kingdom. Think of it! A Great Britain and Ireland called forth from the wilderness, as if by magic, in less than the span of a man's few days upon earth, almost.

> "As if the yawning earth to heaven,
> A subterranean host had given."

Truly the Republic is the Minerva of nations; full-armed has she sprung from the brow of Jupiter Britain. The thirteen millions of Americans of 1830 have now increased to fifty-six millions—more English-speaking people than exist in all the world besides; more than in the United Kingdom and all her colonies, even were the latter doubled in population!

Startling as is this statement, it is tame in comparison with that which is to follow. In 1850 the total wealth of the United States was but $8,430,000,000 (£1,686,000,-000), while that of the United Kingdom exceeded $22,500,000,000 (£4,500,000,000), or nearly three times that sum. Thirty short years sufficed to reverse the positions of the respective countries. In 1882 the Monarchy was possessed of a golden load of no less than eight thousand, seven hundred and twenty millions sterling. Just pause a moment to see how this looks when strung out in cold figures; but do not try to realize what it means, for mortal man cannot conceive it. Herbert Spencer need not travel so far afield to reach the "unknowable!" He has it right here under his very eyes. Let him try to "know" the import of this—$43,600,-

000,000 (£8,720,000,000)! It is impossible. But stupendous as this seems, it is exceeded by the wealth of the Republic, which in 1880, two years before, amounted to $48,950,000,000 (£9,790,000,000). What a mercy we write for 1880; for had we to give the wealth of one year later another figure would have to be found, and added to the interminable row. America's wealth to-day greatly exceeds ten thousand millions sterling. Nor is this altogether due to her enormous agricultural resources, as may at first glance be thought; for all the world knows she is first among nations in agriculture. It is largely attributable to her manufacturing industries, for, as all the world does not know, she, and not Great Britain, is also the greatest manufacturing country. In 1880 British manufactures amounted in value to eight hundred and eighteen millions sterling; those of America to eleven hundred and twelve millions*—nearly half as much as those of the whole of Europe, which amounted to twenty-six hundred millions. Thus, although Great Britain manufactures for the whole world, and the Republic is only gaining, year after year, greater control of her own markets, Britain's manufactures in 1880 were not two-thirds the value of those of the one-century-old Republic, which is not generally considered a manufacturing country at all.

In the savings of nations America also comes first, her annual savings of two hundred and ten millions sterling exceeding those of the United Kingdom by fifty-six millions, and those of France by seventy millions sterling. The fifty million Americans of 1880 could have bought up the one hundred and forty millions of Russians, Austrians, and Spaniards; or, after purchasing

---

*British returns do not include flour mills and saw-mills, but sixty millions sterling, a sum far beyond their possible value, have been allowed for these in the above estimate.

wealthy France, would have had enough pocket money to acquire Denmark, Norway, Switzerland, and Greece. The Yankee Republican could even buy the home of his ancestors—the dear old home with all its exquisite beauty, historical associations, and glorious traditions, which challenge our love—and hold it captive.

> "The cloud-capp'd towers, the gorgeous palaces,
> The solemn temples,"

aye, every acre of Great Britain and Ireland could he buy, and hold it as a pretty little Isle of Wight to his great continent; and after doing this he could turn round and pay off the entire national debt of that deeply indebted land, and yet not exhaust his fortune, the product of a single century! What will he not be able to do ere his second century closes! Already the nations which have played great parts in the world's history grow small in comparison. In a hundred years they will be as dwarfs, in two hundred mere pigmies to this giant; he the Gulliver of nations, they but Lilliputians who may try to bind him with their spider threads in vain.

The shipping of the Republic ranks next to that of the world's carrier, Britain. No other nation approaches her for second place. In 1880, the carrying power of Great Britain was eighteen millions of tons; that of the Republic nine millions, being about one-half the motherland's commercial fleet, but more than that of France, Germany, Norway, Italy, and Spain combined, these being the five largest carrying powers of Europe after Britain. The Western Republic has more than four times the carrying capacity of its European sister France, and quite four times as much as Germany. Her ships earned nearly twenty per cent. of the total shipping earnings of the world in 1880. France and Germany each earned but a shade over five per cent. The exports and imports of America are already equal to those of either of those countries—about £300,000,000 sterling. Notwithstanding those facts, which are corroborated by Mulhall, and are known to be correct, the general impression is that the Republic, gigantic as she is on land, has very little footing upon the water. This is one of many popular delusions about the "kin beyond sea." But while she is next to Britain herself as a maritime power, it is when we turn to her internal commerce—her carrying power on land—that she reverses positions with her great mother. The internal commerce of the United States exceeds the entire foreign commerce of Great Britain and Ireland, France, Germany, Russia, Holland, Austria-Hungary, and Belgium combined. For railway freight over a hundred and ten millions sterling are annually paid, a greater sum than the railway freightage of Great Britain, France, and Italy collectively, and more than is earned by all the ships in the world, exclusive of America's own earnings from ships. The Pennsylvania Railroad system alone transports more tonnage than all Britain's merchant ships.

In military and naval power the Republic is at once the weakest and the strongest of nations. Her regular army consists of but twenty-five thousand men scattered all over the continent in companies of fifty or a hundred. Her navy, thank God! is as nothing. But twenty years ago, as at the blast of a trumpet, she called into action two millions of armed men, and floated six hundred and twenty-six war-ships. Even the vaunted legions of Xerxes, and the hordes of Attila and Timour were exceeded in numbers by the citizen soldiers who took up arms in 1861 to defend the unity of the nation, and who, when the task was done, laid them quietly down, and returned to the avocations of peace. As Macaulay says of the soldiers of the Commonwealth: "In a few months there remained not a trace indicating that the most formidable army in the world had just been absorbed into the mass of the community." And the character of the Republic's soldiers, too, recalls his account of this republican army of Cromwell's. "The Royalists themselves confessed that, in every department of honest industry, the discarded warriors prospered beyond other men, that none was charged with any theft or robbery, that none was heard to ask for alms, and that if a baker, a mason, or a wagoner, attracted notice by his diligence and sobriety, he was in all probability one of Oliver's old soldiers." This was when the parent land was free from hereditary rulers and under the invigorating influence of republican institutions. Thus do citizens fight on one side of the Atlantic as on the other, and, grander far, thus return to the pursuits of peace. Not for throne, for king, or for privileged class, but for *Country*. For a country which gives to the humblest every privilege accorded to the greatest, one says instinctively,

> "Where's the coward that would not dare
> To fight for such a land!"

Britons as republicans were of course invincible. What chance in the struggle has a royalist who cries, "My king!" against the citizen whose patriotic ardor glows as he whispers, "My country!" The "God save the King" of the monarchist grows faint before the nobler strain of the republican,

> "God bless our native land!"

Our king, poor trifler, may be beneath consideration. Our country is ever sure of our love. There be words to conjure and work miracles with, and "our country" is of these. Others, having ceased to be divine, have become ridiculous, and "king" and "throne" are of these.

The twenty thousand Englishmen who met in Bingley Hall, Birmingham, to honor the sturdiest Englishman of all, John Bright, dispersed not with the paltry and puerile "God save the Queen," but with these glorious words sung to the same tune:

> "God bless our native land,
>   May heaven's protecting hand
>   Still guard her shore;
>   May peace her fame extend,
>   Foe be transformed to friend,
>   And Britain's power depend
>   On war no more."

Worthy this of England, blessed mother of nations which now are, and of others yet to be. To hear it was worth the voyage across the Atlantic. Never crept the thrill of triumph more wildly through my frame than when I lifted up my voice and sang with the exulting mass the coming national hymn which is to live and vibrate round the world when royal families are as extinct as dodos. God speed the day! A royal family is an insult to every other family in the land. I found no trace of them at Birmingham.

The Republic wants neither standing army nor navy. In this lies her chief glory and her strength. Resting securely upon the love and devotion of all her sons, she can, Cadmus-like, raise from the soil vast armed hosts who fight only in her defence, and who, unlike the seed of the dragon, return to the avocations of peace when danger to the Republic is past. The American citizen who will not fight for his country if attacked is unworthy the name, and the American citizen who could be induced to engage in aggressive warfare is equally so.

Of more importance even than commercial or military strength is the Republic's commanding position among nations in intellectual activity; for she excels in the number of schools and colleges, in the number and extent of her libraries, and in the number of newspapers and other periodicals published.

In the application of science to social and industrial uses, she is far in advance of other nations. Many of the most important practical inventions which have contributed to the progress of the world during the past century originated with Americans. No other people have devised so many labor-saving machines and appliances. The first commercially successful steamboat navigated the Hudson, and the first steamship to cross the Atlantic sailed under the American flag from an American port. America gave to the world the cotton-gin, and the first practical mowing, reaping, and sewing machines. In the most spiritual, most ethereal of all departments in which man has produced great triumphs, viz.: electricity, the position of the American is specially noteworthy. He may be said almost to have made this province his own, for, beginning with Franklin's discovery of the identity of lightning and electricity, it was an American who devised the best and most widely used system of telegraphy, and an American who boldly undertook to bind together the old and the new land with electric chains. In the use of electricity for illuminating purposes America maintains her position as first wherever this subtile agent is invoked. The recent addition to the world's means of communication, the telephone, is also to be credited to the new land.

Into the distant future of this giant nation we need not seek to peer; but if we cast a glance forward, as we have done backward, for only fifty years, and assume that in that short interval no serious change will occur, the astounding fact startles us that in 1935, fifty years from now, when many in manhood will still be living, one hundred and eighty millions of English-speaking republicans will exist under one flag and possess more than two hundred and fifty thousand millions of dollars, or fifty thousand millions sterling of national wealth. Eighty years ago the whole of America and Europe did not contain so many people; and, if Europe and America continue their normal growth, it will be little more than another eighty years ere the mighty Republic may boast as many loyal citizens as all the rulers of Europe combined, for before the year 1980 Europe and America will each have a population of about six hundred millions.

The causes which have led to the rapid growth and aggrandizement of this latest addition to the family of nations constitute one of the most interesting problems in the social history of mankind. What has brought about such stupendous results—so unparalleled a development of a nation within so brief a period! The most important factors in this problem are three: the ethnic character of the people, the topographical and climatic conditions under which they developed, and the influence of political institutions founded upon the equality of the citizen.

Certain writers in the past have maintained that the ethnic type of a people has less influence upon its growth as a nation than the conditions of life under which it is developing. The modern ethnologist knows better. We have only to imagine what America would be to-day if she had fallen, in the beginning, into the hands of any other people than the colonizing British, to see how vitally important is this question of race. America was indeed fortunate in the seed planted upon her soil. With the exception of a few Dutch and French it was wholly

., as will be shown in the next chapter, the
of to-day remains true to this noble strain and
chs British. The special aptitude of this race for
co.   .tion, its vigor and enterprise, and its capacity
for governing, although brilliantly manifested in all parts
of the world, have never been shown to such advantage
as in America. Freed here from the pressure of feudal
institutions no longer fitted to their present development,
and freed also from the dominion of the upper classes,
which have kept the people at home from effective management of affairs and sacrificed the nation's interest for
their own, as is the nature of classes, these masses of the
lower ranks of Britons, called upon to found a new state,
have proved themselves possessors of a positive genius
for political administration.

The second, and perhaps equally important factor in
the problem of the rapid advancement of this branch of
the British race, is the superiority of the conditions under
which it has developed. The home which has fallen to
its lot, a domain more magnificent than has cradled any
other race in the history of the world, presents no
obstructions to unity—to the thorough amalgamation
of its dwellers, North, South, East, and West, into one
homogeneous mass—for the conformation of the American continent differs in important respects from that of
every other great division of the globe. In Europe the
Alps occupy a central position, forming on each side
watersheds of rivers which flow into opposite seas. In
Asia the Himalaya, the Hindu Kush, and the Altai
Mountains divide the continent, rolling from their sides
many great rivers which pour their floods into widely
separated oceans. But in North America the mountains
rise up on each coast, and from them the land slopes
gradually into great central plains, forming an immense
basin where the rivers flow together in one valley, offer-

ing to commerce many thousand miles of navigable streams. The map thus proclaims the unity of North America, for in this great central basin, three million square miles in extent, free from impassable rivers or mountain barriers great enough to hinder free intercourse, political integration is a necessity and consolidation a certainty.

Herbert Spencer has illustrated by numerous examples the principle that "mountain-haunting peoples and peoples living in deserts and marshes are difficult to consolidate, while peoples penned in by barriers are consolidated with facility." Nations so separated, moreover, regard those beyond the barrier as natural enemies; and in Europe the ambition and selfishness of ruling dynasties have helped to make this belief the political creed of the people. Cowper has seized upon this idea in the well-known lines:

> "Mountains interposed
> Make enemies of nations, who had else
> Like kindred drops been mingled into one."

Europe has thus been kept in a state of perpetual war or of preparation for war among some of its several divisions, entailing much misery and loss of life as well as of material wealth, and retarding civilization.

Besides the rivers, the great lakes of America, estimated to contain one-third of all the fresh water in the world, are another important element in aid of consolidation. A ship sailing from any part of the world may discharge its cargo at Chicago in the north-west, a thousand miles inland. The Mississippi and its tributaries traverse the great western basin, a million and a quarter square miles in extent, and furnish an internal navigable system of twenty thousand miles. A steamer starting from Pittsburgh in Pennsylvania, four hundred and fifty

miles inland from New York, and two thousand from
the mouth of the Mississippi, passing through these
water highways, and returning to its starting place at
that smoky metropolis of iron and steel, will sail a distance much greater than round the world. Nor will it
in all its course be stopped by any government official,
or be taxed by any tariff. The flag it carries will ensure
free passage for ship and cargo, unimpeded by any fiscal
charge whatever, for the whole continent enjoys the
blessings of absolute freedom of intercourse among its
citizens. In estimating the influences which promote the
consolidation of the people much weight must be given
to this cause. Fifty-six millions of people, occupying an
area which includes climatic differences so great that
everything necessary for the wants of man can be readily
produced, exchange their products without inspection or
charge. Truly here is the most magnificent exhibition of
free trade which the world has ever seen. It would be
difficult to set bounds to the beneficial effects of the wise
provision of the national Constitution which guarantees to every member of the vast confederacy the blessings of unrestricted commercial intercourse.

Not only from an economical point of view, but from
the higher stand-point of its bearing upon the unity and
brotherhood of the people, this unrestricted freedom of
trade must rank as one of the most potent agencies for
the preservation of the Union. Were each of the thirty-
eight States of the American continent to tax the products of the others we should soon see the dissolution of
the great Republic into thirty-eight warring factions. If
any one doubts that free trade carries peace in its train
let him study the internal free trade system of America.

The railway system, although an artificial creation,
must rank as even more important than the great natural
water-ways, in its influence upon the unification of the

people. A hundred and thirty thousand miles of rail
—more than in the whole of Europe—traverse the country in all directions, and bind the nation together with
bonds of steel. From the Atlantic to the Pacific, three
thousand miles apart, or from New York to New
Orleans, the traveller passes without change in the same
moving hotel. In it he is fed and lodged, and has every
want supplied.

Seven hundred and sixty thousand miles of telegraph,
enough to put thirty girdles round the earth—the very
nerves of the Republic—quiver night and day with social
and commercial messages. The college-bred youth of
Massachusetts is not separated from the paternal home
and its associations when on his ranche in Colorado; nor
is the Eastern young lady removed from the home influences of New York when she marries the Southern
planter and goes forth to create a similar home in Texas.
Constant communication between the families and frequent visits animate them with kindred ideas and keep
them united. They carry the Stars and Stripes with them
wherever they settle, and preserve the unity of the nation.

In the course of her short career the Republic has had
to face and overcome two sources of great danger, either
of which might have overtaxed the powers and stability
of any political fabric, resting upon a less wide and indestructible base than the perfect equality of the citizen.
The infant state was left with the viper, human slavery,
gnawing at its vitals, and it grew and strengthened with
the growth and strength of the Republic until sufficiently
powerful to threaten its very life. Coiled round and
into every joint and part of the body-politic and sucking
away the moral strength of the nation, the slave power,
in an effort to extend its baneful influence, fortunately
committed one morning what is, in the soul of every

...ardonable sin. It fired upon the
...it was required to bring home
...ence the knowledge that not only
...ery antagonistic social forces which
..., but that slavery as a political in-
...stent with the republican idea. The
shot fired ... t, sunny morning at the ensign, floating like a thing of joy over the ramparts of Fort Sum-
ter, left the patriot no recourse. A thrill passed through
the Free States, and once again for unity, as before for
independence, men of all parties pledged their lives, their
fortunes, and their sacred honor to uphold the Republic.

How nobly that pledge was redeemed is known to the
world. Not only until every slave was free, but not until
every slave was a citizen, with equal voice in the State,
was the righteous sword of the Republic sheathed.

The second source of danger lay in the millions of
foreigners who came from all lands to the hospitable
shores of the nation, many of them ignorant of the English language, and all unaccustomed to the exercise of
political duties. If so great a number stood aloof from
the national life and formed circles of their own, or if
they sought America for a period only, to earn money
with which to return to their original homes, the injury
to the State must inevitably be serious.

The generosity, shall I not say the incredible generosity, with which the Republic has dealt with these people met its reward. They are won to her side by being
offered for their *subject*ship the boon of citizenship. For
denial of equal privileges at home, the new land meets
them with perfect equality, saying, be not only with us,
but be of us. They reach the shores of the Republic *subjects* (insulting word), and she makes them citizens;
serfs, and she makes them men, and their children she
takes gently by the hand and leads to the public schools

which she has founded for her own children, and gives
them, without money and without price, a good primary
education as the most precious gift which even she has,
in her bountiful hand, to bestow upon human beings.
This is Democracy's "gift of welcome" to the new comer.
The poor immigrant cannot help growing up passion-
ately fond of his new home and, alas, with many bitter
thoughts of the old land which has defrauded him of the
rights of man, and thus the threatened danger is averted
—the homogeneity of the people secured.

The unity of the American people is further power-
fully promoted by the foundation upon which the political structure rests, the equality of the citizen. There is
not one shred of privilege to be met with anywhere in
all the laws. One man's right is every man's right. The
flag is the guarantor and symbol of equality. The people
are not emasculated by being made to feel that their
own country decrees their inferiority, and holds them
unworthy of privileges accorded to others. No ranks, no
titles, no hereditary dignities, and therefore no classes.
Suffrage is universal, and votes are of equal weight. Representatives are paid, and political life and usefulness
thereby thrown open to all. Thus there is brought about
a community of interests and aims which a Briton, accustomed to monarchical and aristocratic institutions, dividing the people into classes with separate interests, aims,
thoughts, and feelings, can only with difficulty understand.

The free common school system of the land is probably, after all, the greatest single power in the unifying
process which is producing the new American race.
Through the crucible of a good common English education, furnished free by the State, pass the various racial
elements—children of Irishmen, Germans, Italians, Spaniards, and Swedes, side by side with the native American,

all to be fused into one, in language, in thought, in feeling, and in patriotism. The Irish boy loses his brogue, and the German child learns English. The sympathies suited to the feudal systems of Europe, which they inherit from their fathers, pass off as dross, leaving behind the pure gold of the only noble political creed: "All men are created free and equal." Taught now to live and work for the common weal, and not for the maintenance of a royal family or an overbearing aristocracy, not for the continuance of a social system which ranks them beneath an arrogant class of drones, children of Russian and German serfs, of Irish evicted tenants, Scotch crofters, and other victims of feudal tyranny, are transmuted into republican Americans, and are made one in love for a country which provides equal rights and privileges for all her children. There is no class so intensely patriotic, so wildly devoted to the Republic as the naturalized citizen and his child, for little does the native-born citizen know of the value of rights which have never been denied. Only the man born abroad, like myself, under institutions which insult him at his birth, can know the full meaning of Republicanism.

It follows, from the prevailing system of free education, that the Americans are a reading people. Arising out of this fact we find another powerful influence promoting unity of sentiment and purpose among the millions of the Republic—the influence of the American press. Eight thousand newspapers scattered throughout the land receive simultaneous reports. Everybody in America reads the same news the same morning, and discusses the same questions. The man of San Francisco is thus brought as near to a common centre with his fellow-citizen of St. Paul, New Orleans or New York, as is the man of London with him of Birmingham, Manchester, Liverpool, or Edinburgh, and infinitely nearer than the man of Belfast or Dublin. The bullet of the lunatic which killed President Garfield, could it have traveled so far, would have been outstripped by the lightning messengers which carried the sad news to the most distant hamlet upon the continent. The blow struck in the afternoon found a nation of fifty-six millions bowed with grief ere sunset. So, too, the quiet intimation conveyed one evening by Secretary Seward to the Minister of France, that he thought Mexico was a very healthy country for the French to migrate from, called forth at every breakfast table the next morning the emphatic response—"I rather guess that's so!" Fortunately, the Emperor was of the same opinion.

It is these causes which render possible the growth of a great homogeneous nation, alike in race, language, literature, interest, patriotism—an empire of such overwhelming power and proportions as to require neither army nor navy to ensure its safety, and a people so educated and advanced as to value the victories of peace.

The student of American affairs to-day sees no influences at work save those which make for closer and closer union. The Republic has solved the problem of governing large areas by adopting the federal, or home-rule system, and has proved to the world that the freest self-government of the parts produces the strongest government of the whole.

Chapter II
THE AMERICAN PEOPLE

"From biological truths it may be inferred that the eventual mixture of the allied varieties of the Aryan race forming the population, will produce a finer type of man than has hitherto existed, and a type of man more plastic, more adaptable, more capable of undergoing the modifications needful for complete social life. I think that, whatever difficulties they may have to surmount and whatever tribulations they may have to pass through, the Americans may reasonably look forward to a time when they will have produced a civilization grander than any the world has known."—HERBERT SPENCER.

FORTUNATELY for the American people they are essentially British. I trust they are evermore to remain truly grateful for this crowning mercy. The assertion of the historian of the Norman Conquest that the chief difference between the Briton and the American is that the former has crossed but one ocean, the latter two, is something more than a mere dictum; it is capable of actual demonstration. Two and a half centuries ago the American population was British with a very small intermixture of French and Dutch. In 1776, when the colonies informed the world of the great truth that "all men are created equal," and set up an independent republic, without king or aristocracy, or any other of the political evils of the past, the population had reached three millions. In 1840 it had grown, almost entirely by natural increase, to fourteen millions of white people.

18

There were then three million colored slaves. That these fourteen million whites were almost purely of British origin is shown by the small amount of immigration up to that date. Previous to 1820, when immigration returns were first made, it is estimated that the total number of immigrants to that date had not exceeded a quarter of a million, and most of these were British. Between 1820 and 1830 there arrived only a hundred and forty-four thousand; and during the next decade six hundred thousand, nearly all British, for the German and other Continental exodus had not then begun. It was not till after 1840 that immigration began on a large scale.

Beginning then in 1840, with an almost purely British race, let us trace the ingredients which up to the present time have gone to make the American of to-day, differentiated as he is and yet only British "with a difference."

The total number of immigrants to the United States between 1840 and 1880 was a little more than nine millions, fifty-five per cent. of whom were British. Just note this surprising truth. Lead into one the rivulets which swell the American population from all other parts of the world, and out of the little British Isles comes a stream mightier than all the others in its flow. Glorious mother! with her own heart's blood she feeds her child.

The position may then be stated in round figures* in the following form:

*These figures are arrived at by taking the number of native whites and of immigrants each year, beginning 1840, and adding three per cent., which is about the natural rate of increase. The number of native births and of immigrants arriving the following year is then added, three per cent. again allowed, and so on up to 1880. The figures have been carefully verified, and it is believed that by this mode the truth has been reached, since the result corresponds with the census of 1880, which shows 43,475,000 whites.

Of almost purely British origin in 1840 14,196,000
Increase at 3 per cent. per annum to 1880 .   .   . 11,850,000
British immigration 1840 to 1880, with natural in-
    crease estimated at 3 per cent. per annum upon
    each year's arrivals up to 1880 9,175,000
        Total British blood 35,221,000
Other than British immigration, 1840 to 1880 with
    increase estimated at 3 per cent. per annum . 7,506,000
                                  42,727,000

Thus the American of to-day is certainly more than four-fifths British in his ancestry. The other fifth is principally German; for more than three millions of these educated, thrifty, and law-abiding citizens were received between 1840 and 1880, almost as many as from Ireland. From all countries other than Britain and Germany, the immigration is scarcely worth taking into account; for during the forty years noted the total number was little more than a million; France and Sweden and Norway contributed about three hundred thousand each. But this non-British blood has even less than its proportional influence in forming the national character, especially in its political phase; because the language, literature, laws, and institutions are English. It may, however, safely be averred that the small mixture of foreign races is a decided advantage to the new race, for even the British race is improved by a slight cross. Give me a British foundation, the beef-eater, to begin with, the stolid, or—if you will—stupid mind of the Philistine of dear Matthew Arnold's aversion, only partially open to the sweetness and light of life, slow as an elephant, tough as a rhinoceros, awkward as a mule and just as cantankerous, but possessed of an honest, courageous, well-meaning, and, above all, truth-telling nature. A strange combination of the lion and the lamb, this

Islander,—savage and sentimentalist in one. "It's a fine day, let's kill something," roars the savage—his daily remark for months at a time, and his daily practice too, for even the best educated Briton (with a few exceptions of the Spencer, Balfour, and Arnold type) has not yet risen in his recreations beyond shooting half-tame birds, "for the fun of the thing." And yet their typical hero, dying on the deck of the *Victory,* murmurs, "Kiss me, Hardy," as sweetly as a woman, and passes to the abode of heroes with a warrior's kiss upon his lips. And Nelson's antipode, fat Jack Falstaff—to show how extremes meet—so true to nature is Shakespeare—"ababbled o' green fields," as he left us! There's genuine tenderness and love in all these island mastiffs. And theirs is the one trait *par excellence* without which we say to a man or race—"unstable as water, thou shalt not excel." The Briton is stable. What he sets about to do he does, or dies in the attempt. Concentration is his peculiarity. He may not gain very fast, but he is a veritable ratchet wheel; every inch he gains he holds. There's no slip back in him. Nor does he lose in the race by lateral motion. The tortoise beats the hare, of course; the hare zigzags. No zig-zag in John Bull. He does not like to go round a mountain even when it is the easier way; he digs through. The hunter who found temporary safety when attacked by a bear in catching it by the tail and swinging round with the would-be too affectionate monster, called to his companions to come and "help him to let go." By this sign we know he wasn't a Britisher, for it never occurs to the true Briton that in the nature of things he can voluntarily let go of anything. He would have been in with that bear for the whole war, "bound to fight it out on that line if it took all summer," as General Grant put it. And note it, fellow-citizens, he was a Grant. There came in the Scotch blood of that tenacious, self-con-

tained, stubborn force, which kept pegging away, always
certain of final victory, because he knew that he could not
divert himself, even if he wished, from the task he had
undertaken. His very nature forbade retreat. Thus stood
the sturdy, moody Scotch-American of steady purpose,
fighting through to the finish with no "let go" in his com-
position, as that English-American Lincoln did—for
Uncle Abe's family came from Norfolk—in the wider
field of national policy when he, too, "kept his course un-
shaked of motion." This master trait of the British race
shows resplendently in Lincoln, the greatest political
genius of our era—greatest, judged either by the inherent qualities of the man, or by the material results of
his administration. Even Bismarck's reorganization of
Germany dealt with far less imposing, far less gigantic
forces than those which Lincoln was called upon to control. Nor has Bismarck achieved the highest degree of
political success; he has not harmonized—fused into one
united whole the people he has consolidated, as Lincoln
did. His weapons have been those of force alone—blood
and iron his cry; even in peace a master solely by brutal
force. Lincoln was as generous, as conciliatory, as gentle
in peace as he was always sad and merciful; yet ever immovable in war. Bismarck excited the fears of the masses;
Lincoln won their love. The one a rude conqueror only;
the other not only that, but also the guider of the highest and best aspirations of his people. With monarchical
Bismarck "might made right"; with republican Lincoln
"right made might." That's the difference. Hence the
fame of one is to be ephemeral; that of the other immor-
tal.

   The American fortunately has, in the German, French,
and other races which have contributed to his make-up,
the lacking ingredients which confer upon him a much
less savage and more placable nature than that of the

original Briton. To this slight strain of foreign blood, and to the more stimulating effects of his brighter climate (which caused an English friend once to remark that temperance is no virtue in the American since he breathes champagne), together with the more active play of forces in a new land under political institutions which make the most of men, we must attribute the faculty observed in him by Matthew Arnold, of thinking straighter and seeing clearer, and also of acting more promptly than the original stock, for the American is nothing if not logical. He gets hold of the underlying principle, and, reasoning from that, he goes ahead to conclusion. He wants everything laid down by square and compass, and in political institutions something that is "fair all around," neither advantages nor disadvantages, but universal equality.

Toleration in the Briton is truly admirable; the leading Radical and the leading Tory-Democrat are found dining with each other, perhaps may be found in the same cabinet one of these days, since extremes meet. Well, the American is even more tolerant. Politics never divide people. Once in four years he warms up and takes sides, opposing hosts confront each other and a stranger would naturally think that only violence could result whichever side won. The morning after the election his arm is upon his opponent's shoulder and they are chaffing each other. All becomes as calm as a summer sea. He fights "rebels" for four years and as soon as they lay down their arms invites them to his banquets. Not a life is sacrificed to feed his revenge. Jefferson Davis, educated at the National Military Academy and a deserter from the State, is allowed to drag on his weary life in merited oblivion. No drop of martyr's blood embitters the wayward South and breeds the wish for revenge. "We shall give mankind," said Secretary Seward, "an example of such magnanimity as it has never seen." He had no monarchy, no aristocracy, no military class urging sacrifice to appease its offended majesty; he had the democracy behind him with its generous instincts preaching forgiveness, and hence no drop of blood was shed. The American never cherishes resentment, but is willing always not only to forgive but to forget, the latter not less than half the struggle, for as our humorist very justly observes: "the man who forgives but don't forget is trying to settle with the Lord for fifty cents on the dollar." Brother Jonathan pays the full dollar.

The generally diffused love of music which characterizes America is largely the outcome of the German and Continental contingent for, with all the phlegm of the Briton, there is in the German a part of his nature "touched to fine issues." He loves music, is highly sociable, very domestic at home, and at his best in the bosom of his family. Most valuable of all he is well educated and has excellent habits, is patient, industrious, peaceful, and law-abiding. Another important characteristic of this race is the alacrity with which they adopt American ideas. The vast majority have already done so ere they sailed westward. The German loves his native country, but hates its institutions. Prince Bismarck's yoke is neither light nor easy. Universal military service, the blood-tax of monarchies, is calculated to set the best minds among the bone and sinew to thinking over the political situation, and O, America! how bright and alluring you appear to the down-trodden masses of Europe, with your equal laws, equal privileges and the halo of peace surrounding your brow! What a bribe you offer to the most loyal-minded man to renounce his own country, to share a heritage so fair! The emigrant may not succeed in the new land, or succeed as the Irishman did, who replied to the inquiry of his friend as to whether the Republic was the country for the poor man: "It is, indade; look at me, when I came I hadn't a rag to my back, and now I'm just covered with them." Many new arrivals fail, many would succeed better in their old homes. America is only a favored land for the most efficient; drones have no place in her hive, but in whatever the emigrant may fail, whether in securing wealth, or home, whether he remain poor or lose health, whether his lot be happy or miserable, there remains one great prize which cannot escape him, one blessing so bright, so beneficent, as to shed upon the darkest career the glory of its entrancing rays and compensate for the absence of material good. Upon every exile from home falls the boon of citizenship, equal with the highest. The Republic may not give wealth, or happiness; she has not promised these, it is the freedom to pursue these, not their realization, which the Declaration of Independence claims; but, if she does not make the emigrant happy or prosperous, this she can do and does do for every one, she makes him a citizen, a *man*.

The Frenchman is not a migrating animal. It is much to the credit of America that it has attracted even three hundred thousand of these home-keeping Gauls. The number is so small that their influence upon the national character cannot be otherwise than trifling. They are the cooks and the epicures of the world and to them America may well be grateful for the standard maintained by the "Delmonicos," the French restaurants of the principal cities. No country has experienced so clearly as this, till recently, that while God sent the victuals, the cooks came from another source. These were not from France, nor under French influence in the former days. Even yet, west of Chicago, the cookery is shameful, but thanks to the Frenchman, the better modes travel westward rapidly. Nature never furnished to any nation so great a variety of food, yet no civilized people ever cooked so badly.

In women's dress, for the few male "dudes" affect English fashions, our Gallic brethren give evidence of their influence in the direction of good taste. The verdict of my English friends invariably is that the American woman dresses so well—so much better than her English sister. We must credit the French citizen with this flattering verdict.

No other race than the French and the German (including Swedes and Norwegians, who are also Teutons) has reached these shores in sufficient numbers to impress even a trace of its influence upon the national character.

The inability of the American race to maintain itself and its dependence upon immigration for its future have furnished texts for certain foreign writers. But the facts are against them. Of the fifty-six million Americans now living, seven-eighths, or forty-nine millions, are native born. One-eighth, or seven millions, first saw the light in foreign lands. The colored population is about equal to the foreign born. The census returns show that the rate of increase among native-born Americans has been as follows: 1850 to 1860, 32⅓ per cent.; 1870 to 1880, 31¼ per cent. In no European country does the rate of increase approach these figures, which are about the average rate of increase for the entire population of America, native and foreign, which proves that the native American is as prolific as the foreign born in America, while both are more prolific than the inhabitants of any European country. Notwithstanding the enormous number of immigrants which yearly flow into the country, the native births are seven to eight times greater in number than the foreign arrivals. Besides this, as we have seen, more than half of the foreign arrivals are British; so that the American people are ever becoming more purely British in origin.

The value to the country of the annual foreign influx, however, is very great indeed. This is more apt to be under than overestimated. During the ten years between 1870 and 1880 the number of immigrants averaged two hundred and eighty thousand per annum. In one year, 1882, nearly three times this number (789,000) arrived. Sixty per cent. (473,400) of this mass were adults between fifteen and forty years of age. These adults were surely worth $1,500 (£300) each—for in former days an efficient slave sold for this sum—making a money value of $710,000,000 (£142,000,000), to which may be safely added $1,000 (£200) each, or $315,000,000 (£63,000,000) for the remaining forty per cent. of the host. Further, it is estimated that every immigrant brings in cash an average of $125 (£25). The cash value of immigrants upon this basis for the year 1882 exceeded $1,125,000,000 (£225,000,000). True, 1882 was an exceptional year, but the average yearly augmentation of the Republic's wealth from immigrants, who seek its shores to escape the enormous taxation and military laws of monarchical governments, and to obtain under Republican institutions entire political equality, is now more than twice as great as the total product of all the silver and gold mines in the world. Were the owners of every gold and silver mine in the world compelled to send to the Treasury at Washington, at their own expense, every ounce of the precious metals produced, the national wealth would not be enhanced one-half as much as it is from the golden stream which flows into the country every year through immigration.

But the value of these peaceful invaders does not consist solely in their numbers or in the wealth which they bring. To estimate them aright we must take into consideration also the superior character of those who immigrate. As the people who laid the foundation of the American Republic were extremists, fanatics, if you will —men of advanced views intellectually, morally and politically, men whom Europe had rejected as dangerous —so the majority of emigrants to-day are men who leave their native land from dissatisfaction with their surroundings, and who seek here, under new conditions, the opportunity for development denied them at home. The old and the destitute, the idle and the contented do not brave the waves of the stormy Atlantic, but sit helplessly at home, perhaps bewailing their hard fate, or, what is still more sad to see, aimlessly contented with it. The emigrant is the capable, energetic, ambitious, discontented man—the sectary, the refugee, the persecuted, the exile from despotism—who, longing to breathe the air of equality, resolves to tear himself away from the old home with its associations to found in hospitable America a new home under equal and just laws, which insure to him, and what, perhaps, counts with him and his wife for more, insure also to their children the full measure of citizenship, making them free men in a free state, possessed of every right and privilege.

The true value of the men who emigrate is well understood by the ruling classes of the old world, who make every effort to prevent the exodus of so many able-bodied citizens. This is not from any fear of a depletion of population at home, for it has been conclusively shown that emigration does not tend to diminish the rate of increase in the country emigrated from, provided, of course, that the drain be not in excess of the natural fecundity of the human race, but rather from a well-grounded knowledge that it takes away the best of the population, the very bone and sinew of the race. Fortunately for America, these efforts have proved of little avail, and the steadily flowing stream of Britons, Teutons, and Latins, is assuming greater proportions as the years roll on, and will be limited in future not by the emigrating capacity of European nations, but by the superior attractions which the Republic can offer. So long as America presents to the world the spectacle of a country with a strong yet free government, where social order prevails, where taxation is at a minimum, where education is every man's birthright, where higher rewards are offered to labor and enterprise than elsewhere, and where equality of political rights is secured, so long will the best of the workers seek its shores. A portion of the stream may be diverted in time to other countries, when such offer equal advantages, political and material, but the United States have the advantage in this—that the current has set this way for more than half a century, and emigrants are apt to follow the course of those who have preceded them, those already established attracting their friends and relatives, and often providing the means for them to cross the ocean.

Besides being ambitious, energetic, and industrious, the emigrant is physically a strong and healthy man. The halt, the deaf, and the blind are not prompted to leave their European homes, nor does the confirmed invalid often seek a grave in a foreign land. This influence, which has been potent since the days of the Pilgrim Fathers, has resulted in a freedom from physical defect in America that is very noteworthy. Statistics show that the proportion of blind, deaf, and dumb to the total population is less than half what it is in Europe.

The capacity of America to absorb the population which is flowing into her, as well as the great natural increase of her people, cannot be more strikingly illustrated than by a comparison. Belgium has four hundred and eighty-two inhabitants to the square mile, Britain two hundred and ninety, the United States, exclusive of Alaska, less than fourteen. In the ten years from 1870 to 1880, eleven and a half millions were added to the population of America. Yet these only added three persons to each square mile of territory; and should America continue to double her population every thirty years instead of every twenty-five years as hitherto, seventy years must elapse before she will attain the density of Europe. The population will then reach two hundred and ninety millions. If the density of Britain ever be attained, there will be upwards of a thousand million Americans, for at the present every Briton has two acres and every American forty-four acres of land as his estate.

These forecasts are not only possible, they are extremely probable. The progress made since 1880 in the settlement of new regions is putting every preceding period into the shade. It is simply marvellous, and even those who are in the midst of it have difficulty in realizing how great it is. Look at the great North-west. Scarcely a decade has passed since it was represented as a barren, icy plain, wild, inhospitable and scarcely habitable. The railway has changed it as by a wizard's touch. Minnesota has more than a million inhabitants. The population of Dakota has quadrupled in five years, and is now half a million. Towns are springing up with magical rapidity. Its wheat crop last year was thirty million bushels—twice as great as the whole crop of Egypt. Montana is barely known by name in England. Last year —in twelve short months—her population increased from eighty-five thousand to one hundred and ten thousand; her cattle interests from four hundred and seventy-five thousand to eight hundred and fifty thousand, and her output of minerals from less than $10,000,000 to more than $23,000,000 (£2,000,000 to £4,600,000). Her taxable property is $50,000,000 (£10,000,000). Wyoming,

Idaho, Washington, and Oregon, are being developed
almost as rapidly. Other parts of the West have advanced at even a greater pace. The aggregate population
of seven States tributary to Kansas City increased in one
year (1879–80) from fewer than five and a half millions
to more than seven millions. Since 1880, the value of
cattle in the same region has advanced from $9,000,000
to $14,500,000 (£1,800,000 to £2,900,000), and of
sheep from $6,000,000 to $9,500,000 (£1,200,000 to
£1,900,000). At these rates of advance the "Wild West"
is rapidly become a thing of the past, and in a few years
it will be a thickly-settled land.

Figures are poor aids to the comprehension of great
truths. The comparative chart printed herewith by kind
permission of its author, Mr. Edward Atkinson, will
help the reader to a conception of the possibilities of this
great continent. It represents the area of Texas in con-
junction with the areas of other American States and
European countries. How petty some of the latter seem
beside majestic Texas! And yet Texas is but one of the
forty-six territorial divisions of the Republic. Observe
Montenegro, which at various times has excited all
Europe, and provoked enormous bloodshed; it would
hardly make a fly-speck on the map of Texas, and note
that the whole United Kingdom could be planted in this
one State of the Union, and still leave plenty of room
around it. Notice, too, gentle reader, how all the world's
cotton could be grown in the State of Texas alone, without greatly affecting its capacity for other productions. It
is scarcely overdrawing the picture to imagine that in a
few decades two or three hundred million republicans
will be living in amity, under one government, on the
great American Continent.

In view of these startling probabilities, it would seem
advisable that the statesmen of the old home, instead of

bestowing so much of their attention on the petty States of Europe, should look thoughtfully westward sometimes to the doings of their own kith and kin, who are rapidly building up a power which none can hope to rival.

We must not pass without mention our fellow-citizens of African descent, who, as we have seen, are equal in number to the entire foreign population—one-eighth of the whole. These, as the world knows, were all slaves a few years ago; but Abraham Lincoln, with one stroke of the pen, raised them from the condition of slavery to that of free men. They now exercise the suffrage just as other citizens do. There is not a privilege possessed by any citizen which is not theirs. The English poet says:

"Slaves cannot breathe in England; if their lungs
Receive our air, that moment they are free;
They touch our country, and their shackles fall."

No more can they exist in England's child-land; and the Declaration of Independence, asserting the freedom and equality of men, is no longer a mockery.

Grave apprehensions were entertained that freedom suddenly granted to these poor slaves would be abused. Those best acquainted with their habits, the Southern slave-holders, predicted, as a result of freedom, universal idleness, riot, and dissipation. It was asserted that the negro would not work save under the lash of the overseer. None of these gloomy predictions have been fulfilled—every one of them has been falsified. There is now more cotton grown than ever, and at less cost. Under the reign of freedom the material resources of the South have increased faster than ever before. Indeed, so surprised were most Americans by the result of the last census that it was insisted mistakes had been made: the figures could not be right, and in some districts the enumeration was made a second time, with the result of

verifying the former figures. The number of Congress-
men to each State is determined every ten years by the
population shown by the census. When the census of
1880 was made the general expectation was that the
Northern States would increase their proportionate representation; but the Southern States not only held their
own, but actually gained. The ninety-eight Southern
representatives were increased by thirteen, while the one
hundred and ninety-five Northern representatives gained
only eighteen—only half the Southern ratio of increase.
Even the unexampled growth of the North-western
States was insufficient to give the Northern States a proportionately increased legislative power. So much for
freedom versus slavery!

The universal testimony is that the former slaves
rapidly develop the qualities of freemen and exhibit, in
a surprising degree, the capacity to manage their own
affairs. Many of them at once arranged with their former
masters to work a part of the plantation upon shares.
Others bargained for the purchase of strips of land.
They are now quite orderly and well-behaved, and much
more industrious than before.

It seems to the writer but yesterday since he was compelled to listen to arguments from good men in favor of
the system of slavery, as he is yet doomed sometimes to
hear defences of monarchy and aristocracy, and to hear
them contend that it was best for the black race. Their
contentedness and happiness under masters were always
boldly asserted. A well-known judge in Ohio was noted
for his defence of slavery, upon the ground that the
slaves knew what was best for themselves, and should be
allowed to remain in the condition which admittedly
brought them a degree of happiness seldom, if ever,
attained by laborers in the North. His conversion to the
opposite opinion was suddenly brought about by an inter-

view with a run-away who had crossed the Ohio River
from Kentucky, and entered the village in which our
friend resided. Said the judge to the fugitive:

"What did you run away for?"

"Well, Judge, 'wanted to be free."

"Oh! wanted to be free, did you? Bad master, I suppose."

"O no; berry good man, massa."

"You had to work too hard, then?"

"O no; fair day's work."

"Well, you hadn't a good home?"

"Hadn't I, though! You should see my pretty cabin
in Kentucky!"

"Well, you didn't get enough to eat?"

"Oh, golly! not get enough to eat in Kentucky! Plenty
to eat."

The Judge, somewhat annoyed: "You had a good master, plenty to eat, wasn't overworked, a good home. I
don't see what on earth you wanted to run away for."

"Well, Judge, I left de situation down dar open. You
can go right down and get it."

The result was a five-dollar note given to help the
unreasonable slave who had left well-being behind to become a man. Henceforth the Judge was an ardent aboli-
tionist, recognizing that

> "Freedom hath a thousand charms to show,
>   That slaves, howe'er contented, never know."

The proportion of the colored to the white element
steadily grows less and less. In 1790 it was twenty-seven
per cent. of the whole, in 1830 it had fallen to eighteen
per cent., in 1880 it was only thirteen per cent. While the
total white population of the country has risen from ten
and a half to forty-three and a half millions in fifty
years, the number of the colored population has only

risen from two and a quarter to six and a half millions.
This steady decrease results from two causes. First, the
colored race receives no immigrants, but is restricted
wholly to native increase for its growth; and, second, it
has been proved that although their birth rate is greater
than that of the whites, it is more than balanced by their
higher death rate. The increase of colored people from
1860 to 1880 was but forty-eight per cent., against sixty-
one per cent. increase of the whites.

It is too soon yet to judge whether, with superior
knowledge and more provident habits flowing from freedom, this excessive death rate will not be considerably
reduced; but the conclusion seems unavoidable that the
colored race cannot hold its own numerically against the
whites and must fall farther and farther behind. Adap-
tive as man is, we can scarcely expect the hotter climate
of the Southern States, in which the colored people live,
to produce as hardy a race as that of the cooler States of
the North.

We close, then, showing in the Republic a race essentially British in origin, but fast becoming more and more
American in birth, the foreign-born elements sinking into
insignificance and destined soon to become of no greater
relative magnitude, perhaps, in proportion to the native-
born American than the foreign-born residents of Britain
are at present to the native born. The American republican can never be other in his blood and nature than a
true Briton, a real chip of the old block, a new edition
of the original work, and, as is the manner of new editions, revised and improved, and, like his prototype in
the thousand and one ways, some of them grotesque in
their manifestations, which link the daughter to the
mother, who, seen together, impress beholders not so
much as two separate and distinct individualities as two
members of the one grand family.

Chapter III
CITIES AND TOWNS

"It is indeed a thrilling thought for a man of the elder England to see what a home the newest home of his people is. The heart swells, the pride of kinship rises, as he sees that it is his own folk which has done more than any other folk to replenish the earth and to subdue it. He is no Englishman at heart, he has no true feeling of the abiding tie of kindred, who deems that the glory and greatness of the child is other than part of the glory and greatness of the parent."—FREEMAN.

AMERICA forms no exception to the rule that population in civilized lands gravitates towards great centres. Though her immense agricultural development might have been expected to arrest this movement and divert population to the rural districts, such has not been the case. Despite the temptations to rural life offered by fertile land at nominal prices, towns have grown during the last half century much faster than the country. The dull, dreary round of life upon the farm is found intolerable by the young man whose intellectual faculties have been awakened by education. The active mind seeks companionship with other minds and the pleasurable excitements of city life. Most great men, it is true, have been born and brought up in the country, but it is equally true that very few great men have remained there beyond their teens. The country is just the place for the extremes of life—at the beginning in childhood and early youth, when the body is to be nurtured, and also at the end,

"when nature turns again to earth" in ripe old age and
retires from the fray to

> "Ruminate in sober thought
> On all he's seen, and heard, and wrought."

In 1830 only six and a half per cent. of the population lived in towns of eight thousand inhabitants and
upwards; in 1880 the proportion had risen to twenty-
two per cent. Thus, nearly one person in every four in
America is now a member of a hive of more than eight
thousand human beings. Fifty years ago this was true
of but one in fifteen, for fourteen out of fifteen lived in
the country or in small villages.

This is a stupendous change and marks the development of the Republic from the first stage of homogeneity of pastoral pursuits into the heterogeneous occupations of a more highly civilized state. The nation is
now complete, as it were, in itself, and ready for independent action. Its mechanical and inventive genius has
full scope in the thousand and one diversified pursuits
which a civilized community necessarily creates, and
which necessitate the gathering of men together in
masses.

The American, however, need not fear the unhealthy
or abnormal growth of cities. He need not imitate the
example of those who advocated legislative measures to
prevent the growth of London, which Cobbett called a
wart upon the hand of England. The free play of economic laws is keeping all quite right, for the town gained
upon the country population only one-fourth as fast during the last decade (1870 to 1880) as in the previous
one.

Oh, these grand, immutable, all-wise laws of natural
forces, how perfectly they work if human legislators

would only let them alone! But no, they must be tinkering. One day they would protect the balance of power in Europe by keeping weak, small areas apart and independent—an impossible task, for petty States must merge into the greater—political is as certain as physical gravitation; the next day it is silver in America, which our sage rulers would make of greater intrinsic value. So our governors, all over the world, are at Sisyphus's work—ever rolling the stone uphill to see it roll back to its proper bed at the bottom.

That the country held its own so well in the competition with the towns during the last decade is partly due to the fact that the enormous profits made under an improved system of agriculture held the rural population to the soil. The general depression of manufactures also checked settlement in towns, and forced population into the country. The commercial panic of 1873 drove hundreds of thousands from the crowded cities of the East to the unoccupied plains of the West. Train-load after train-load of native emigrants were to be seen passing west to become farmers. With a return to normal conditions we may expect to find the towns absorbing much more than an equal share.

It is always a result of industrial depression in America that the towns are relieved of surplus population which in older countries remains in poverty and distress to swell the ranks of the unemployed. Horace Greeley's advice, "Go West, young man!" is followed. One needs however to add to it, "and stay there," to complete the matter. The equilibrium is thus restored between producers and consumers, and prosperity to both follows. If there be too much food it is unprofitable to grow more cereals, and fewer people become farmers; if the market be overstocked with manufactures, manufacturing becomes unprofitable and fewer engage in it. The population, meanwhile increasing at the rate of nearly two millions per annum, soon requires the surplus, be it food or manufactures. America possesses hundreds of thousands of acres of virgin soil ready for the plough. Like the fabled Antæus, her power of recuperation lies in the earth: let her touch but that and her giant strength is restored. This will continue to be so until her population becomes as dense as that of Europe.

According to Dr. Swainson Fisher, there were not, in 1835, five thousand white inhabitants in all the vast territory between Lake Michigan and the Pacific Ocean, a region half as large as Europe. Now it is covered with an agricultural population, and contains many populous cities, including Chicago, Milwaukee, and St. Paul, to say nothing of the cities of the Pacific coast. Of the State of Wisconsin, occupying a part of this territory, a member of the Wisconsin Historical Society wrote, thirty years ago:

"In the summer of 1836, with a comrade, I camped at the head of Mendota or Fourth Lake, within six miles of the spot where the Capitol now stands (1856), at which time there was not within twenty miles of that point a single white inhabitant, and none within the present limits of Dane County, an area of twelve hundred and forty square miles, except one family."

Dane County, then an uninhabited wilderness, contained in 1880 a population of more than sixty thousand, while Wisconsin itself had a million and a half. In 1880 the density of population in this young State exceeded that of Maine and nearly equalled that of such old settled States as Georgia, Alabama, and West Virginia.

The United States had no city in 1830 which could boast a population of a quarter of a million. Even New York had but two hundred and two thousand. In that

year there were but fourteen towns with more than
twelve thousand inhabitants each; in truth, but fifty-five
years ago, the Republic could boast only of a few villages. In 1880 there were one hundred and seventy-six
such towns, and to-day the number exceeds two hundred.

New York City in 1880 was the only millionaire in
heads, though Philadelphia now claims that she has
reached that distinction. The census of 1880 accredits
the Empire City with fewer than a million and a quarter
inhabitants; but if the population within a radius of eight
miles of the City Hall were included, she would be
credited with fully two and a quarter millions. Brooklyn,
Jersey City, and other suburbs, divided from the city by
rivers, are under separate municipal governments, but
they are none the less outgrowths of the great centre.
Thus New York ranks next to monster London as a busy
hive of human beings. Every decade sees an addition of
half a million people to each of these two vast aggregations of humanity. The increase of New York in actual
figures is equal to that of London, which makes the ratio
of increase to population double. While London has
taken since 1840 to double her population, New York,
including the suburbs, has doubled hers in half that time.
So that if the present rate of increase be maintained,
forty years hence London will have doubled her present
population once and New York twice: their populations
will then be about equal. It is a neck and neck race between the two emporiums which the world of 1920 is to
see, with the odds in favor of New York. It is easier for
her to twice double her two than for London to double
her four millions, and besides, the goddess Fortune, true
to her sex, may confidently be expected to breathe her
secret prayers for the younger aspirant. She is fond of
youth and fickle, and really seems disposed to be off with
the old love, dear old smoky London, and on with the

new, bright, rosy, gallant New York. Let us hope she may illustrate another phase not inconsistent with her sex, and continue as hitherto to smile upon both suitors. If Jack has his favorite in every port, surely our goddess may be allowed one in the East and one in the great West.

Of the fifty largest cities of the Union, the least with a population of 36,000 in 1880, fifteen had no existence in 1830; they were not born. Their sites were either the unbroken prairie or an Indian settlement, with a fort and a few log huts. Chicago is the most famous example. Fifty-five years ago it was a trading post, where trappers and Indians bartered their pelts for fire-water and ammunition. I knew one of Chicago's first settlers well; and have often heard him speak of the little fort and the scattering log huts which marked the city's site some sixty years ago. There was scarcely a white woman in the settlement when he began trading with the Indians. In 1833 the streets of the projected town had been staked out, but no grading had been done, not even a dirt road thrown up. Such, however, was the growth of "this little mushroom town," as an early writer calls it, that in 1846 it was noted that "eight years ago (1838) the ground upon which the entire city of Chicago stands could have been bought for a sum now (1846) demanded for a front of six feet on one of the streets." Tradition tells of an early settler who averred that he had seen the time when he could have bought the "hull tarnation swamp" for a pair of old boots. To the inquiry —"Why didn't you?" he had the entirely adequate reply: "Ah, stranger, I hadn't the boots." How many chances in life do we miss just for the want of the boots. Moral: Get the boots.

In 1840 the population of Chicago was 4,500; ten years later, 30,000; in ten years more, 112,000. It now exceeds 700,000. This splendid city, "the Queen of the West," leads the world in three branches of industry; she is pre-eminent as a lumber market, as a provision market, and, strange antithesis, as a manufactory of steel rails. Such a combination of "greatnesses" surely the world has not seen. Her statistics show the receipt of nearly two thousand million feet of lumber and nine hundred million shingles per annum. Her yearly receipts of grain approach two hundred million bushels. Twenty-six million bushels can be laid away in her twenty-eight elevators,—a store which dwarfs the ostentatious garnering of the ancient Pharaohs as much as her enormous shipments outnumber the sacks of corn which Joseph's brethren carried away. Last year she received nearly two million cattle, a million sheep, and five million hogs, more than twenty-five thousand animals per day. So that there marches into Chicago every day in the year—Sundays and Saturdays included—a procession of victims, two miles and a half long—ten animals abreast. The cattle and hogs are mostly transformed into provisions before leaving Chicago. The year 1881 was an exceptionally good year for pork-packers, but a bad one for the hogs. Five and three quarter millions fell in Chicago alone,—an average of nineteen thousand a day:

> "The fittest place for man to die
> Is where he dies for man."

The fittest place for a hog is evidently Chicago, for every minute of time, night and day—all the year round —thirteen of them, "die for man," at that place of slaughter.

Chicago has moreover three steel rail mills within the city limits, and a fourth within thirty miles. Their combined capacity exceeds 500,000 tons annually—sufficient to put a light steel rail "girdle round the earth." There will probably be as many steel rails made in and about Chicago alone next year as one-half the total rail product of Great Britain. Her coat of arms should be: Barry of alternate steel rails and pine planks, proper; over all, a pig rampant, gules. Motto, "The Whole Hog."

San Francisco is another mushroom. In 1844 fifty people were settled in log huts on a barren tract of the Pacific coast. A few whalemen and north-east traders occasionally called at this settlement, and bartered food and clothing for tallow, hides, and horns. Gradually the embryo village grew; and in 1847 certain plots of ground on the water front were sold, the prices ranging from £10 to £20 per lot. Six years later, such was the rapid enhancement of values, inferior lots brought from £1,600 to £3,200; from £20 to £2,000 in fourteen years; four small building plots bringing £240,000, equal to £60,000 per block. This was in the palmy days depicted by Colonel Mulberry Sellers, when you had but to lay out a town site into lots, every one of them a corner lot, and sit down and figure just how much money you wanted and then rake it in. Thirty-seven years sufficed to raise the settlement of fifty persons to a magnificent city with a quarter of a million inhabitants. The bartering of a few hides has grown into an annual trade exceeding twenty millions sterling.

Jersey City, opposite New York, furnishes another example of rapid city growth. In 1840 the population was only 3,072; in 1880 it was 120,722. But Brooklyn, the corresponding suburb on the other side of New York harbor, has eclipsed every city, except Chicago, its population of 12,000 in 1830 having grown to 566,000 in 1880. The growth of Cleveland, Ohio, has not been slow. In 1830 it had only 1,000 inhabitants; now it boasts 160,000. The finest avenues of residences are in this city. After seeing all that the rest of the world has to offer in that respect, I pronounce Euclid and Prospect Avenues in this lake city of Cleveland the grandest and most beautiful; though the smaller Prospect Avenue in Milwaukee, and Delaware Avenue in Buffalo, and that in Detroit are very handsome indeed, and are open for second and third prizes.

The city of Milwaukee, with a present population of 125,000, consisted in 1834 of two log houses. In 1835 it was laid out as a village; and the next year we find it described as a hamlet of about two hundred inhabitants. At that time the only roads leading into the city were a few Indian trails. Once in a while a wagon came winding through from Chicago. But even at this infantile age Milwaukee had begun to display the enterprise which has continued to distinguish it. In 1840 the town could boast of one brick building—a small one-story dwelling-house. There were then eleven stores in the place. During the next ten years the population increased from 1,712 to 20,061. In 1841 began the shipment of grain— a trade which has since attained an enormous development. In that year four thousand bushels of wheat—the first ever sent out of Wisconsin—was exported; but such was the imperfect provision for loading that this small shipment required three days to put on board ship. The trade thus begun, grew apace; and three years later we find that Mr. Higby, a pioneer merchant, *imported* a grain warehouse from Sheboygan. The character of this structure is shown by the fact that it was afterward carried about to several other places. The whole receipts for grain shipments at Milwaukee in that year did not equal those received in a single day fifteen years later, or, remarkable fact, *in a single hour at present!* The receipts of grain at Milwaukee now approximate forty million bushels a year. It is taken out of ships and cars, carried to the top of the elevators, and weighed and poured into bags and bins at the rate of seven thousand bushels an hour, without any manual labor. Automatic machines are the giants who do the work.

A unique man resides in Milwaukee, one so closely identified with its wonderful growth that he is thought of whenever that city is mentioned—Alexander Mitchell, who left Aberdeen, a young Scotch lad, some fifty years ago. He has one proud distinction of which he can never be deprived, for it can scarcely ever be expected in the history of the race that any development of material resources can equal that of the American railway system. Alexander Mitchell has built more miles of railway than any man who has lived, is living, or who is ever to live. He began the work at Milwaukee as President of the Milwaukee & St. Paul Railway, a position which he still holds. It is scarcely necessary to add that the said Mitchell has not failed to hold on to a fair proportion of this gigantic property, for it has been noted that he is Scotch. When we reached Chicago with our Scotch guests two years ago we found his special car—a much grander hotel than any saloon-carriage—waiting there subject to our orders. The conductor said his instructions were to go where we wished, stop and start on any train desired, and when we were done with him he was to return with his car to Milwaukee. We spent days in that car, visited St. Paul in the North, and Davenport in the West, and did not traverse one mile of line which that Scotch boy had not built, and over which his word was not law. "Scotland forever!" Mr. Mitchell is one of the dozen richest men in the world, a credit to Aberdeen, a credit to his native Scotland, a credit to his adopted America. A grand Republican he is, too. Staunch as Aberdeen granite there. No royal family or hereditary legislators for him, mind you. He is not the stuff out of which a "loyal subject" to another human being can be made; or, if made, not the man to occupy that degrading position long. He holds himself, as man, the equal of any monarch. A man whom all men honor.

The adjoining State of Minnesota contained in 1880 about 800,000 people, of which 88,000 resided in the capital, St. Paul, and its twin sister town, Minneapolis. In 1885 the State population had increased to eleven hundred thousand—43 per cent. in five years. Greatest wonder of all, however, is the five years' growth of the city of Minneapolis. In 1880 its population was 47,000; in 1885, 130,000, a gain of over 176 per cent.! St. Paul increased from 41,000 to 111,000—a gain of 168 per cent. Yet in 1848 this region was a wilderness, the entire territory, nearly twice the size of the present State, having only about 3,000 inhabitants. A trading house was built on the site of St. Paul in 1842, and round it gradually grew a small community of whites and half-breeds, engaged in barter with the Indians and trappers. In 1850 the population numbered 1,135. To quote the words of a writer of that period, "St. Paul is in the wilderness. Look where you will, the primitive features of the surrounding country remain unchanged, and the wild animals and Indians still haunt the grounds to which ages of occupancy have given them a prescriptive right." A few miles away, a group of houses might have been seen clustering around the Falls of St. Anthony. There, in 1848, a saw-mill was put in operation by the aid of a temporary dam built across the east channel of the river. As the forests fell before the lumberman's axe, and emigrant farmers brought in the plough, flouring mills were built at the falls, and Minneapolis emerged from the country-village state. Checked in their growth by the war in 1861, and more seriously by the Sioux massacre of 1862, Minneapolis and St. Paul experienced renewed prosperity in 1864 and 1865, and since then the two towns have gone forward, marching across the dividing forest to meet each other, and will eventually mingle their suburbs, and form a city a dozen miles across, with a population of a million souls. The child is living who will see all this and more.

As we have Alexander Mitchell dominating Milwaukee, so no one can think of Minneapolis without recalling that notable family the "Washburn Brothers." Their career is typically American. These Washburns are a family indeed, seven sons, all of them men of mark. Several have distinguished themselves so greatly as to become part of their country's history. The family record includes a secretary of state, two governors, four members of Congress, a major-general in the army, and another second in command in the navy. Two served as foreign ministers, two were State legislators, and one a surveyor-general. As all these services were performed during the Civil War, there were Washburns in nearly every department of the State, laboring in camp and council for the Republic at the sacrifice of great personal interests. All came forth from peaceful avocations to serve their country as their first duty. The Union saved, they are found to-day pursuing their industrial occupations as of old. The nation having no enemies to conquer, they turn their energies to the work of feeding it. Is not this turning the sword into the plough-share and the spear into the pruning-hook? Let the nation be endangered, or an emergency arise where, in the judgment and conscience of such men, they can perform a greater use in public than in private life, and they are once more upon the stage of action. The Republic has such citizens by thousands, and yet the privileged classes of Europe assiduously spread the belief among the masses abroad that the Republic lacks pure and distinguished noble men to guide her councils. Believe me, fellow-citizens, no nation upon earth has such wealth of patriotism, men with such power to conceive, or such ability to execute, as rests quietly in reserve, but ever ready for emergencies, in this democracy. It is this reserve force which has kept the Republic steadily upon her course. It votes or fights as may be necessary, and never shirks a duty. When the ship of State is in smooth waters more important matters require its attention, and the governing power goes below; but, mark you, when the wind blows this captain walks the deck. The Republic has never been allowed to sail far out of the true course, and never will be. Too much science on board, and too many independent observations taken and compared in the full blaze of the sun, not to find the true reckoning and follow it closely, steadily, to the desired haven. This reserve was seen forcibly during the four years during which the Union was imperilled. When a leader was needed one was found in an attorney's office in Illinois,—a great, heaven-born leader, Lincoln. When foreign relations were necessarily dangerous in the extreme, and even our mother country stood threatening, Seward proved himself a diplomatist of the first order. For Secretary of War a genius was taken from the practice of the law in Pittsburgh. No man since the days of Carnot has waged war as did Stanton. "The armies will move now," said a friend, when his appointment was announced, "if they move to the devil." I knew Stanton well, a Cromwell kind of man; he walked straight to his end, either to triumph or to die. His life he could give and would give that the nation should live; that was his duty; victory might come or defeat, that was not his affair. When generals to lead the armies were sought for, the great leader came from a tannery in Galena; the second from teaching in a college. All these were from peaceful occupations, and every one of them resigned power poor men. The families of several of them were provided for by private subscriptions among friends. Politics are but means to an end. When the laws of a country are perfect, and the equality of the citizen reached, there is far more important work to be performed at home than in legislative halls. Hence the ablest and best men in the Republic are not as a class found trifling their time away doing the work of mediocrity. But let great issues rise and see who come to the front—a body of men superior to any found elsewhere in the world.

Already Minneapolis is the greatest wheat market in the West, and unlike other large receiving points, four-fifths of all wheat received there is manufactured into flour before shipment. Last year one and a quarter million bushels were often received in a single week. The total receipts of 1884 were nearly three times as great as those of 1880, aggregating twenty-nine million bushels. The milling trade has also increased at a prodigious rate. One-fifth of all the flour exported from the United States is sent direct from Minneapolis on through bills of lading. The capacity of the mills is over thirty thousand barrels per day; and one of the Washburn Mills alone has made over seven thousand barrels of flour in one day. Five and a quarter million barrels were manufactured last year—five times the output of 1876. Surely no worthy second of this can be found elsewhere. Yet flouring is not the only industry of this youthful giant. Three hundred million feet of lumber were cut by the mills last year, besides one hundred and thirty-six million lath and shingles! Minneapolis justifiably boasts that she is "a city of mechanics." Her manufactures exceeded twelve millions sterling in 1884, while her trade, exclusive of flour and lumber, reached almost an equal sum. The total receipts and shipments of

Minneapolis in the year 1884 comprised two hundred and forty-six thousand nine hundred and eighty-five carloads. A local statistician has reckoned that "if all these cars were made up into trains of twenty cars each they would make twelve thousand three hundred and forty-seven trains, requiring that number of engines to move them; if cars and engines were continuously coupled together they would make a train one thousand seven hundred miles in length; or, if made into four trains, each train would reach from Minneapolis to Chicago; or the line of freight cars would be sufficient to completely fence in England and Scotland, and then form a wall across the middle of the country at its widest part.

Some idea of the enormous amount of flour manufactured by the mills of Minneapolis can be obtained if we estimate it at the rate of two hundred and fifty loaves of bread to the barrel, which would give us twenty-five loaves for each of the fifty-six million people of the United States. If the flour made by Minneapolis in one year were put into barrels and these set end to end and roped together, they would make a pontoon bridge from New York to Ireland.

A similar phenomenal growth is going on in another region. In 1870, only fifteen years ago, except Superior and Duluth, the former a "straggling little hamlet!" and the other "laid out on speculation in the woods on the lake shore," there was not a town, village, or hamlet westward on or near the line marked out for the Northern Pacific Railroad for more than a thousand miles. Between the head of the lake and the mining camps among the Rocky Mountains in Montana, no abodes of civilized men existed, save two or three military posts and Indian agencies, and a few isolated trading stations. Northern Minnesota was a forest into which even the lumberman had not yet penetrated, save for a few miles

back of Lake Superior. At present the whole line of the
railway is dotted with thriving towns. "The town laid
out on speculation in the woods," is deserving of a moment's attention.

Duluth, even in the embryonic state, displayed a pre-
cocity that brought upon it the ridicule of a famous
orator. With scathing sarcasm, but unconscious prophecy, he dubbed it "the zenith city of the unsalted seas."
There is a scream from the American eagle for you; but
is it not poetic? The juvenile city is now the terminus of
ten thousand miles of railway. Its receipts of wheat for
1884 approached fourteen million bushels. Saw-mills are
getting almost as plentiful as blackberries; and in a single year they cut two hundred and five million feet of
lumber besides eighty-five million lath and shingles. The
clearances show that seven hundred steamers and nearly
six hundred sail-craft arrived at Duluth in 1884. Banking transactions amounted to thirty-four million dollars
a year. Storage capacity for grain is nearly ten million
bushels. Lastly, the population of this magic city has
bounded from two thousand five hundred in 1875 to
eighteen thousand in 1884. Was ever the like known except in the triumphant Republic?

Indianapolis, with its present population of ninety
thousand inhabitants, has also a history which the "oldest inhabitant" can recite from personal experience.
Practically its history as a city dates from the opening of
the Madison Railway in 1847. Before that date it was
but a small country town, so isolated that its trade was
compared to that of the two boys who, when locked up
in a closet, made money by swapping jackets. The slowness of its growth before the advent of the railway is
shown by the following facts extracted from Hollo-
way's "Local History." The town was laid out in 1821.
Ten years later three-fourths of the town site remained

unsold. The legislature managed to get rid of most of the lots by putting a minimum price of $10 upon them, and when the sales were closed in 1842, it was found that the whole of Indianapolis had brought but $125,000 (£25,000). The city thus sold out was but a forest, except where a clearing here and there had opened the ground to the light. To get the streets cleared it was proposed to give the timber to anybody who would cut it. A man by the name of Lismund Basye took the contract for Washington Street, expecting to make a "good thing" of such a superb lot of timber trees, and then began to calculate. There were no mills and his trees were of no use without them, so he rolled his splendid logs together and burned them as well as his fingers. The street thus opened, a hundred and twenty feet wide, is now lined with fine buildings; and a single block on this handsome thoroughfare would now fetch more than the sum for which the whole city was originally sold. Indianapolis has claims to be considered one of the greatest railway centres in the world. Fourteen railways centre there, and about a hundred and twenty passenger trains pass in and out of the city every day.

Kansas City is another example of Western phenomenal growths. Thirty years ago (1855) its population was three hundred; in fifteen years (1870) it had increased more than a hundredfold, to thirty-two thousand; by 1880 it had again doubled to sixty-three thousand, and at the time of writing it is about one hundred and twenty-five thousand. The assessed valuation of property has increased from $500,000 (£100,000) in 1846 to $34,000,000 (£6,800,000) in 1884. The exchanges, as shown by the returns of the city clearinghouse, have advanced from $20,000,000 (£4,000,000) in 1875 to $177,000,000 (nearly £36,000,000) in 1884. The business of the post-office increased during the same

period fivefold. About twenty-four million bushels of
grain were received in 1884, against one million bushels
in 1871. One and a quarter million hogs are annually
turned into pork—about a fourth of monster Chicago's
herd, and fifteen hundred cattle are also weekly shipped
as provisions. The trade in live stock is also very great;
nearly two and a half million cattle, hogs, sheep, horses
and mules pass through its markets—a procession, five
abreast, that would reach from Inverness to London.

Numerous other examples might be cited. Allegheny
City, an off-shoot of Pittsburgh, has grown from a village of twenty-eight hundred inhabitants in 1830 to a
city of seventy-nine thousand in 1880; while the population of Pittsburgh itself increased during the same period
from twelve thousand to one hundred and fifty-six thousand. Buffalo during the same fifty years advanced from
eighty thousand to one hundred and fifty-five thousand
inhabitants; Philadelphia increased from eighty thousand
to nearly eight hundred and fifty thousand; Cincinnati
from twenty-four thousand to two hundred and fifty-five
thousand; Detroit from two thousand to one hundred
and sixteen thousand; Rochester from fifteen persons in
1812 to eighty-nine thousand in 1880; Toledo from
twelve hundred and twenty-two in 1840 to fifty thousand
in 1880; Scranton from three hundred and sixty-three
in 1840 to forty-six thousand in 1880.

Of the growth of these towns we have an excellent
picture in the following paragraphs, the first from the
pen of Capt. Basil Hall, the "best-hated Englishman"
in America some fifty years ago, and the second by
the Norwegian, Arfedson, descriptive of Columbus,
Georgia:

"The first thing to which our attention was called was a long
line cut through the coppicewood of oaks. This our guide begged

us to observe was to be the principal street; and the brushwood having been cut away so as to leave a lane four feet wide, with small stakes driven in it at intervals, we could walk along it easily enough. On reaching the middle point, our friend, looking around him, exclaimed in rapture at the prospect of the future greatness of Columbus: 'Here you are in the centre of the city!' After threading our way for some time amongst the trees, we came in sight here and there, of huts partly of planks, partly of bark, and at last reached the principal cluster of houses, very few of which were above two or three weeks old. As none of the city-lots were yet sold, of course no one was sure that the spot on which he had pitched his house would eventually become his own. Many of the houses were in consequence of this understanding built on trucks, a sort of low strong wheels, such as cannon are supported by, for the avowed purpose of being hauled away when the land should be sold. At some parts of this strange scene the forest was growing as densely as ever; and even in the most cleared streets some trees were left standing. As yet there had been no time to remove the stumps of the felled trees, and many that had been felled were left in their places; so that it was occasionally no easy matter to get along. Anvils were heard ringing away merrily at every corner, while saws, axes, and hammers were seen flashing amongst the woods all around."

Columbus in 1832, only four years later:

"It may already be called a flourishing town. The population exceeded two thousand, and among them were several that might be denominated wealthy. The number of inhabitants is augmenting monthly, and the increase of commerce, I was assured, was in the same proportions. Carpenters, masons, and workmen of every kind were never without employment, and could not erect houses fast enough. Streets, which in 1828 were only marked out, were now so filled with loaded wagons that it was next to impossible to pass. The principal street which traverses the city, following the course of the river, is like the rest, not paved, but has so many shops filled with a variety of goods, such a number of neat houses, and finally, in the mornings, such a concourse of people, Christians and Indians, that it can hardly be believed that it is the same street which was only marked out in 1828. Most of the houses are of wood, and some of brick; a few in the English style, others again in the Grecian taste."

If we compare the preceding accounts of the rise and progress of recently established cities with the slow movements of old Boston, the contrast is great indeed. Boston was first settled in 1630. Fifty years later the first fire-engine was procured, and the first fire-company organized—a sign of progress attained by a modern town in as many weeks. In 1704 appeared the *Boston News Letter,* the first newspaper ever published in the British colonies of North America. Now the printing press is set up almost in the first plank house erected; and a town of a few miners must have its own newspaper. In 1710, eighty years after the settlement of the town, a post-office was established, and mails were forwarded once a week to Plymouth and to Maine, and once a fortnight to New York. In 1786 the citizens undertook their first great enterprise, and constructed a bridge over the Charles River; so that Boston required a hundred and fifty years to attain a position which is now often reached by modern towns of the prairies in as many months.

Examples without number of phenomenal growth of cities and towns might be cited, for the line stretches on, one seemingly miraculous till the other comes. From East to West, from North to South, up and down and across the map of the Republic the student may pass in imaginative flight, sure of meeting everywhere these cities and towns which, springing up like mushrooms, have nevertheless taken root like the oak.

A beautiful tribute to the mother land is found in the names of towns and cities in the new. As even on the crowded, tiny May Flower the stern Puritan found room to bring and nurse with tender care the daisy of his native land, so the citizen driven from the dear old home ever sighs, "England, with all thy faults I love thee still." Surely, why not? Her faults are as one, her virtues as a thousand. And having a new home to christen, with swelling heart and tearful eye, and a love for the native land which knows no end and never can know end while breath clings to the body, he conjures up the object of his fondest love and calls his new home Boston, York, Brighton, Hartford, Stratford, Glasgow, Edinburgh, Durham, Perth, Aberdeen, Dundee, Cambridge, Oxford, Canterbury, Rochester, London, Newcastle, Manchester, Birmingham, Chester, Coventry, Plymouth, or other dear name of the place where in life's young days he had danced o'er the sunny braes, heard the lark sing in the heavens, and the mavis pour forth its glad song from the hedge row. There is scarcely a place in the old land which has not its namesake in the new. Take Pittsburgh, which is itself named after the great Pitt, and within a few miles' radius the English visitor can walk the streets of Soho, Birmingham, and Manchester. All these were suburban places a few years ago, and now they are as crowded as their prototypes. Brighton, Rochester, Newport, Middlesex, Newcastle are only a few miles away. This love of the old household words is carried even farther. The Englishman travels through the Republic living in a succession of hotels, Victorias, Clarendons, Windsors, Westminsters, Albemarles. He might think himself at home again except that the superior advantages of the new hostelries serve to remind him at every turn that things are not as he has been accustomed to. So that our household gods are not only the same in the new as in the old land, but we call them by the same names and love them. The exile's heart is always sad when he thinks of the one spot of mother earth which alone can be in the deepest sense his home. Who then shall keep apart the land of his home and the land of his domicile? And what American worthy of the name but shall reverence the home of his fathers, and wish it God-speed? When the people reign in the old home as they do in the new, the two nations will be one people, and the bonds which unite them the world combined shall not break asunder. The republican upon this side of the Atlantic extends his hand to his fellow upon the other. They' clasp hands. Democracy cries to democracy, "We stand for the rights of man, the day of kings and peers is past. Down, privilege, down. Ring in the reign of the people, the equality of the citizen." No peal so grand as that, save one, that which proclaims the substitution of peaceful arbitration for war the world over. And that too is involved in republicanism. All parties in the Republic already stand pledged to the doctrine. Patience, my fellow-citizens, patience. Democracy goes marching on. The reign of the masses is the road to universal peace. Thrones and royal families, and the influences necessarily surrounding them, —the vile brood they breed—make twenty wars while Triumphant Democracy makes one.

Chapter IV
CONDITIONS OF LIFE

"The ideal State is one in which every citizen is content with the laws under which he lives. If any body of men in a State agitate for a change of laws, dissatisfaction is proven to exist, and by this much is the State disordered and unenviable. To produce universal satisfaction is possible only by meting out to every citizen the same measures. The slightest inequality produces disturbance, for only under equality are the parts free from strain, and hence in repose. The State in equilibrium has then reached perfection in its political system."—EIGENRAC.

AMID so much that is marvellous in American history, nothing stands out with greater prominence than the rapid amelioration of the conditions of life. A century ago the continent of America was for the most part a wilderness. A long strip of the Atlantic coast was sparsely populated, and a few towns were unevenly sprinkled over the narrow territory. But behind this the country was in the same wild condition as when the Pilgrim Fathers landed, a hundred and fifty years before. There were few roads through the backwoods, and the inhabitants of Massachusetts were as widely divided from those of Virginia as from those of the old home, all intercommunication of the colonies being by coasting vessels. After Independence (1776), however, the young nation, full of the enthusiasm and hot blood of youth, vigorously applied itself to the development of the

country. Canals and turnpike roads were built, and by
1830 there were open for use one hundred and fifteen
thousand miles of highway, and upwards of two thousand miles of canals, the latter costing upwards of $65,-
000,000 (£13,000,000). Canals and turnpikes were then
the mighty forces of civilization, the wonderful means
of locomotion.

Eight miles per hour by the mail-coach and six miles
per hour by the express packet upon the "raging canal!"
What was the world coming to!

Notwithstanding this, the country was very backward,
and there was little, considered in the light of modern
comforts, to make life worth living. In the newspapers
of the time, and in books written by travellers, we get
faint glimpses of the inconveniences under which the past
generation labored; but the full significance of many a
little statement written fifty years ago, is not to be realized in these days of luxurious refinement and elegant
ease. Here, for example, is an extract from *Niles's
Register,* March 20, 1830:

"A letter written in Baltimore has been replied to from Norfolk in forty-one hours, a distance of about four hundred miles—
by steam!"

The note of exclamation appended to the statement
seems oddly incongruous in these days of telegraphs,
telephones, and penny postage. The difficulty of communication in those early days is further exemplified by
the statement in the *American Quarterly Observer* for
July, 1834, that:

"A package of books can be more readily sent from Boston to
London than to Cincinnati. A book printed in Boston has been
republished in Edinburgh before it has reached Cincinnati."

And here are a few passages from Miss Martineau's "Society in America," date 1834–5:

"The great cities are even yet ill supplied from the country. Provisions are very dear: . . . butcher's meat throughout the country is far inferior to what it will be when an increased amount of labor, and means of transport, shall encourage improvements in the pasturage and care of stock. While fowls, butter, and eggs, are still sent from Vermont into Boston, there is no such thing to be had there as a joint of tender meat. In one house in Boston, where a very numerous family lives in handsome style, and where I several times met large dinner parties, I never saw an ounce of meat, except ham. The table was covered with birds, in great variety, and well cooked; but all winged creatures. The only tender, juicy meat I saw in the country, was a sirloin of beef at Charleston, and the whole provision of a gentleman's table in Kentucky. At one place, there was nothing but veal on the table for a month; in a town where I staid ten days, nothing was to be had but beef; and throughout the South the traveller meets with little else than pork, under all manner of disguises, and fowls."

Miss Martineau, writing from Philadelphia, further remarks that,

"All the ladies of a country town, not very far off, were wearing gloves too bad to be mended, or none at all, because none had come up by the canal for many weeks.

"At Washington, I wanted some ribbon for my straw bonnet; and in the whole place, in the season, I could find only six pieces of ribbon to choose from. (She would find sixty shops to-day each filled with ribbon.)

"Throughout the entire country (out of the cities), I was struck with the discomforts of broken windows which appeared on every side. Large farm-houses, flourishing in every other respect, had dismal-looking windows. Persons who happen to live near a canal, or other quiet watery road, have baskets of glass of various sizes sent to them from the towns, and glaze their own windows. But there is no bringing glass over a corduroy, or mud, or rough limestone road; and those who have no other highways must get along with such windows as it may please the weather and the children to leave them."

Even so late as 1845 this isolation was the lot of all who lived at a distance from the coast. Sir Charles Lyell, visiting Milledgeville, Georgia, in that year, relates that the landlady of the hotel regarded Lady Lyell as quite a curiosity because she did not know how to make soap; and the good dame told her how the maids "make almost everything in the house, even to the caps I wear." And it appears from contemporary records that soap and candles were home-made for many years after, and home-spun cloth was largely worn by the people. In the rural districts of New England at present many houses still have in their garrets the old family spinning-wheel and loom.

William Cobbett, writing in 1823, of Long Island, says:

"There, and indeed all over the American States, north of Maryland, and especally in the New England States, almost the whole of both linen and woollen used in the country, and a large part of that used in towns is made in the farm houses. There are thousands and thousands of families who never use either, except of their own making. All but the weaving is done by the family. There is a loom in the house, and the weaver goes from house to house. I once saw about three thousand farmers, or rather country people, at a horse-race in Long Island, and my opinion was that there were not five hundred who were not dressed in homespun coats. As to linen, no farmer's family thinks of buying linen."

The discomforts of life to those in settled districts were few and slight compared with those experienced by settlers who went West. Of these a writer in *De Bow's Review*, in 1825, says:

"Their journey was made after long preparation, and was toilsome, slow, and expensive. They were compelled to bring their heavy tools and bulky implements of husbandry, their kitchen utensils and fragile furniture, by a difficult navigation and over heavy roads; several years were required to make a small clearing, rude improvements, and enough coarse food for domestic use."

And after all this effort the conditions of life often accorded with those indicated in the following laconic dialogue:

"Whose land was that you bought?"

"Moggs'."

"What's the soil?"

"Bogs."

"What's the climate?"

"Fogs."

"What do you get to eat?"

"Hogs."

"What do you build your house of?"

"Logs."

"Have you any neighbors?"

"Frogs."

Though this is a playful exaggeration, there were many settlers whose lot was scarcely more enviable than that of the man who lived amid the bogs he bought of Moggs. Far removed from all means of communication, the western pioneer was practically cut off from the world. No ubiquitous postal system enabled him to keep up communication with his friends "down East," or in the "old country." Newspapers rarely penetrated into the wild regions where he lived; and if he wished to visit his nearest neighbor he had to ride many miles across a rough and often hostile country. The traveller on the western rivers occasionally saw a solitary individual, perhaps a woman, paddling up stream in a canoe to visit a neighbor twenty or thirty miles off. Letters to the settlers were sent to the nearest town, perhaps a hundred miles away, where they lay for months until the person they were destined for, or some neighbor, could find time to go for them.

The rates of postage in those days were very high. A letter of one sheet was carried any distance not exceeding thirty miles for six cents; and this sum was doubled or trebled if the letter consisted of two or three sheets. For any distance exceeding four hundred miles the charge was twenty-five cents (one shilling) per sheet —a sum which then had double the purchasing power it has to-day.

Primitive simplicity prevailed in municipal arrangements where these existed. A notice copied from the walls of the bar-room of the village inn at Sandisfield, Massachusetts, in 1833, well illustrates this:

"All persons who have neglected to pay their taxes or bills committed to Josiah H. Sage, collector, are hereby notified that, in consequence of the sickness of the said collector, the bills are at my house, where those who are willing can have opportunity to pay their taxes if they improve it *soon;* and those who neglect may expect to pay a constable with fee for collecting."

Scavenging was done by pigs which were allowed to run at large through the streets. Sir Charles Lyell describes them as going about Cincinnati in large numbers, no person in particular claiming ownership of them. Even in New York these scavengers were long tolerated on the side-walks because of their supposed usefulness. It was no uncommon thing thirty-five years ago for pedestrians to be thrust into the road by the dirty snout of some city hog; a newly imported Irishman declared, on being so pushed into the gutter, that it was "a sthrange counthry were the pigs were all loose and the stones all tied."

The streets of towns were usually unlighted at night. New York, however, used in 1830 thirty-five thousand gallons of oil for two hundred and ninety-nine street lamps, "besides gas." In a description of Cincinnati in 1831 a writer in the *New England Magazine* says:

"Every citizen, who ventures abroad when the moon is absent, carries his own lantern or runs the risk of breaking his neck. It is a curious sight to see the lights hurrying in all directions, passing, repassing, and flitting to and fro, as if dancing at a masquerade of genii."

New York, in 1837, was destitute of a supply of good and wholesome water. There were numerous wells with pumps in all parts of the city; but the pump water was generally considered deleterious. Rain water was largely used by the citizens, most of the houses being provided with good cisterns. A contemporary writer says:

"Many parts of the city are now supplied with water for the table brought from the upper wards in casks. On the East and North Rivers, in some instances, it is pure, and in others its goodness is but little better than the present well water. The tables of the wealthy are supplied from this source, while the poorer classes have to resort to such wells and pumps as are in their neighborhood. It has been ascertained that there are now brought to the city by water-carts, six hundred hogsheads, for which there is paid one dollar and twenty-five cents for each hogshead (or about one cent per gallon) amounting to $750 per day, or $273,750 per annum, for water from that source."

It is not surprising that under such conditions New York, now one of the best-watered cities in the world, suffered several severe epidemics of cholera, which in 1832 "raged to a fearful extent, nearly depopulating it." The water supply of New York is equal to that of monster London; so that the New Yorker uses more than double the quantity of water used by the Londoner. The stupendous character of the works undertaken in America is shown by this water supply question of New York. A sub-way, averaging two hundred and fifty feet below the surface, large enough for a double-track railway, and more than thirty miles long, is now being constructed to increase the supply of the Empire City. Five miles are already done, and it is expected that the entire work will be finished in three years from the date of letting the contract. In a couple of years, therefore, the water supply of ?Iew York will be four hundred million gallons per diem, or four times that now consumed by London. The world has long heard of a projected channel tunnel between Dover and Calais. Here is a longer tunnel of equal size being quietly constructed, and scarcely anything said about it.

Other towns were as badly off in regard to water supply; a circumstance which acquires prominence when viewed in connection with the great fires which periodically destroyed large portions of the towns of the Union. Contributing to these frequent disasters was the imperfect apparatus at that date for extinguishing fires. So inoperative were the fire-engines, that in the report of a fire at New Orleans, in *Niles's Register* for May 8, 1830, it is related that though within one hundred yards of the Mississippi, little water was to be had. It was not until 1853 that the steam fire-engine was made a practical machine, and it was much later before it came into general use. Now, the equipment of the fire brigade of America is the most perfect in the world. Electric communication between all quarters of towns, and between many houses and numerous fire-stations exists everywhere; and a minute after a fire is reported by pressing an electric button, half a dozen steam fire-engines are speeding from different quarters towards the fire. In many towns the same pressure of an electric button, which is made to sound an alarm on gongs in a dozen different fire-stations, also starts machinery which releases the horses from their halters, allows the harness to fall on their backs, and raises the stable-gates.

In the early days, when men had an entire continent to bring into subjection, and when the work of doing this was doubly difficult through the imperfection of machinery, the business of life was work—work in its most Carlylean sense of intense, unrelaxed labor. Men had no time to waste in fashionable frivolity; and even the graver kinds of amusement were, except in the older cities of the East, little indulged in. Mrs. Trollope, a name long discordant to American ears, commented on this circumstance:

> "I never saw any people who appeared to live so much without amusement as the Cincinnatians. Billiards are forbidden by law, so are cards. To sell a pack of cards in Ohio subjects the seller to a penalty of $50. They have no public balls, excepting, I think, six during the Christmas holidays. They have no concerts. They have no dinner parties."

To this emphatic *"never,"* is probably required the Sullivan-Gilbert qualification "hardly ever." To say that the people of Cincinnati, fifty years ago, *never* went to balls, *never* attended concerts, *never* dined out, is obviously straining the literal truth. Still it is unquestionable that social recreations were few and far between in those days.

Although facts prove that the general standard of comfort was necessarily very much lower in the early part of the period we are considering than now, there yet prevailed a degree of general well-being unknown at the same time in Europe. Arfedson, a Swedish traveller, who visited the country in 1832–34, has thus placed on record his impressions:

"A European, travelling in this direction (New York State), cannot help admiring the general appearance of comfort and prosperity so singularly striking. To an inhabitant of the Scandinavian peninsula, accustomed to different scenes, it is peculiarly gratifying to witness, instead of gorgeous palaces by the side of poor huts, a row of neat country houses, inhabited by independent farmers."

A Swedish servant, lately arrived in America, at the date in question, on looking round and perceiving the happy state so generally diffused, exclaimed, with surprise and characteristic simplicity, "Sir, have the goodness to inform me where the peasantry live in this country?"

In works on America written about this period, we everywhere find expressions of surprise at the absence of beggars. Sir Charles Lyell, inquiring in his "First Visit" in 1840, "to what combination of causes the success of national education is to be attributed," and replying to his own query, makes a statement which is here relevant. He says:

"First there is no class in want or extreme poverty here, partly because the facility of migrating to the West, for those who are without employment, is so great, and also, in part, from the check to improvident marriages, created by the high standard of living to which the lowest people aspire, a standard which education is raising higher and higher from day to day."

As a further result of this universal prosperity, there was less crime than in the older countries, where life was difficult.

"The number of persons apprehended by the police of the city of London, in 1832, was seventy-two thousand eight hundred and twenty-four. The population of London being twenty times that of Boston, the same proportion would give for Boston, thirty-six hundred and forty-one, instead of the actual number, nineteen hundred and four."

But probably the greatest contrast of all was that between the low status of the factory operatives in England and the high status of the same class in America. In England, forty years ago, the factory hand was a mere machine—a drudge, ill-fed, ill-housed, addicted to low pleasures, with no hope on earth, and scant knowledge of heaven. In America the female operatives were usually farmers' daughters, who entered the factory to make a little money with which to set up housekeeping when they married. Their intellectual status is shown by the fact that at Lowell, Massachusetts, a magazine was published consisting entirely of articles and poems written by girls employed in the factories. By a judicious superintendence their morals were cared for, none being permitted to live in unauthorized lodging houses; and the result was that the girls of the Lowell factories were celebrated as much for their virtue as for their intellectual superiority. Unfortunately all this is changed. Immigrant operatives from Europe came in, and supplanted those of New England; and at the present time the condition of the American factory hand, though decidedly better than that of the European operatives, is said to be not nearly so high as it was forty years ago.

The glimpses we are thus able to obtain of this period of fifty-five years ago (1830) show us a people scattered for the most part along the Atlantic seaboard. A few aggregations of people at Boston, New York, Philadelphia, and Baltimore had made good their claim to rank as cities. The roads of America, still, with some exceptions, the worst perhaps in the civilized world, were then only dirt lanes, almost impassable during the rainy sea-

son, but excellent in summer and during the hard frosts
of winter. Stage-coaches ran between the cities at intervals which to us seem absurdly rare; and sailing packets,
propelled by steam, and on the canals express packets,
drawn by horses, divided the passenger traffic with the
stage-coaches. Enterprising pioneers had pushed westward beyond the Alleghanies into the Ohio valley, and
even as far as the plains of Illinois. The emigrant travelled in his own wagons to his new home in the then "far"
West. During the long and hazardous journey, his family lived the life of roaming gypsies.

The people's dress was of the cheapest and simplest
character. A rough casinet cloth was used for the best
dress of the men, and few women out of the principal
cities aspired to a silk gown. In 1830 cotton calico was
worn by most women, even of the well-to-do class. The
servant problem, to-day such a difficult one to the American housewife, was much easier of solution then; for, as
there were fewer foreign women available for domestic
service, native Americans had to be employed. These
were not called servants, but "help"; and it was the custom for them to sit at the family table, and in other ways
to be treated as equals and members of the family. Such
an arrangement was hardly an inconvenience where so
much simplicity of life prevailed. A repugnance then existed to all distinctions in dress. No coachman was ever
seen in livery, nor did servants dress in any prescribed
fashion. Concerning this trait Miss Martineau writes:

"One laughable peculiarity at the British Legation (at Washington) was the confusion of tongues among the servants, who
ask you to take fish, flesh, and fowl in Spanish, Italian, German,
Dutch, Irish, or French. The foreign ambassadors are terribly
plagued about servants. No American will wear livery, and there
is no reason why any American should. But the British ambassa-
dor must have livery servants. He makes what compromise he

can, allowing his people to appear without livery out of doors, except on state occasions; but he is obliged to pick up his domestics from among foreigners who are in want of a subsistence for a short time, and are sure to go away as soon as they can find employment in which the wearing a livery is not a requisite."

Such was the repugnance to livery that policemen dressed like ordinary citizens. Even New York City did not give its police a distinctive dress until 1845. Other cities followed later, until now it would be difficult to distinguish the police force in any American city from the metropolitan police of London. Coachmen's liveries are less gaudy in America than in Europe. We have not yet adopted powdered-haired coachmen and flunkeys with stuffed calves, nor brilliantly colored coaches.

I remember well that when the Pennsylvania Railroad Company decided that conductors and passenger-train men upon its lines should be distinguished from passengers by a uniform official dress, serious doubts were entertained whether the requirement would not lead to universal refusal to wear livery. In this case, as with the police force, the obvious advantage of the men in authority being known at once by their uniform was finally recognized by the employees.

It is a sentiment well worth humoring, however,—this dislike to distinctive badges, except when clearly useful. Unless so, let republican citizens be independent and differ even in dress.

There was scarcely a private carriage in Western cities in those days. People rode on horseback or in rude wagons, or, at best, in one-horse chaises. An old lady, living not long since, and one whom I knew well and honored, kept the first carriage in Pittsburgh; and the lady who first had a coachman in livery (he was a colored man fond of display) died only recently. If the dress, conveniences, and homes of the people were of the simplest character, so was the food. It was, however, very cheap. Eggs were three half-pence a dozen, and a leg of lamb cost only a shilling. Foreign wine was so rare and costly as to be almost unknown. The importations of wine in 1831 amounted to only a million and a half dollars. Barter was a common mode of payment. Workmen, even in cities, received orders upon a store for their labor. Wages were generally low. Laborers received sixty-two cents (three shillings) per day, and two dollars (eight shillings) per day was long considered remarkably high wages, and was given only to very skilful workmen. Salaries were even lower in proportion. The late President of the great Pennsylvania Railway received only $1,500 (£300) per annum as late as 1855, when he was superintendent of the western division of the line. I was overwhelmed when, as his successor, I received £50 more per annum. Notwithstanding low wages, the regularity of work and the simplicity of life enabled the people to save considerable sums every year.

Such as there was of fashion was in the direction of the plainest living, and in opposition to ostentation in residence, furniture, dress, food, or equipage. It was republican to be plain, simple, unaffected, and of the people. Kid gloves, dress coats, and silk dresses were hardly known west of the Alleghanies. There were no millionaires in those days. Men with fifty or a hundred thousand dollars (£10,000 to £20,000) were spoken of throughout the country as the millionaire is now. Indeed, there are probably more millionaires in New York City to-day than there were men in the whole country in 1830 who were worth a hundred thousand dollars. The first pianoforte manufactory was founded in 1822, but was so insignificant that in 1853 it turned out only fifteen pianos a week. Few carriages were made till 1840. Works of art were rarely seen. The first picture gallery of any consequence was that of the Pennsylvania Academy, Philadelphia, opened in 1811. Other cities remained till a recent date without important art collections. Libraries existed in colleges and in the public buildings of the State capitol, but few collections of books were accessible to the people. Previous to 1830 only three or four cities had such libraries, and these were unimportant.

In those days every village and country district had its universal genius who could turn his hand to anything, from drawing a tooth to mending a clock. The doctor of divinity had usually the functions of doctor of medicine as well. The doctor of the body had no brother doctor of the soul; he was both himself. The lawyer was attorney, counsellor, real estate agent, banker, and barrister in one. With increasing population, handicrafts and professions have become specialized; and communities, however small, are now generally well supplied with men trained to their special vocations, to which they confine themselves.

A community of toilers with an undeveloped continent before them, and destitute of the refinements and elegancies of life,—such was the picture presented by the Republic fifty years ago. Contrasted with that of to-day we might almost conclude that we were upon another planet and subject to different primary conditions. If the roads throughout the country are yet poor compared with those of Europe, the need of good roads has been rendered less imperative by the omnipresent railroad. It is the superiority of the iron highway in America which has diverted attention from the country roads. Macaulay's test of the civilization of a people by the condition of their roads must be interpreted, in this age of steam, to include railroads. Communication between places is now cheaper and more comfortable than in any other country.

Upon the principal railway lines the cars—luxurious
drawing-rooms by day, and sleeping chambers by night
—are ventilated by air, warmed and filtered in winter,
and cooled in summer. Passenger steamers upon the lakes
and rivers are of gigantic size, and models of elegance.
The variety and quality of the food of the people of
America excels that found elsewhere, and is a constant
surprise to Europeans visiting the States. The dress of
the people is now of the richest character—far beyond
that of any other people, compared class for class. The
comforts of the average American home compare favorably with those of other lands, while the residences of
the wealthy classes are not equalled anywhere. The first-
class American residence of to-day in all its appointments
excites the envy of the foreigner. One touch of the electric button calls a messenger; two touches bring a telegraph boy; three summon a policeman; four give the
alarm of fire. Telephones are used to an extent hardly
dreamed of in Europe, the stables, gardeners' houses,
and other outbuildings being connected with the mansion; and the houses of friends are joined by the talking
wire almost as often as houses of business. Speaking
tubes connect the drawing-room with the kitchen; and
the dinner is brought up "piping hot" by an elevator.
Hot air and steam pipes are carried all over the house;
and by the turning of a tap the temperature of any room
is regulated to suit the convenience of the occupant. The
electric light is coming into use throughout the country
as an additional home comfort. Indeed there is no palace
or great mansion in Europe with half the conveniences
and scientific appliances which characterize the best
American mansions. New York Central Park is no unworthy rival of Hyde Park and the Bois de Boulogne in
its display of fine equipages; and in winter the hundreds
of graceful sleighs dashing along the drives form a pic-

ture prettier than anything London can boast. The opera houses, theatres, and public halls of the country excel in magnificence those of other lands, if we except the later constructions in Paris and Vienna, with which the New York and Philadelphia opera houses rank. The commercial exchanges, and the imposing structures of the life insurance companies, newspaper buildings, hotels, and many edifices built by wealthy firms, not only in New York but in the cities of the West, never fail to excite the European's surprise. The postal system is equal in every respect to that of Europe. Mails are taken up by express trains, sorted on board, and dropped at all important points without stopping. Letters are delivered several times a day in every considerable town. The uniform rates of postage for all distances, often exceeding three thousand miles, is only two cents (one penny) per ounce.

In short, the conditions of life in American cities may be said to have approximated those of Britain during the fifty years of which we are speaking. Year by year, as the population advances, the general standard of comfort in the smaller Western cities rises to that of the East. Herbert Spencer was astonished beyond measure at what he saw in American cities. "Such books as I had looked into," said he, "had given me no adequate idea of the immense developments of material civilization which I have everywhere found. The extent, wealth, and magnificence of your cities, and especially the splendor of New York, have altogether astonished me. Though I have not visited the wonder of the West, Chicago, yet some of your minor modern places, such as Cleveland, have sufficiently amazed me, by the marvellous results of one generation's activity. Occasionally, when I have been in places of some ten thousand inhabitants, where the telephone is in general use, I have felt somewhat ashamed of our own unenterprising towns; many of which, of fifty thousand inhabitants and more, make no use of it."

There is little difference between the municipal institutions of the new and the old lands, but no contrast can be greater than that between their country districts. The unfortunate people of monarchies have reason to envy the American in many respects, but in none more keenly than for the perfection of his local township and county organizations. If my American readers were generally informed of the chaos prevailing throughout the country districts of England, they would be at a loss to understand how a people who speak the English tongue could have tolerated it so long. The Church has a certain share in local matters, especially as regards education; and the clergymen, vicars, rectors, and curates are found upon the select boards which manage all local affairs. Then the "lords of the manors," the owners of lands, have also a share. The squire and the parson are really the powers which attend to everything, and manage all to their own liking. The palace of my lord duke is assessed to pay taxes less in amount than the moderate-sized villa of the new man, who is not in the ruling coterie. Every little country district has its "ring." For in place of one "ring" in the Republic there are twenty in the Monarchy. The offices are naturally distributed to the favorites of the landlords and the parsons. The people of the district have no voice whatever in the matter, since they are excluded from voting for county officials; only those who are possessed of a certain amount of property, or who reside in large houses and pay large rents, and who are consequently of the ruling classes, are permitted to vote. The majority of the people, therefore, have no interest in the community as a community. There is no soil for the growth of local patriotism.

In the British towns, however, a pleasing contrast to

this sad picture is presented. In these manhood suffrage prevails and, in many if not all cases, women possessed of property are also entitled to vote. The result is a degree of attention to municipal affairs upon the part of the best citizens of the towns which is rarely found even in America beyond the borders of the old settled States, if at all. The proceedings of the town council, including the speeches of every member, are regularly published at length in the local newspapers. Sometimes as much as four columns are occupied by the report of this local parliament, and no reading is so much enjoyed, or excites a deeper interest in the community. It is true, one outside of the boundaries smiles to read of really able men, the local manufacturers and merchants of the place, disputing upon the correctness of a charge of five pounds six and eight pence for repairing the town-house clock, or an increase of ten pounds in the salary of the town clerk; but the Imperial Parliament itself is not seldom engaged upon trifling matters, and it is this attention to details which insures a proper disposition of the public funds, and an excellent government of the municipality.

The magistrates and town councillors are held in the highest honor, and one hears in Britain of Provost Matthieson or Provost Donald, premiership and local improvements being characterized as during this or that "administration." The resident of the town hears the names of prominent public men, but these are mere abstractions to him, and furnish no material basis for admiration; but when the provost passes he sees in him concentrated glory, the pride of power, the "real presence" as it were.

From the town councils the nation is drawing some of its foremost leaders. Mr. Chamberlain and Alderman Kenrick began their education in that of Birmingham; Mr. Storey his in that of Sunderland, and the late

George Harrison his in Edinburgh. My experience of the town community in Britain gives me the highest possible estimate of the power of the masses to produce beneficial changes through the selection of men best qualified for the work.

The time has not yet arrived for as complete and effective municipal institutions throughout the Republic as those of Britain, but we see in the more settled parts that we are arriving at similar results. While, therefore, the municipalities of the old land are not excelled by any in the new, and are upon the average better, the country districts of Britain have institutions which are a disgrace to a people. The stolid ignorance of the masses, their seeming contentedness with a life befitting the swineherds of early Saxon times, their dependence upon what they call their "betters," and the sycophantic vices which aristocratic rule ever produces in the poor, are positively sickening to the American, who naturally contrasts the situation with that at home, and especially contrasts the men and women produced by the two systems.

"You see then," says the narrow, uninformed Tory squire, as he shows his American visitor the condition of the masses around him; "you see how utterly unfit these people are for what you call self-government and the equality of the citizen. Bless you! if we didn't look after them they couldn't live." He does not often hear the proper reply, but I flatter myself he does sometimes. "Give these people all the rights and privileges you possess in this district, and before you die, unless you drop off suddenly, the result will surprise you. Never can they be transformed from practical serfdom except by imposing upon them the duties of citizens, and then educating them to the proper performance of those duties. You are just like the foolish mother who would not permit her boy to go near the water till he had learned to swim. Throw him in. Be at his side to see that he does not quite drown, but be careful not to assist too much. Don't bolster him up until he is exhausted and ready to sink." This same Tory squire will descant at dinner upon the mission his country holds for the improvement of inferior races throughout the world, wholly oblivious to the fact that it would be difficult to find among any subject race in any part of the world a more ignorant, debased, and poverty-stricken community than that which the autocratic system of his class has produced within a few miles of his own gate. No man can see so clearly the mote in his brother's eye and be so blind to the beam in his own as the country magnate of England. He feels, at least he professes to feel, for every people but his own.

A short description of the republican country organizations will probably be interesting to the British people, and even to the American who is too apt to enjoy his blessings without paying much attention to their sources. The subdivisions of States into counties, and of counties into townships for purposes of local self-government, have not been made upon a uniform plan; the earlier States present many points of difference in these divisions, but the newer States of the West and Northwest, which combine much the greater area of the country, may be said to follow the same general mode. It is that alone which I think worth while to describe, since it is the recent and distinctively American practice.

Iowa is one of the most creditable communities in the Union, and I shall give a glimpse into her local governments. The genesis of these home parliaments is very simple. First comes a settler, axe in hand, who erects a log cabin, clears the ground, and plants whatever seeds he may be blessed with. Then comes another and another who do the same upon adjoining land until a dozen or

more families are near together. Two wants are now felt
—roads or paths between these houses, and from the
hamlet to the nearest market town or railway station,
and a school for the children. There is no central
authority to provide these, and finally the hardy settlers
resolve to have a meeting and talk matters over. They
vote to tax themselves and construct them. Somebody
must be designated to assess the tax, somebody to collect
it, some one to supervise the work, and some one to keep
the accounts, etc. Here are the beginnings of the tax as-
sessor, collector, county supervisor, and town clerk, and
after a while to these are added the constable and the
justice of the peace.

Many a township record begins like that of Burlington in Calhoun County, Michigan.

"Organized in 1837, and held its first township meeting April 3
of that year, electing Justus Goodwin, supervisor; O. C. Freeman, town clerk; Justus Goodwin, Gibesia Sanders, and Moses S.
Gleason, justices of the peace; Leon Haughtailing, constable and
collector; established six road districts; voted $100 to build a
bridge across the St. Joseph River, and $50 for bridging Nottawa
Creek; voted $50 for common schools, and $5 bounty for wolf
scalps."

Ah, that $50 for common schools! That was the vote
of votes, gentlemen. Just see, wherever we peer into the
first tiny springs of the national life, how this true pana-
cea for all the ills of the body politic bubbles forth—
education, education, education. Through all the history
of the land runs this care for the golden thread of knowledge, upon which to string the blessings and achievements
of an educated, triumphant Democracy.

And will you note also that no mention is made of
the "birth" or "rank" of these village Hampdens. It
may safely be inferred that neither was thought of in

that democratic meeting. The fittest and best man was what the occasion demanded, and no doubt wise choice was made upon the only sensible basis:

"The tools to those who can best use them."

The township is, as a rule, six miles square, as all the territories are divided into such areas by the government surveyors. As population increases, twelve to fifteen townships band together and form the greater political division, the county, the larger Home Rule circle.

The county officials are usually elected for terms of two years, although in many States annual elections are held. Suffrage is invariably universal, and electoral districts equal. All officials are paid, but their salaries are extremely moderate. The county town is selected, of course, in democratic fashion by a fair vote. By vote of the people are elected at short intervals not only all county political officials, including the sheriffs and other magistrates having authority, and the county superintendent of education, the road supervisors, and guardians of the poor, but the judges themselves, and why not? Who are so deeply interested in the able and pure administration of justice as the masses of the people, the poorer classes of the people who may be trusted to elect the men least likely to lean unduly to the side of the rich, the powerful, and the strong? If judges must have leanings, and being but human, they must be influenced, even unconsciously, by their environments, by all means let their failings lean to virtue's side, which is with very rare exceptions the side of the poor and the weak.

Many counties at last form the third and largest circle of Home Rule, the State, which in turn with other States constitute the Federal system of the Republic. Thus there are centres within centres of Home Rule, and the experience gained of their healthfulness in matters political is such as to bring about the general rule that the central authority shall do nothing which the State can do for itself, the State nothing which the county can do for itself, and the county nothing for the township which it can do for itself. As sure as the sun shines, in proportion as government recedes from the people immediately interested, it becomes liable to abuse. Whatever authority can be conveniently exercised in primary assemblies should, therefore, be placed there, for there it is certain to produce satisfactory results.

Jefferson was indeed a far-seeing statesman, and he says:

"These wards, called townships in New England, are the vital principle of their governments; and have proved themselves the wisest inventions ever devised by the wit of man for the perfect exercise of self-government and for its preservation."

The American believes in Home Rule down to the smallest divisions, and has shown an admirable dislike of centralization. He will not call upon any authority to help him as long as he can help himself. Divide society into as many and as small divisions as you please, the smallest still remains a complete epitome—a microcosm of the whole. The council of a city is a perfect miniature of the Imperial Assembly. The observer recognizes its pocket editions of Cleveland, Gladstone, Blaine, and Salisbury; in the life of the city there stand the local Beecher and the local Spurgeon, the Spencer, Fiske, Huxley, Marsh, the Drs. Flint, Dennis, Mackenzie, the Black and the Howells. Yes, it has even its Arnold, Holmes, Lowell, Browning, and Whitman—all in miniature, no doubt, as befits the small stage upon which these tiny actors perform. Men and women divide into a few classes, and in every village these classes exist, and the smaller the body the more clearly defined the line be-

tween them in society. Oh, yes, there is even society in
these villages, and leaders of fashion too—all the absurd
things as well as the good things are present, not one
missing; for as each grain composing the block of marble has within itself all that makes marble marble, so
each gathering of men and women, no matter how small,
has all that makes empires empires. Statesmen have but
to allow free play to these forces to produce harmonious
action. The American always does this in town and country. The Briton has pursued a different course, except
recently in the towns, and the effect of exclusion from
the management of their local affairs upon the character of the masses throughout the country districts has
been deplorable. They are not yet men, they are in spirit
only serfs. But as the right to vote for members of Parliament was granted them last year, and they have just
voted *en masse* against the ruling class, the tide has begun to turn at last, and there must soon arise among them
an irresistible movement for Home Rule within their
own small divisions.

The truest account I have found of the condition of
the masses of the American people who live in the villages and small towns, as distinguished from the large
cities and from the country, is that concerning New England in Professor Fiske's excellent little book, "American
Political Ideas." I give my readers this description, and
certify of my own knowledge to its entire truthfulness:

"As a rule, the head of each family owns the house in which
he lives, and the ground on which it is built. The relation of
landlord and tenant, though not unknown, is not commonly met
with. No sort of social distinction or political privilege is associated with the ownership of land, and the legal differences between
real and personal property, especially as regards ease of transfer,
have been reduced to the smallest minimum that practical convenience will allow. Each householder, therefore, though an absolute

proprietor, cannot be called a miniature lord of the manor, because there exists no permanent dependent class such as is implied
in the use of such a phrase. Each larger proprietor attends in
person to the cultivation of his own land, assisted perhaps by his
own sons, or by neighbors working for hire in the leisure left over
from the care of their own smaller estates. So, in the interior of
the house, there is usually no domestic service that is not performed by the mother of the family and the daughters. Yet, in
spite of this universality of manual labor, the people are as far as
possible from presenting the appearance of peasants. Poor or
shabbily-dressed people are rarely seen, and there is no one in the
village whom it would be proper to address in a patronizing tone,
or who would not consider it a gross insult to be offered a shilling.
As with poverty, so with dram-drinking and with crime; all alike
are conspicuous by their absence. In a village of one thousand
inhabitants there will be a poor-house, where five or six decrepit
old people are supported at the common charge; and there will be
one tavern, where it is not easy to find anything stronger to drink
than light beer or cider. The danger from thieves is so slight that
it is not always thought necessary to fasten the outer doors of the
house at night. The universality of literary culture is as remarkable as the freedom with which all persons engage in manual
labor. The village of a thousand inhabitants will be very likely to
have a public circulating library, in which you may find Professor
Huxley's *Lay Sermons,* or Sir Henry Maine's *Ancient Law;* it
will surely have a high-school, and half a dozen other schools for
small children. A person unable to read and write is as great a
rarity as an albino, or a person with six fingers. The farmer who
threshes his own corn and cuts his own firewood has very likely a
piano in his family sitting-room, with the *Atlantic Monthly* on the
table, and Milton and Tennyson, Gibbon and Macaulay, on his
shelves, while his daughter, who has baked bread in the morning,
is, perhaps, ready to paint on china in the afternoon. In former
times theological questions largely occupied the attention of the
people; and there is probably no part of the world where the
Bible has been more attentively read, or where the mysteries of
Christian doctrine have, to so great an extent, been made the subject of earnest discussion in every household. Hence, we find in

the New England of to-day a deep religious sense, combined with singular flexibility of mind and freedom of thought."

Such is the Democracy; such its conditions of life. In the presence of such a picture can it be maintained that the rule of the people is subversive of government and religion? Where have monarchical institutions developed a community so delightful in itself, so intelligent, so free from crime or pauperism—a community in which the greatest good of the greatest number is so fully attained, and one so well calculated to foster the growth of self-respecting men—which is the end civilization seeks?

>"For ere man made us citizens
>God made us men."

The republican is necessarily self-respecting for the laws of his country, in full accord with the laws of God, begin by making him a man indeed, the equal of other men; and believe me, my readers, the man who most respects himself will be found the man who most respects the rights and feelings of others.

The rural Democracy of America could be as soon induced to sanction the confiscation of the property of their richer neighbors, or to vote for any violent or discreditable measure, as it could be led to surrender the President for a king. Free institutions develop all the best and noblest characteristics, and these always lead in the direction of the golden rule. These honest, pure, contented, industrious, patriotic people really do consider what they would have others do to them. They ask themselves what is fair? Nor is there in Britain so conservative a body of men; but then it is the equality of the citizen—just and equal laws—republicanism, they are resolved to conserve. To conserve these they are at all times ready to fight and, if need be, to die; for, to men who have once tasted of the elixir of political equality, life under unequal conditions could possess no charm.

To every man is committed in some degree, as a sacred trust, the manhood of man. This he may not himself infringe or permit to be infringed by others. Hereditary dignities, political inequalities, do infringe the rights of man and hence are not to be tolerated. The true democrat must live the peer of his fellows, or die struggling to become so.

It only remains for those still held in the toils of feudalism in the parent land to vindicate their right to rise to the full stature of equal citizenship, since by the greater part of the English speaking race this position has been already acquired through the Triumphant Democracy.

Chapter V
OCCUPATIONS

"All nations have their message from on high,
Each the Messiah of some central thought
For the fulfilment and delight of Man:
One has to teach that labor is divine."—LOWELL.

SUCH is the mission of the Republic, for there are few drones in the republican hive, and these are not honored. If a man would eat he must work. A life of elegant leisure is the life of an unworthy citizen. The Republic does not owe him a living, it is he who owes the Republic a life of usefulness. Such is the republican idea.

During the colonial period the industries of America were cramped and repressed by the illiberal policy of the imperial government. The occupations of the people were necessarily confined to those connected with the cultivation of the soil. The varied pursuits which now distinguish the Republic were unknown. "The colonies have no right to manufacture even so much as a horse-shoe nail," was the dictum of a leading English statesman; and in accordance with this doctrine, the early settlers were hampered by restrictions which, but for their injurious effect on American industries, would appear ludicrous to us of modern times. The manufacture of hats was forbidden; the making of paper gave offence; and even the weaving of homespun cloth for domestic use was regarded as indicating a rebellious spirit. Iron could not be manufactured beyond the condition of pig; and none but British vessels were permitted to trade with the colonies.

But do not let us reflect upon our mother-land for this. Even in pursuing this policy she was not behind her day. What were colonies for unless to be of direct advantage to the country which created and fostered them? Why should Britain undertake new outlets for her people and her commerce, if her children were to prove ungrateful and defeat the only end the parent-land had in view in nursing them into life? Such was the accepted view of the time in regard to colonial possessions. It is to the credit of Britain that she now sees how futile is the attempt to extend commerce through colonization, or to interfere with the internal affairs of her children. She permits them to foster what they please, to trade freely with all nations upon any terms the colonies fix for her own trade with them. True it must be said that her offspring are not very grateful children; they turn against their mother with surprising harshness. When desired financial aid requires it, our Canadian friends flatter the dear old lady into opening her purse-strings, to give the spoiled child what she begs. Canada is very dutiful upon such occasions, but she taxes her mother's products all the same to foster manufactures upon her own soil.

The Republic boldly puts on a tariff and announces that she means to have within herself the manufacturing facilities which distinguish her parent, and to beat her in manufacturing if possible; and she has become the greatest manufacturing nation the world has ever known. I like this boldness; having set up for herself and being a free and independent State, the Republic has a right to do as she pleases. Canada's hypocritical and ungrateful conduct merits and inspires only contempt. She has no business to tax her good mother's manufactures to pro-

tect her own, but if she does it, she should at least cease
her loyal whine and announce in honest fashion that she
intends to assume the responsibilities of national existence and no longer to rely upon her mother's assistance.

But why talk of Canada, or of any mere colony? What
book, what invention, what statue or picture, what anything has a colony ever produced, or what man has
grown up in any colony who has become known beyond
his own local district? None. Nor can a colony ever give
to mankind anything of value beyond wood, corn, and
beef. If Canada and the Australian colonies were free
and independent republics, the world would soon see the
harvest of democracy in noble works, and in great minds,
and for the mother of these nations the result would be
infinitely better even as to trade. Besides she would be
far prouder of her progeny, which in itself is not a bad
return for a fond mother like her.

If Lord Rosebery were to succeed in his amusing Imperial Federation fad (which, happily, is impossible),
these nations in embryo would be stifled in their cradles.
Imagine the great democratic continent of Australia
really subject to the little island, and to the funny monarchy and its antiquated forms. I have heard of the tail
which wagged the dog, but it must have been a very big
tail and a very small dog. Britain will form a very
diminutive tail to the Australia of the next generation.
No; the English-speaking continents of America and
Australia and the parent, Britain, will be separate political communities, but one day linked together in a league
of peace, one provision of which will be that all international disputes shall be settled by it.

With the independence of the Republic came the natural reaction of the suppression of occupations just spoken
of. The reaction has not quite spent its force even to this
day, so hard is it to eradicate national bitterness which

springs from oppression. With surprising energy the people began to turn their condition of colonial dependence into a condition of national independence, industrial as well as political. The long European wars which followed fostered the embryo industries of the Republic by hindering the importation of European manufactures, a result further assisted by a tariff; and, though disaster followed this system of over-stimulation, the eventual condition reached was eminently satisfactory. By the year 1830 many industries were firmly established, and since that period their development has proceeded with a regularity which even the terrible Civil War was unable to check.

The occupations of the people of half a century ago appear strangely primitive when contrasted with those of present times. Indeed, the difference is more like that of five centuries than of five decades. Take as an example the shoe manufacture at Lynn, Massachusetts. Fifty years ago a visitor to this village would have heard the beat, beat, beat of many hammers issuing from small wooden sheds erected against the sides of the houses. These were the sounds of the disciples of St. Crispin working away, with last upon knee, and making perhaps one pair of shoes per day. During the summer the same men became farmers or fishermen, and the village ceased to resound with the shoemakers' hammers. The present city of Lynn, with forty-five thousand inhabitants, has numerous fine buildings of great height and length, which are the lineal descendants of the little wooden sheds of fifty years ago. In these, boots and shoes are made by the million, and with hardly any handling by the sons of St. Crispin. Machines now do all the cutting, the hammering, and the sewing. Massachusetts is the shoe State *par excellence*. In 1835, according to Mulhall, there were in the State thirty thousand more bootmakers than in 1880, yet in the latter year the factories produced boots worth $70,000,000 (£14,000,000) more than they did in 1835.

Changes equally great took place in the nature of work in textile industries. In 1830, woollen, linen, and cotton manufactures were largely conducted in the household. In Hinton's "Topography of the United States" we read that "many thousands of families spin, and make up their own clothing, sheets, table-linen, etc. They purchase cotton yarn, and have it frequently mixed with their linen and woollen; blankets, quilts, or coverlets, in short, nearly all articles of domestic use, are chiefly made in the family. It is supposed that two-thirds of all the clothing, linen, blankets, etc., of those inhabitants who reside in the interior of the country are of household manufacture. It is the same in the interior with both soap and candles." But many forces were at work revolutionizing the industrial methods of the day. The steam-engine was gradually replacing the water-wheel, or supplementing it when winter bound fast the rivers, thereby insuring to employees regularity of work in factories, and releasing manufacturers from the incubus of idle capital during half the year. Then railroads and canals were rapidly increasing the facilities for distributing the products of manufacturing centres. Further great improvements in machinery placed manual labor more and more at a discount. Thus, in 1834, a spindle would spin on an average from one-sixth to one-third more than it did a few years previous. Indeed, it was said in 1834, "that a person could spin more than double the weight of yarn in a given time than he could in 1829." And so there resulted a complete change in the manner of life of the people. Instead of working with the old-fashioned spinning-wheel in country farm-houses, or the hand-loom in the rural cottage, spinners and weavers gathered together in large towns. And here we have one cause of the great growth of towns as compared with the country, which has been referred to in a previous chapter.

A large proportion of the people fifty years ago were engaged in agriculture, another pursuit in which mechanical appliances have since worked a complete revolution. The transformation is shown with startling vividness by two extracts:

"Among new inventions to increase the pauperism of England, we observe a portable steam threshing machine."—*New York Evening Star,* August, 1834.

"Dr. Glin, of California, has forty-five thousand acres under wheat. On this farm is used an improved kind of machinery; each machine can cut, thresh, winnow, and bag sixty acres of wheat in a day."—*Mulhall's Progress of the World,* p. 499 (date, 1880).

In view of such a contrast we hardly need the assurance of Mr. H. Murray, who, writing in 1834, says: "Agriculture is in its infancy in the United States." The statement which follows is also interesting: "The country," he adds, "is covered with dense dark woods. Even the State of New York is still three-fourths forest." Since that period the expansion of agriculture has been phenomenal. The farms of America equal the entire territory of the United Kingdom, France, Belgium, Germany, Austria, Hungary, and Portugal. The corn fields equal the extent of England, Scotland, and Belgium; while the grain fields generally would overlap Spain. The cotton fields cover an area larger than Holland, and twice as large as Belgium. The rice fields, sugar, and tobacco plantations would also form kingdoms of no insignificant size. And such is the stage of advancement reached by American agriculturists, that Mulhall estimates that one farmer like Dr. Glin or Mr. Dalrymple, with a field of wheat covering a hundred square miles, can raise as much grain with four hundred farm servants as five thousand peasant proprietors in France.

Notwithstanding this, it is pleasing to know that not even with the advantage here implied are these gigantic farms able to maintain the struggle against the smaller farms owned and cultivated by families.

The Republic to-day is, as it ever was, a nation of workers. The idlers are few—much fewer than in any other great nation. A continent lies before the American, awaiting development. The rewards of labor are high; and prizes are to be won in every pursuit. The family which strikes out boldly for the West, settles upon the soil and expends its labor upon it, may confidently look forward to reach independent circumstances long before old age. The mechanic with skill and energy rises first to foremanship and ultimately to a partnership or business of his own. As the country fills, these prizes naturally become more and more difficult to secure; but the very knowledge of this acts as an additional incentive, and impels men to "make hay while the sun shines."

The American works much harder than the Briton. His application is greater; his hours are longer; his holidays fewer. Until recently, a leisure class has scarcely been known; and even now a man who is not engaged in some useful occupation lacks one claim to the respect of his fellows. The American must do something, even if disposed to be idle; he is forced to join the army of toilers from sheer impossibility to find suitable companions for idle hours. One conversant with the mother and child lands is particularly struck with the difference between Britons and Americans in this regard. If a party of educated and agreeable gentlemen are wanted to join in a pleasure excursion, twenty are available in Britain to one in this high-pressure America. The American has always so much to do. Even when the family leaves home in the summer, the man returns to town every few days to hammer away at something. The English gentleman, on the contrary, seems always to have a few days he can call his own for pleasure. Ladies are equally available upon both sides of the ferry. The American woman seems to have quite as much leisure as her English sister. I must not fail to note, however, the signs of change which begin to appear. A small number of the best men of this generation, especially in the Eastern cities, having inherited fortunes, now devote themselves to public cares, not necessarily political, as a Briton would infer, and discard the lower ambition of adding more to that which is enough. The roughest and most pressing work, that of clearing and settling the land, has been done to a great extent; and the influences of refinement and elevation are now patent everywhere. It is thus that a free society evolves that which is fitted for its highest ends.

The census of 1880 shows that the number of persons pursuing gainful and reputable occupations was over seventeen and a quarter millions, or thirty-four and one-half per cent. of the total population. This proportion is greater than that shown by the census of 1870. Each census is no doubt taken in a more thorough manner than the preceding one—the last being the most complete enumeration ever made of any people. But even allowing for this, it is evident that owing to the extensions of the factory system, the increased division of labor, and especially to the greater number of occupations open to women, a larger proportion of Americans are now at work than ever before.

The increased employment of women is very marked. In 1880 the ratio had increased to eleven hundred and ninety as against one thousand in 1870, nearly twelve per cent., while that of men increased only from one thousand to ten hundred and sixty-seven, less than seven per cent. It is clear that the American woman is steadily conquering her right to share with man many occupations from which she has been excluded. But her advance is, I fear, in no less degree indicative of a growing necessity to swell the earnings of the family.

Lowthian Bell, when in America, remarked that he had heard always of great inventions made in manufacturing by the Americans, and of their wonderful aptitude in this department of industry; but he found after all that Britons had done a large part of this work. This is corroborated by the horse-shoe machines of Mr. Burden, a sturdy Scot; Mr. Thomas, a Welshman, who first smelted pig-iron with anthracite coal; Mr. Chisholm, of Dunfermline, Scotland, who has created the extensive steel rail and steel wire mills at Cleveland; Isaac Stead, an enterprising Englishman, who first wove tapestry in Philadelphia; Mr. Wallace, founder of the famous brass mill at Ansonia, and many others. It is, indeed, quite interesting to note how great a proportion of the manufacturing of America is controlled by the foreign-born British. Forty-nine per cent. of all Scotch and English in the United States are engaged in manufactures—a ratio much higher than that shown by any other nationality. Immigrants from British America are also largely occupied in manufacture, the ratio being forty-four per cent. Native Americans are mostly engaged in agriculture, and contribute but nineteen per cent. of their number to manufactures. Forty-three per cent. of the Irish-born are engaged in personal and professional services. So it can still be claimed that Britons do the manufacturing of the world, and we must credit to our race, not only the hitherto unequalled sum of products of our native land, but to a large extent the still greater sum of the Republic's. Only nineteen of every hundred Americans engage in manufacturing occupations against forty-nine

per cent. of these tough Islanders—just three times as
many in proportion to numbers—a ratio which is probably substantially maintained in their progeny. We must
not let the Yankee claim all the credit for the manufacturing supremacy of his country. What would it have
been but for the original stock? Democracy is entitled
to all, for there is not in all the land one who is not a
democrat. But, as between the native and imported
democrat, the strain of British blood, never excelled if
yet equalled, must be credited with more than its due
share. See, my countrymen, of what your race is capable
when relieved from unjust laws and made the peers of
any, under republican institutions. Man is a thing of the
spirit; the Westerner who weighed two hundred pounds
when drowsy, and more than a ton when he was roused,
is exactly like the man born under a king, and denied
equality at birth, compared with himself when he is
invested under the Republic with the mantle of sover-
eignty. The drowsy Briton becomes a force here.

The earnings of the people compare as follows with
those of England, where labor is better paid than elsewhere in Europe:

AVERAGE IN COTTON MILLS		AVERAGE IN WOOLLEN MILLS	
	s. d.		s. d.
In England	19 7 per week.	In England	26 7 per week.
In America	24 1 " "	In America	43 3 " "

ARTISAN AVERAGE

	s. d.
In England	31 0 per week.
In America, New York . .	54 6 " "
In " Chicago . . .	50 6 " "

The average per annum of operatives of all kinds is £35 6s. 1d.
in England against £73 in the United States.

Messrs. Clark & Co. and Coates & Co., the extensive thread manufacturers of Paisley, Scotland, who have similar mills on this side, have stated in evidence that the wages paid in their American mills are fully double those paid in Paisley. In all branches of the iron and steel manufacture wages here are fully double what they are in Britain.

The cost of living has been much greater in the Republic, not that the workingman cannot live here as cheaply as in Britain, but that he will not do so. Large earnings and certainty of steady employment lead to increased wants and to their gratification. The workers demand better houses and furniture, better food, better clothing, more books and newspapers, and spend their larger earnings to secure these. There are one hundred and seventy-five thousand pianos, organs and harmoniums annually made in America, and three-fourths of these remain in the country. Nothing is more suggestive than a fact like this, showing as it does that thousands purchase these instruments, which those in similar positions in other countries would never dream of possessing.

The relative cost of living in Britain and America has been subjected to a great change during the past few years in favor of the latter. It is astonishing how cheap the food and clothing of the masses have become. The food of course never was as high as in Britain, for most of it goes from this side. It was in clothing that the American was at a disadvantage. Articles of similar kind are now asserted to be quite as cheap throughout America as in Britain. House rent has fallen very much indeed.

The best authority we have is Mr. Jos. D. Weeks, Secretary of the Western Iron Association, an Englishman by descent, who spent much time upon the other side investigating this important subject. I give his letter to me:

"Pittsburgh, Pa., December 16, 1885.
"My dear Mr. Carnegie:

"Absence from the city has prevented an earlier reply to yours regarding relative cost of living in the United States and Great Britain.

"The purchasing power of a dollar in the hands of an American workman is considerably in excess of what its equivalent would be in the hands of an English workman. That is, a dollar will buy more food in the United States than 4s. 1½d. will in England. It will buy considerably more flour (as you know but little bread is bought in this country compared with the amount bought abroad, most families here baking their own bread), more meat, provisions, bacon, ham, vegetables, eggs, butter, cheese, farm products of all kinds, tea, coffee, more oil, a little less sugar, in many parts of the country more fuel. As to dry goods and clothing, it will buy more sheeting, shirting, prints or calicoes, and as much of many kinds of clothing such as workingmen wear, but in other cases less. House rents are higher here. It is, of course, to be understood that I am speaking, so far as relates to clothing, of the grades that most workmen buy. Of course imported cloths cost more, as does what is called high class tailoring.

"I made a very careful estimate once with the following result:

Items of Expenditure	Percentage of the Expenditure of a Family of a Workingman with an Income of	
	From $300 to $450 (£60 to £90) a year	From $450 to $600 (£90 to £120) a year
	Per cent	Per cent
Subsistence	64 ⎫	63 ⎫
Clothing	7 ⎬ 97	10.5 ⎬ 95
Rent	20	15.5
Fuel	6 ⎭	6 ⎭
Sundry expenses . .	3 3	5 5
Total . . .	100	100

Note.—Above from Report Massachusetts Bureau of Labor Statistics.

"Now, I estimate that on subsistence the American working-man has an advantage of at least twenty-five per cent.; on clothing, nothing; on rent, the English workingman has an advantage of thirty-three and one-third per cent.; and on fuel and sundry expenses I concede an equality. Then take the table as representing each one dollar expenditure of the American workingman.

	RELATIVE EXPENDITURE OF AN AMERICAN AND ENGLISH WORKMAN			
	Income $300 to $450 per year		Income $450 to $600 per year	
	American	*English*	*American*	*English*
Subsistence . . .	64	80	63	78.75
Clothing	7	7	10.5	10.50
Rent	20	13	15.5	10.37
Fuel	6	6	6	6
Sundry expenses .	3	3	5	5
Total . . .	100	109	100.00	110.62

"That is, if the relative modes of living in England and the United States of two classes of workmen are the same, it will cost ten per cent. more in England than in the United States.

"But the English workman, as a rule, does not live as well as the American, and it is just here that the fallacy exists in the statement that it costs the American workman more to live than it does the English. It does, for he lives better, spends more money; but this is not the true basis of comparison. The real question is: In which country will one dollar, or its equivalent, purchase more of a given article of consumption of a given grade? I answer unhesitatingly, on the whole, in the United States.

"Very truly,

"Jos. D. Weeks."

As a rule, the American workingman is steadier than his fellow in Britain—much more sober and possessed of higher tastes. Among his amusements is found scarcely a trace of the ruder practices of British manufacturing districts, such as cock-fighting, badger-baiting, dog-fighting, prize-fighting. Wife-beating is scarcely ever heard of, and drunkenness is quite rare. The manufacturer in America considers it cause for instant dismissal, and is able to act, and does act upon this theory, thereby insuring a standard of sobriety throughout the works. During all my experience among workingmen I have rarely seen a native American workman under the influence of liquor, and I have never known of any serious inconvenience or loss of time in any works resulting from the intemperance of the men. Even on the Fourth of July the blast-furnaces are run with accustomed regularity, and if the "glorious Fourth" be passed successfully, all other temptations are naturally harmless. It is upon Independence Day, if upon any day in the calendar, that the laboring citizen feels impelled to give vent to his feelings in violent demonstrations of irrepressible joy.

This calls to mind the story of one of the principal iron masters of Western Pennsylvania in days gone by. Passing his mill on the Fourth, on his way to church as a patriotic duty (for in those times churches were open for service on that day, and preachers were accustomed to torture the American eagle till it screamed), he heard the sound of busy hammers clanking rivets up. Stopping his buggy, he listened a moment in doubt, then alighted and walked to the spot, to find a party of men hard at work repairing a leaking boiler. At work on the Fourth of July! Degenerate republicans! when he was on his way to church to thank God for establishing the inalienable rights of man. He was the son of an Englishman, and his father had left England because of his republicanism. He could not stand it, but cleared the mill of every man, swearing he would not have a man about him who would work a stroke upon the sacred day. His remonstrance to the manager was no less emphatic. "What are you doing," he roared, "repairing boilers to-day? Aren't there plenty of Saturday nights and *Sundays* for this kind of work?" To his last day that manager never completely regained the respect and confidence of my dear old patriotic friend. This desecration of the Fourth, although forgiven, was never forgotten. The settlement with the offender, too, was only partial; for my friend, while admitting that the manager was a competent man, always had a qualifying "but" at the end of the eulogy. And the "but," as we all knew, had reference to the one unpardonable offence.

The human bees in the American hive work in four grand divisions. First, seven and three-quarter millions are detailed to tickle Mother Earth with the hoe, that she may smile with a harvest, and to tend the herds and flocks—the cattle upon a thousand hills and the sheep in the dewy fields, through which wander the complaining brooks, making the meadows green. A pleasant, healthful life is this, redolent of nature's sweetest odors, full of the rest and quiet of peaceful primitive days. These toilers grow the roses of life, and are to be much envied; and if the farmer's life in America is a life of toil, it is none the worse for that. It is the idle man who is to be pitied. The farmer is the man of independent mind,

> "Who holds his plough in joy."

Next to these envied out-of-door workers comes the second division—the manufacturers, three million eight hundred thousand strong—about half as many as the devotees of Ceres, these hardy sons of Vulcan. Every form of inventive genius or of mechanical skill finds

fitting occupation in this army. Variety of pursuit is of
vital consequence to a nation, and we find it here. Pent
up in mills and factories from morning to night, begrimed
with smoke and dirt, amid the ceaseless roar of machinery, these cunning toilers fashion the things conceived by the mind of man—from pins to anchors. In this
class are embraced those who literally live in the bowels
of the earth, who down deep in unfathomable mines rob
the earth of her hidden treasures, and drag them forth
for the uses of man. It is notable, that while in agriculture only seven per cent. of the division are females, in
this branch the ratio is no less than sixteen per cent.
Women do so much of the lighter manufacturing work in
America, more than six hundred thousand being so
employed. This division excites our sympathy; their
work is the least pleasing of all. Shut out from the sky,
and closed in mine or factory, they seem banished from
nature's presence. This is the class of whom we should
think most in our Sunday regulations. On that one day
let it be through nature that they look at nature's God.
To shut up within walls on the seventh day the prisoners
who have been incarcerated all the six, would be cruel.
Is there no reformer who will act upon the assertion that
the groves were God's first temples, and take the toilers
there in their only day of liberty? The annual camp-
meeting in the wood is fast dying out, yet it had its advantages. Poor men and women got a glimpse of nature
there.

The service division, which comes next, slightly out-
numbers the preceding class, for it reaches four millions.
The professions—the minister, the doctor, the lawyer,
the author, etc., are all embraced; fortunately, the
"noble" profession of arms (that means the butchering
of men) need not be counted in the Republic. The domestic servants are in themselves a host; the Irish take

to this branch much more generally than any other race. Of course, the percentage of females is here far greater than in any other of the main divisions, one million three hundred and sixty thousand domestic Amazons being enrolled, or one-third of the whole.

The fourth and last industrial corps is that conducting trade and transportation, numbering a million and eight hundred thousand, only sixty thousand of whom are females. These, combined, constitute the seventeen millions of working bees who made the honey of the national hive, in which there is no room for those who "toil not, neither do they spin." In that hive the drones are not stung to death at intervals; they are not suffered to come to life. If a specimen happens to escape the massacre, and walks about doing no useful work to justify his existence, the public regard him much as the countryman did the "dude" (masher) whom he saw for the first time promenading Broadway: "Lor', what lots of queer game one sees when he leaves home without his gun!" There is an inherited suspicion in the republican breast that the only thing good for the useless, idle, fox-hunting, pleasure-loving man, as well as for the State, if not to shoot him, is at least "to bounce him." When the fair young American asked the latest lordling who did her country the honor to visit it, how the aristocratic leisure-classes spent their time, he replied: "Oh, they go about from one house to another, don't you know, and enjoy themselves, you know. They never do any work, you know." "Oh," she replied, "we have such people too—tramps."

> "Allah! Allah! cries the stranger—
>   Wondrous sights the traveller sees;
> But the greatest is the latest,
>   Where the drones control the bees."

It was evidently not the democratic division of the English people which the Eastern traveller visited, but the poor oppressed land of monarchy and aristocracy, where honest labor naturally ranks below hereditary sloth.

Chapter VI
EDUCATION

"There being education, there will be no distinction of classes."
—CONFUCIUS.
"Education is the only interest worthy the deep, controlling anxiety of the thoughtful man."—WENDELL PHILLIPS.

THE fair fabric of justice raised by Numa," says Plutarch, "passed rapidly away because it was not founded upon education." No truer reason can be given for the decay of everything good in a State. Upon no foundation but that of popular education can man erect the structure of an enduring civilization. This is the basis of all stability, and underlies all progress. Without it the State architect builds in vain.

Whether the sturdy Pilgrim Fathers were conversant with the conceptions of the Greek thinkers who were filled with projects for universal education, whether they were versed in the speculations of Pluto's "Republic" or Aristotle's "Politics," is doubtful; but it is certain that they were imbued with the spirit which animated Luther and Knox in regard to the education of the masses. The true parent of modern education was the Reformation, for did not Luther himself say that if he were not a preacher he should be a teacher, as he thought the latter the more important office? John Knox demanded a public school for every parish in Scotland, and it was the Protestant State of Germany that first undertook the education of the whole people. Fortunate indeed for the world that the demand for religious freedom necessarily involved the priceless boon of secular education.

The preamble to the Massachusetts school law of 1642 tells the story:

"It being one chief project of that old deluder, Satan, to keep men from the knowledge of the Scriptures, as in former times, keeping them in an unknown tongue, so in these latter times, by persuading from the use of tongues, so that all at least the true sense and meaning of the original might be clouded and corrupted with false glosses of deceivers; and to the end that learning may not be buried in the grave of our forefathers, in church and commonwealth, the Lord assisting our endeavors:

"It is therefore ordered by this Court and authority thereof, that every township within this jurisdiction, after the Lord hath increased them to the number of fifty householders, shall then forthwith appoint one within their town to teach all such children, as shall resort to him, to write and read, whose wages shall be paid, either by their parents or masters of such children, or by the inhabitants in general, by way of supply, as the major part of those who order the prudentials of the town shall appoint; provided that those who send their children be not oppressed by paying much more than they can have them taught for in other towns."

In 1700 the State of Connecticut enacted its system of public instruction, which embraced the following as its first obligation:

An obligation on every parent and guardian of children, "not to suffer so much barbarism in any of their families as have a single child or apprentice unable to read the holy word of God, and the good laws of the colony"; and also, "To bring them up to some lawful calling or employment" under a penalty for each offence.

The right of private judgment presupposes a judgment to judge with. This presupposes knowledge, and knowledge is the result of education. Hence, the first

duty of the State, as the Fathers saw it, was to educate
the children thereof. Our Pilgrim Fathers carried with
them from their old to their new home a realizing sense
of the importance of this subject. It may well be said of
them as Froude has said of the Scotch—"With them
education was a passion," for scarcely had they got roofs
over their heads in the forest before we find them establishing public schools and appointing schoolmasters. Here
is a copy of one of the earliest records of Boston:

"The 13th of ye 2nd month, 1635. It was then generally agreed
upon yt our brother Philemon Purmount shall be intreated to
become schoolmaster for ye teaching and nourturing of all children with us."

Next year, only six years after the first settlement of
Boston, four hundred pounds was appropriated towards
the establishment of a college. This sum exceeded the
entire tax levy of the colony for the year.

Eleven years later the State of Massachusetts made
the support of schools compulsory and education universal and free; and we read that "in 1665, every town
had a free school, and, if it contained over one hundred
families, a grammar school. In Connecticut every town
that did not keep a school for three months in the year
was liable to a fine."

Such was the policy adopted by the men of the people
who sought these northern shores that they might establish and enjoy the blessings of civil and religious liberty.

Far different was the policy of the aristocratic element
with which Virginia was cursed. Twenty years after the
establishment of free schools by law in New England, Sir
William Berkeley, Governor of Virginia, wrote:

"I thank God there are no free schools or printing, and I hope
we shall not have them these hundred years. For learning has

brought heresy and disobedience and sects into the world, and printing has divulged them, and libels against the best government. God keep us from both."

Even in the early part of the eighteenth century, says Sir Charles Lyell, "there was not one bookshop in Virginia, and no printing-presses," though "there were several in Boston, with no less than five printing offices, a fact which reflects the more credit on the Puritans, because at the same period (1724) there were no less than thirty-four counties in the mother country, Lancashire being one of the number, in which there was no printer."

Thus are the ideas and methods of democracy and aristocracy contrasted! The former is ever seeking the education of the masses; the latter from its very nature is ever seeking to restrain education to the few, well knowing that privilege dies as knowledge spreads. It was death to teach a slave to read. The instinct which led the slave-holder to keep his slave in ignorance was a true one. Educate man, and his shackles fall. Free education may be trusted to burst every obstruction which stands in the path of the democracy towards its goal, the equality of the citizen, and this it will reach quietly and without violence, as the swelling sapling in its growth breaks its guard. "Ballots not Bullets" is the motto of educated republicanism, and "Obedience to Law" its fundamental requirement.

Owing to the incompleteness of early censuses it is not easy to ascertain the exact condition of education in 1830. But contemporary writers sometimes make estimates which are accessible. From these we learn that in 1831 the proportion of school children to population in America was fifteen per cent., or double the European average, and second only to that of Prussia. It would have been as high as twenty-two per cent. (much beyond the Prussian average) but for the slave States, where the negro slaves were not educated. In 1832 a European visitor said:

"The State of New York stands foremost on the list of school children. It counts in the proportion of one to three and one-half of the number of its inhabitants; the New England States one to five; Pennsylvania and New Jersey, one to eight; Illinois one to thirteen; Kentucky, one to twenty-five and so on. By way of comparison, I may just mention that Wurtemberg has one to six; Bavaria and Prussia, one to seven; Scotland, one to ten; France, one to seventeen and one-half; Russia, one to three hundred and sixty-seven."

The condition of the country in regard to education in 1834 is summed up by a contemporary as follows:

"In the New England States there are not less than five hundred thousand children educated at the common schools, and in 1830 there were four hundred and seventy-three thousand, five hundred and eight white persons in these States between the ages of five and fifteen, and allowing for the increase of population, we may say that the benefits of elementary education are universally diffused.

"In the States to the south and west of New York, however, there is reason to believe that there were one million two hundred and ten thousand children without the knowledge and benefits of education."

Many English readers will no doubt be surprised to learn that the general government has nothing whatever to do with the education of the people. This duty belongs to the different States, and is fulfilled by them each in its own way. A system of public education is in operation in every State and Territory in the Union, and twenty-eight out of the thirty-eight States have provided normal schools for the training of teachers. There are

ninety-eight of these institutions. All have recognized
the duty of providing for every child a free common
school education; and in furtherance of this end the general government has frequently made liberal grants of
public lands to the various States. Even as early as the
Continental Congress the question of affording aid to
education was discussed; and in 1785, immediately after
the close of the War of Independence, Congress passed
an act reserving for school purposes the sixteenth section
of each township of the public land of the Territories.
When the Territories were admitted as States they were
made trustees of these lands. Under this and subsequent
laws, twelve of the new States came into the Union possessed of magnificent educational endowments. In 1848,
Congress granted an additional section in each township for the same purpose. Nearly sixty-eight million
acres of land have been given in this manner to twenty-
seven States. Further special grants of land have from
time to time been made for the creation of State universities; and in 1862 each State received a grant either of
land within the State or an equivalent amount of scrip,
for the purpose of establishing and endowing schools of
agriculture and the mechanical arts. The total amount
of land hitherto devoted by the general government to
educational endowments exceeds seventy-eight millions
of acres, an area greater than the whole of England,
Scotland, and Ireland combined.

Throughout the history of the Republic great liber-
ality has been displayed in the grants for educational
purposes. The people who cannot be induced to make the
salaries of officials half as large as those of the officials
of the petty powers of Europe, nevertheless urge their
representatives to vote millions upon millions for educational purposes. The ratio of money spent on the army
to that spent on education is in startling contrast to that

of Europe. America is the only country which spends more upon education than on war or preparation for war. Great Britain does not spend one-fourth as much, France not one-eleventh, or Russia one-thirty-third as much on education as on the army. Here are the figures, which the patient democracies of Europe will do well to ponder. How long yet will men, instigated by royal and aristocratic jealousies, spend their wealth and best energies upon means for slaughtering each other!

ANNUAL EXPENDITURES ON

	ARMAMENTS	EDUCATION
United Kingdom	£28,900,000	£6,685,000
France	35,000,000	3,200,000
Germany	20,000,000	6,900,000
Russia	33,000,000	1,000,000
Austria	13,400,000	2,900,000
Italy	18,900,000	1,100,000
Spain	6,300,000	1,200,000
Other European States . .	8,300,000	2,100,000
	£163,800,000	£25,085,000
United States	£9,400,000	£18,600,000

Thus for every pound spent by Great Britain for the education of her people, more than four pounds are squandered upon the army and navy. The Republic reverses this practice and spends nearly two pounds upon education for every one spent for war.

Truly has Longfellow written:

"Were half the power that fills the world with terror,
Were half the wealth bestow'd on camps and courts,
Given to redeem the human mind from error,
There were no need of arsenals nor forts.

The warrior's name would be a name abhorred!
And every nation that should lift again
Its hand against a brother, on its forehead
Would wear forevermore the curse of Cain."

While the New England States fully embraced the idea of free and universal public instruction very early in their history, the great State of New York adjoining them only reached this height after a struggle of many long years. It was not until 1851 that the popular vote sanctioned the principle that the State must educate all its children. The State now spends eleven millions of dollars per annum (more than two millions sterling) upon education. A free college in the city of New York is filled with the best students from the public schools; a free normal college provides higher education for female teachers, and in every part of the State normal schools produce great numbers of accomplished teachers.

The amounts expended upon education by each State, *per capita* of school population, range from $18.70 (£3 15*s*.) in Navaded, to 85c. (3*s*. 6½*d*.) in North Carolina, and 81c. (3*s*. 4½*d*.) in New Mexico. It is an interesting fact that the States which spend most *pro rata* on education are not the old settled States of New England, but the young, vigorous States of the Northwest. Thus Iowa spends almost double in proportion to its wealth what Massachusetts does; and Idaho, not yet admitted as a State, excels all the States in this respect. Wisconsin, Minnesota, Kansas, and Nebraska are all far in advance of the New England States. The Southern States rank last, though not so far behind as might be expected. Indeed, several of them, such as Maryland, Virginia, West Virginia, and South Carolina, exceed the average of the New England States.

The United States have not escaped entirely the religious difficulty in their march to universal free education, but fortunately opposition to the system has been confined to one sect—the Roman Catholic—all others having united in giving to it enthusiastic support. The dissatisfied Catholics have not been strong enough even in the city of New York, where they are much more powerful than elsewhere in the Union, to disturb the complete exclusion of dogmatical teaching which everywhere characterizes the public schools of America. A few verses from the Bible are generally read without comment in the schools as a public exercise once each day. At this no one takes offence, and every one, with the exception of the Roman Catholics, is satisfied, as all feel that the public school is not the proper place for religious instruction.

So vitally important to the child is education considered throughout America that not even the rigid discipline of the Roman Catholic Church is strong enough to restrain Catholic parents from sending their children to the public schools. Remonstrances against this soul-destroying practice were recently made simultaneously in all the Catholic churches of Pittsburgh, Penn., and so vehement were the denunciations hurled at offenders that the *Commercial Gazette* had a thorough canvass made to determine to what extent Catholics were availing themselves of the public schools. Statements were asked from the principals of fifty-six schools, and replies received from twenty-four. The others declined from conscientious scruples to inquire into the religious beliefs of the scholars. Most significant this of the complete toleration which prevails in this country upon the subject of religion, and surely not without value as proving to Britain how slight is the religious difficulty, if it be a difficulty at all, in the path of free secular education. For this reason, some of the strongest Catholic districts were unreported; nevertheless, it was clearly proven that one-half as many Catholic children attend the public schools as the denominational schools, notwithstanding the fulminations of the priests and the command of the Vicar of Christ, the supreme pontiff, which is quoted in the recent attack in Pittsburgh against the godless public schools. I was so much surprised at the result here stated, that before quoting it I applied to the highest authorities for confirmation, among them, to my distinguished fellow-countryman, Mr. William Wood, who has long been one of the Commissioners of Education in the city of New York, and he not only affirms that the result at Pittsburgh may be taken to represent the average situation throughout the country, but that in New York and other large cities Catholic children receive their education even in greater numbers side by side with Protestant children in the State schools. So let the Church continue to issue its mandates against free, godless education in the Republic. The Pope, being infallible, must be consistent, and this is his nineteenth century bull against the comet, and will probably be as efficacious as the older one.

The public schools are supported mainly by direct taxation, and no tax is so willingly paid as "the school tax." In 1880, eighty-two and a half million dollars (sixteen and a half millions sterling) were raised for schools—four-fifths by direct tax, the other fifth being derived from rents, or sale, or proceeds of school lands.

Following the public schools, in which every child is entitled to receive a common school education free of expense, we come to the various institutions for higher education with which the State has nothing to do. These are mainly private schools and depend for maintenance upon fees from scholars. Some of them are authorized by State legislative enactments to grant degrees and diplomas, but as the standards of States differ greatly, a school entitled in Tennessee to call itself a university or college might not rank as either in Massachusetts. We must, therefore, caution our readers not to be misled by figures which show so many more colleges and universities in the former than in the latter.

Schools higher than primary public schools in the United States number three thousand six hundred and fifty, and contain nearly half a million students. Of these, three hundred and sixty-four are universities and colleges, with fifty-nine thousand five hundred and ninety-four students.

The number of public schools in the country is estimated at one hundred and seventy-seven thousand one hundred, making in all one hundred and seventy-nine thousand eight hundred and eighty-four schools, and the army of teachers number two hundred and seventy-three thousand, of whom one hundred and fifty-four thousand three hundred and seventy-five are women. A glorious army this. Let me quote from the report which the Rev. Mr. Fraser made to the British Government some years ago:

"American teachers are self-possessed, energetic, and fearless, admirable disciplinarians, firm without severity, patient without weakness; their manner of teaching lively, and their illustrations fertile. No class could ever fall asleep in their hands. They are proud of their position and fired with a laudable ambition to maintain the credit of the school; a little too sensitive of blame, and a little too greedy of praise, but a very fine and capable body of workers in a noble cause."

The position of America in regard to reading and writing in 1880 is this: out of thirty-six and three-quarter million persons of ten years of age and over, nearly five million, or thirteen per cent., are unable to read, and six million and a quarter, or seventeen per cent., are unable to write. In 1870 the percentage was sixteen and twenty per cent. respectively so that the march against ignorance is still onward. The gain in the number able to write is significant. For every thousand inhabitants who could not read in 1870 there were but eight hundred and fifty-three in 1880, and for every thousand who could not write in 1870 there were but eight hundred and twenty-six who could not do so in 1880. In this improvement the colored population participated to almost as great an extent as the white, which encourages the friends of that race to look hopefully to their future. A satisfactory feature is the great reduction of illiteracy in the foreign born element, for of every thousand foreign born who were illiterate in 1870 there were but seven hundred and fifty-nine in 1880, which testifies to the well-known fact that the character of recent immigration has been far higher than ever before. Of course the native illiterate are found mainly in the Southern States and among the colored people. Of colored people more than ten years of age in 1880, no less than seventy per cent. were unable to write, while of the native white born (Southern as well as Northern) there were only eight and seven-tenths per cent. in this class. In the Southern States, taken as a whole, not more than sixty out of every hundred inhabitants over ten years of age can write.

That the condition of the colored population is due to circumstances and not to any inherent lack of capacity or disposition, we have the best evidence in the fact that while seventy-five and six-tenths per cent. of this class in the Southern States are illiterate, the Northern States of the North Atlantic group present an average of illiteracy as low as twenty-three and two-tenths per cent., or not one-third as great.

Throughout the whole North, where the mass of the

people reside, it may be said that the native born American, male and female, can read and write; for the percentage returned as unable to do so does not exceed an average of five per cent. Five persons in every hundred most of whom, no doubt, are mentally incapacitated for instruction.

If we compare the number of white males of twenty-one years and over who cannot read or write, with those of ten years and over, we see at once how education has advanced in recent years. The percentages of all the States rise a grade in every instance when those educated within the ten year period only are considered, those showing between two and five per cent. of the latter, show between five and ten per cent. when the twenty-one years class is embraced. In other words, the children of to-day are more generally educated than those of the preceding decade.

The average percentage of white males of twenty-one years and over who cannot read and write is seven and eight-tenths, and of white females to total white females is eleven per cent., only three more women than men in every hundred, showing that women in the Republic are not far behind. In 1870 the percentages were as follows: male illiterates eighteen and twenty-six hundredths per cent., female illiterates twenty-one and eighty-seven hundredths per cent. The decrease of illiteracy in ten years is one of the most surprisingly clear marks of the country's progress.

Schools for the superior instruction of women numbered in 1880 two hundred and twenty-seven and contained twenty-five thousand seven hundred and eighty students. In 1870 there were but one hundred and seventy-five such schools and eleven thousand two hundred and eighty-eight students. These statistics show a rate of increase far beyond that of any other branch, and prove how rapidly women are being advanced in education.

The average wages per month paid teachers in the public schools vary greatly in the different States. Nevada pays her female teachers $77 (£15 8s. 0d.), and her male teachers $101.47 (£20 5s. 10d.), which is the highest; Massachusetts $30.59 (£6 2s. 4d.), and $67.54 (£13 10s. 2d.); South Carolina $23.89 (£4 15s. 7d.), and $25.24 (£5 1s. 0d.).

The ratio of average attendance to school population by States in 1880 ranged from sixty-four in Maine to nineteen in Louisiana, and the average number of school days from fifty-four in North Carolina to one hundred and ninety-two in New Jersey.

As we have already seen, the public schools of America cost in 1880 over sixteen millions sterling. This is very unequally distributed among the States. Virginia City, Nevada, spends most per head upon her scholars, namely $34.81 (almost £7). Then comes Sacramento, California, with $34 (£6 16s.) per head. The city of Boston, Massachusetts, ranks third with $33.73 (£6 15s.) per head, which is more than three times that expended by London.

While the American living is ever mindful of the cause of education he does not forget it at death, and often bequeaths large sums to his favorite school or college. In 1880 such benefactions exceeded five and a half millions of dollars (£1,100,000).

Now let us just pause a moment to ask how monarchical and aristocratic institutions affect the minds of wealthy people in this respect. Great Britain is, next to her child, the richest country in the world. Her aristocracy, as a class, is by far the richest in the world. There is none comparable to it in the Republic. But who ever heard of a nobleman leaving large sums for the higher education of his fellows, or indeed for any public use whatever? A great physician in London, Erasmus Wilson, dies and leaves a hundred thousand pounds, half his entire fortune, to the College of Physicians and Surgeons, to be used to extend its usefulness. Who can point to a member of the aristocracy who has risen beyond his own family, which is only another name for himself! The vain desire to found or maintain a family or to increase its revenues or estate is the ignoble ambition of a privileged order. What they give or leave as a class, with few exceptions, is "nothing to nobody." We can say of the average peer or aristocrat:

> "The wretch concentred all in self,
> Living shall forfeit fair renown,
> And doubly dying shall go down
> To the vile dust from whence he sprung,
> Unwept, unhonored, and unsung."

The few illustrious exceptions, all the more notable for their rarity, are wholly insufficient to redeem their order from the just reproach of grasping from the too indulgent State all that can be obtained, and using it only for aims which end with self. They can justly plead, perhaps, the influence of example in the highest quarters where surely better things might have been expected—even thrones hoard for self in these days. But his is but the legitimate outcome of the monarchical and aristocratic idea. No fair fruit is to be expected from privilege.

The Republic has a remarkable list of educational institutions bestowed upon it by its millionaires, among them Johns-Hopkins University, Cornell University, Vanderbilt University, Packer Institute, Vassar College, Wellesley College, Smith College, Bryn Mawr College, and the Stevens Institute. These have each cost several millions

of dollars, Johns-Hopkins alone having an endowment
of $5,000,000 (£1,000,000), the gift of one man. Only
a few days ago the announcement was made that Leland
Stanford, President of the Central Pacific Railway and at
present United States Senator from California, has transferred property valued at seven million dollars to establish a worthy university on the Pacific coast.

The ratio of population to students enrolled by classes
of institutions in 1880 shows that one out of every five
attends the public schools, while secondary education is
received by one out of every four hundred and fifty-five;
university and college education by one out of every eight
hundred and forty-two; commercial and business education by one out of every one thousand eight hundred and
forty-eight; a scientific education by one out of every
four thousand three hundred and twenty-one; a theological education by one out of every nine thousand five hundred and sixty-eight; and a legal education by one out of
every sixteen thousand and one. Such is the record of
the educational establishments of all kinds in the country
as given by the census of 1880.

The moral to be drawn from America by every nation
is this: "Seek ye first the education of the people and all
other political blessings will be added unto you." The
quarrels of party, the game of politics, this or that measure of reform, are but surface affairs of little moment.
The education of the people is the real underlying work
for earnest men who would best serve their country. In
this, the most creditable work of all, it cannot be denied
that the Republic occupies the first place.

It is and ever has been with all Americans as with
Jefferson: "A system of general instruction which shall
reach every description of our citizens from the richest
to the poorest, as it was the earliest so shall it be the
latest, of all the public concerns in which I shall permit

myself to take an interest." There speaks the inspired voice of triumphant Democracy, which holds as its first duty the universal education of the people. Of all its boasts, of all its triumphs, this is at once its proudest and its best. We say to the old Monarchies of the world: Behold Democracy produces as its natural fruit an educated people.

Chapter VII
RELIGION

"The religion of a people, prevailing at any time or place, is the highest expression of which that people is then and there capable."

The relation of the Church to the State is one of the problems which the Republic may be said to have solved. It is decided that it has no relation whatever.

The State has as much relation to religion as to medicine, and no more; and it might as well establish homœopathy as its medical system, as episcopacy as its religion. It might as well undertake the health of the body as of the soul—indeed, far better, since it is a much less complex task.

In the Republic the regulation of religious beliefs by the State would be regarded as absurd as the regulation of dress. It is not even admitted that the State has a right to patronize one form of religion—much less one sect —to the prejudice of other forms. Buddhism, Confucianism, or the crudest Fetichism, stand in exactly the same relation to the State as any of the sects which derive their creeds from the teachings of Christ. No form of worship, no religious creed is selected by the State for special favor. The "heathen Chinee" in New York may worship his ancestors with a restful consciousness that the black-coated Christian, passing with gold-edged book to church, is not more favored by the State.

And how does this system of perfect religious equality work? Perfectly, as to all sects in general; much better than the advocates of the State Church system in the mother-land could believe for the Anglican Church in particular, which is vigorous to a degree which might well be envied by the parent stem. So far from religion being neglected by the people, the number of religious edifices in proportion to population is far greater in America than in Britain, and the congregations frequenting them are quite as large. In England there are thirty-five thousand churches, or one hundred and forty-four to each one hundred thousand inhabitants; in the United States there are ninety-two thousand churches, or one hundred and eighty-one to each one hundred thousand inhabitants. Of the latter, more than eighty thousand are owned by Protestants.

The steps leading to this remarkable result display the same general character as every other kind of advancement in America: progress by leaps and bounds. At the beginning of the century, students of Yale and Harvard were accustomed to call themselves by the names of French and German infidels; and only a small proportion of the students in colleges were church members. All this has been changed. From 1870 to 1880, Harvard, the most advanced of all universities, graduated more than fourteen hundred young men, only two of whom publicly registered themselves as "sceptics." In 1800, when the population of the United States was about five millions, the number of communicants in the various churches was three hundred and sixty-four thousand, an average of one to fifteen of the population. In 1880, with a population of fifty millions, the number of Protestant communicants was more than ten millions, an average of one in five. If the members of the Roman

Catholic Church be included, the proportion will be largely increased.

The multiplication of handsome religious edifices is equally remarkable. Many American churches are noted for their beauty. All the large cities have examples of church architecture which would not discredit towns having a history as old as that of Coventry; and in rural districts the church spire rises above the cottages and trees as frequently as they tower over the hamlets in the old country. One of the grandest churches of modern times is undoubtedly the Roman Catholic Cathedral of Fifth Avenue, New York, a massive Gothic structure of white marble; and in the same avenue are quite half a dozen other churches of great beauty and architectural merit.

It is estimated that thirty millions, or nearly three-fifths of the entire population of the country, are within the pale of the Christian Church. Twenty-four millions of these are Protestants, of whom the Methodist and Baptist claim the largest proportion; next in numerical order come the Presbyterian, Roman Catholic, Lutheran, Christian (Disciples of Christ), Congregational, Episcopal, United Brethren, and a host of sects which it would tire one to enumerate. The buildings and other property belonging to these various bodies are estimated to be worth in the aggregate upwards of $350,000,000 (£70,000,000).

The clergy in the United States, upwards of seventy-seven thousand in number, are maintained solely by the worshippers. The government, of course, gives nothing to any. There is no "dissent," because no sect is preferred.

The leading part which religion played in the settlement of this continent had an effect which continues to mark the American of to-day. He is a church-going person and a liberal contributor to the cause of the Church, though he has outgrown the strict and narrow creeds of early days, and is religious, not theological.

As late as 1705 aristocratic Virginia decreed three years' imprisonment, and many political disabilities upon any one who should a second time assert disbelief in the Trinity and the Scriptures; but the government of New Amsterdam was rather more advanced, for in 1664 it decreed that no person who professed Christianity should be molested, fined, or imprisoned for difference of religious opinions. The revolutionary struggle quickened the march towards complete religious toleration. The fear that England would establish the Episcopal Church in America, if the colonies should be subdued, drew together all the other sects and all favorable to religious equality, and therefore opposed to the claims of the English Church. "This," says John Adams, "contributed as much as any other cause to arouse the attention, not only of the inquiring mind, but of the common people, and urge them to close thinking on the constitutional authority of Parliament over the colonies." And the intensity of colonial opposition to the State Church is shown by the special instructions of the Assembly of Massachusetts to its agent in London, in 1768: "The establishment of a Protestant episcopate in America is very zealously contended for (by a party in the British Parliament); and it is very alarming to a people whose fathers, from the hardships they suffered under such an establishment, were obliged to fly their native country into a wilderness in order peaceably to enjoy their privileges— civil and religious. We hope in God that such an establishment will never take place in America; and we desire you would strenuously oppose it!" In addition, therefore, to the dissatisfaction which the State Church produces at home, it is justly to be charged with being one of the chief causes which led to the loss of the colonies abroad.

When the colonies triumphed and a Constitution had to be made for their government as a nation, there was but one course possible. Since no sect could be given a preference, and especially not the Episcopal sect, which had been the least loyal of all to the cause of Independence, it followed that perfect equality must be established. The State must protect all religions alike; and accordingly the Constitution provides that Congress shall make no law respecting an establishment of religion or prohibiting the free exercise thereof. Such is the charter under which Jew and Gentile, Christian, Mahometan and Hindoo stand equal and secure in their rights. The various States soon followed the spirit of this law, Virginia taking the lead. Provision for the support of the clergy was erased from their Constitutions, and yet the variety of healthy and vigorous religious life in the United States to-day is greater than anywhere else in the world. So much for a free Church in a free State.

We are unable to make comparisons between the amounts contributed each year for religious purposes fifty years ago and those of to-day because the census returns are silent upon this point. At the time of the Revolution (1776) there were one thousand four hundred and sixty-one ministers and one thousand nine hundred and fifty-one churches, which gave one minister for every two thousand and fifty-three souls and a church for every one thousand five hundred and thirty-eight. In 1880 there was a minister for every six hundred and sixty and a church for every five hundred and fifty-three. This shows that although the country has increased in population at a pace unknown before in the history of mankind, its churches and ministers have not only kept abreast of this movement but have actually exceeded it.

Wherever the American settles he begins at once the erection of his school house and his church.

The principal sects, according to the census of 1880, number as follows:

Methodist	3,286,158
Baptist	2,430,095
Presbyterian	885,468
Lutheran	569,389
Disciples of Christ . . .	556,941
Congregational	384,800
Episcopal	336,669

The Roman Catholic Church claimed in 1883 to have 6,832,954 adherents of that faith in the United States, but church membership is not reported. This estimate includes all the members of those families which are in any way connected with it; the adult membership may therefore be estimated at two-fifths of the above—nearly two and three-quarter millions.

The American reader knows that in Britain the State continues to establish and endow one among the numerous Protestant sects which it calls *The* Church of England and another called *The* Church of Scotland; with delightful impartiality the State indorses the Episcopal form as *The Church, i. e.* the true, divine system, south of the Tweed, and is equally assured that north of that small river the aristocratic apostolic succession becomes inoperative and the democratic Presbyterian idea constitutes *The Church.* Parliament is supreme over both, and her Majesty is the defender not only of *the* faith, but of both faiths. In England she is a devout Episcopalian, in Scotland a Presbyterian; but as all Scotland is of the latter faith, and the sects represent only the minor differences which inevitably crop up among the polemical Scots in any institution, secular or religious, the State

Church, although partaking of the nature of privilege, and hence insulting to the other sects as implying their inferiority, is not, in Scotland, to the same degree the irritating and almost intolerable grievance which it is in England. A Presbyterian family in Scotland may not belong to the Established Church and yet retain its social position. In England it would be almost, if not quite impossible, for the "Church people" constitute society. Episcopacy is the only fashionable form of religion—the only form that is "good form." It is the rule, and exceptions to it are not numerous, for Episcopal clergymen in the country districts to decline to meet the ministers of other denominations who are not clergy at all in the estimation of these the only true successors of the Apostles. Instead of being a bond of peace among people in England, religion is made by a State-preferred sect a bone of contention, and produces more discord than the Episcopal Church heals. These bitter quarrels do not even end at the grave; most unseemly and discreditable disputes occur even there over the right or non-right of the members of other churches to be buried among their own people in the only graveyard of the district. One cannot but marvel that a people so given to the observance of the outward proprieties of life should permit scenes which I am sure have not their like in even the most ignorant lands. A recent Burials Act of Parliament does something to remedy the evil but the matter is still far from being upon a proper footing.

The sale of livings is another scandal which Americans will hear of with perhaps equal surprise. There frequently goes with a land purchase the right of appointing the clergyman of a district, and as the emoluments may be great, this post has a marketable value. It ranks just as so many additional acres in appraising the estate, and we constantly see advertisements offering for sale a clergyman's position to such and such a "living." It matters not what the character or attainments of the purchaser may be if in orders; if he has the cash and buys his appointment then he is the lawful minister of the unfortunate congregation and it is powerless.

This system results in another evil. The rich purchaser may not have the slightest idea of pursuing his holy calling. He buys a revenue of say one thousand pounds per year, and he hires a poor curate for one hundred and fifty pounds, and the difference is his profit upon the investment. One step further, if my American reader is in a state to believe anything more monstrous, in the path of this Established Church. The right to appoint a minister at the death of a present incumbent is often sold by public sale. A poor, faithful clergyman is old and must soon die. How much bid for his place, gentlemen? Going, going, gone!

This is church life in England. I often wonder how one of our bishops of the Episcopal Church can cordially take by the hand his fellow-bishops of England, the receivers of the disreputable fruits of this system. Archdeacon Farrar has just been good enough to tell us he does not wish it disturbed. Of course not, but he is not in a position to judge impartially since he cannot be held to have quite clean hands himself.

The evils of the State Church flow from its parent, the Monarchy, of which it is the legitimate offspring. Its archbishops and bishops residing in palaces and rolling in wealth are the religious aristocracy; the thousands of poor curates who drag out existence upon pittances represent the masses. The revenues of the State Church exceed five million pounds sterling. The Church owns all kinds of property and is squeamish about none. An editorial in the *London Times* recently called attention to the charge that the Archbishop of Canterbury, walking between certain of his residences or churches in London, would pass a hundred gin palaces erected upon land owned by the Church, upon which the rents were raised from time to time as the vile trade flourished; but Church people who will sell the right to cure the souls of men naturally do not hesitate to sell the right to destroy their bodies, both strictly for sash. The present Church of England, of the Monarchy, is in the respects I have noted unworthy of fellowship with its purer offspring of the Republic. But my readers will not have failed to observe that all the evils which cling to it flow from its degrading connection with the State, as our own Episcopal Church abundantly proves that they are not inherent in the system. When the political aspect of the matter be settled as it is settled here, the branch of the Episcopal Church in Britain will become as pure as the other.

After a trial of free and independent existence nothing is more certain than that a proposition from the government to give to the Protestant Episcopal Church of America the position in the State at present occupied by the Episcopal Church in England would be overwhelmingly rejected by that body as injurious to the life and usefulness of the organization, and derogatory to the true position of religion. If the Church of England enjoyed one year's freedom from State control, in like manner, it could never be induced to return to its present dependence upon the State.

As the British landlords stand to-day, who once stood bewailing the coming ruin from the repeal of the Corn Laws, as the American slave-holders stand, who once stood predicting a saturnalia of bloodshed in the South when the slaves were freed,—so will the English churchman stand who foresees the State Church ruined by separation from the State. Short-sighted man! From the day the Church of England is free and independent of the State its power and influence will begin to grow with redoubled strength, and all the other sects will be stirred to increased effort. Indeed, an independent Church of England, which no longer implies the inferiority of others, may prove itself the power which is finally to absorb within its folds all the sects, and restore to Great Britain the unity of religious form unfortunately lost when the political invaded the religious domain. The breadth of view, the large tolerance, the fading importance attached to mere dogmas of man's own creation, which characterize the present Church, appear admirably suited for a foundation upon which, after the scandals resulting from State control are eliminated, can be built a Church which will draw all religious people to its fold and become in reality as in name *the* Church of England.

We do not yet see in the Republic a tendency to the obliteration of sects. We do see, however, that the preliminary stage toward this has been developed. The sects are mingling more and more one with another in many great works. Co-operation embracing all the sects is noticeable. The Jewish rabbi, the Catholic priest and the Episcopal minister, and those of all the other denominations are constantly seen together occupying the same platform and advocating the same measures. When this stage of progress toward unity is fully developed the next step is not far distant.

Without Church-rate or tithe, without State endowment or State supervision, religion in America has spontaneously acquired a strength which no political support could have given. It is a living force entering into the lives of the people and drawing them closer together in unity of feeling, and working silently and without sign of the friction which in the mother country results from a union with the State, which, as we have seen, tends strongly to keep the people divided one from another.

The power of the Church in America must not be sought, as Burke said of an ideal aristocracy, "in rotten parchments, under dripping and perishing walls, but in full vigor, and acting with vital energy and power, in the character of the leading men and natural interests of the country. If judged by the church accommodation provided and the sums spent upon Church organizations, Democracy can safely claim that of all the divisions of the English-speaking people, it has produced the most religious community yet known.

Chapter VIII

PAUPERISM AND CRIME

"The poor ye have always with you and the criminal classes as well, but the poor can be made few and the criminals less vicious by proper treatment upon the part of the State. No test of the place a State occupies in civilization is surer than the lightness of its punishments and the care taken of its poor. A pitying spirit toward these unfortunate classes and not that represented by the grim authority of the law, is that which in the end lessens crime and pauperism, and best befits an educated community; for the end of all punishment and that alone which justifies it is not the vindication of the outraged law but the desired amendment of the offender."—Thoughts of the Sages.

In the old books, periodicals, and newspapers which have been searched for facts throwing light upon the condition of America half a century ago, frequent reference has been found to the comparative freedom of America from beggars and paupers. A writer in De Bow's *Commercial Magazine* at this period said:

"Throughout the greater part of Virginia and Kentucky pauperism is almost unknown. I passed some time ago the poorhouse of Campbell County, Kentucky, . . . and there was not a solitary inmate. And I have known a populous county in Virginia to have but one." And during a prolonged tour through the States by Captain Alexander, of the British Army, in 1832, "only one beggar was seen."

But with many such indications of the absence of poverty among Americans fifty years ago are found complaints that large numbers of European paupers were brought in. Thus we read in the *New England Magazine* for 1833 that "a memorial was presented to the General Assembly by the Mayor and City Council of Baltimore calling their attention to the evils arising from the influx of foreign paupers. The memorial states that the number of emigrants who arrived at the port of Baltimore in 1831 was four thousand three hundred and eighty-one, and in 1832, seven thousand nine hundred and forty-six; a large proportion of whom were destitute of the means of subsistence. Also that of one thousand one hundred and sixty persons admitted to the almshouse in that city in 1831, four hundred and eighty-seven were foreigners; and that of this number two hundred and eighty-one had been in the country less than six months prior to their admission, and one hundred and twenty-one less than one week."

The Philadelphia *National Gazette* stated in 1834 that "an active and intelligent guardian of the poor in that city has declared, that the support of our own poor would be an insignificant charge, and that *more than three-fourths* of the paupers in the almshouse are exported from Europe. Sometimes a whole family will come almost directly from the ship to the almshouse."

The New York *Advertiser* relates "that in the course of the present season (1834) an Austrian armed ship has been despatched from that country to this, with a large number of persons on board, who were of a character which the Austrian Government did not incline to suffer to remain within their own territories, and therefore sent them out, in the very imposing manner just mentioned, and landed them in the city of New York."

Twenty years later there was the same cause of complaint. It is related in Booth's "History of New York" that "during the winter of 1855 there was much suffering among the poor of New York, who, unable to find work, paraded the streets with banners and mottoes appealing for aid. Soup kitchens were opened in every part of the city, where the hungry were fed from day to day. In the Seventh Ward alone, in one day in January, nine thousand persons were fed by public charity; not one of whom it may be remarked in passing was an American."

And now again there is an outcry against the importation of paupers, which even yet has not ceased.

But poverty was not the only charge brought against foreigners; they formed a large proportion of the criminal class. The criminal statistics of early censuses are so incomplete as to be untrustworthy; but Mulhall's statement of present facts also represents the case in the past. He says: "It is remarkable that although foreigners compose but one-seventh of the population, they supply fourteen thousand offenders, or thirty per cent. of the total."

The proportion of paupers to total population is less in the United States than in any other country. Indeed, the difference is so great as to be almost incredible. Britain has a pauper army of more than a million, or one pauper to every thirty-four persons. America with her greater population has only a quarter of a million, or one pauper in every two hundred of her inhabitants. This statement is fairly representative of the difference between the Republic and other European nations; though in one or two cases the difference in favor of the Republic is even greater, as will be seen by the following:

	No. of Persons Relieved	Ratio to Population	
United Kingdom, . . .	1,037,000	33	per 1000
Italy, ...	1,365,000	48	" "
Prussia, ...	1,310,000	50	" "
Austria, ...	1,220,000	35	" "
France, ...	1,151,000	32	" "
Low Countries, . . .	1,010,000	105	" "
Spain and Portugal, . .	596,000	30	" "
Scandinavia, ...	301,000	38	" "
Switzerland, ...	140,000	54	" "
	8,130,000	41	" "
United States, . . .	225,000	5	" "

Thus it appears that for every pauper in the United States, there are twenty-one paupers in Holland and Belgium, and six in the United Kingdom.

It should be further remarked that of the registered paupers maintained at public expense in America more than one-third are foreigners. The native paupers constitute ten-hundredths per cent. of the native population; the foreign paupers thirty-four hundredths per cent. of the foreign-born element, three times more than their due proportion.

It is gratifying to note that the colored race shows the smallest proportion of pauperism, further discrediting the wild predictions of their idleness and dissipation so common before emancipation. Reduced to percentages of the whole total of each element, the white paupers are fourteen-hundredths and the colored nine-hundredths.

The American poor-law system is very different from that which in England has done so much to foster the idle and improvident at the expense of the industrious and prudent. In many cities bureaus of charity connect the official with the private distribution of alms, and these often procure work for the indigent instead of giving them money. The recipients of relief in America have not been taught to look always to the State for pecuniary help; and the union of public and private charity is useful in maintaining this desirable state of mind amongst the poor. Where paupers regard charity as a right, they are apt to demand it in cases where they would hesitate to ask for favors. The cost of the system compared to that of Great Britain, where fifty million dollars is annually spent on paupers, further commends it. The Republic spends on its poor not a third as much as England.

The causes of the comparative freedom of America from pauperism are not far to seek. In a new country no one who is willing to work need suffer from poverty; and there is no class in America content to remain idle. Then the defective classes bear a smaller proportion to the population than is found in old countries where the conditions of life are harder, and lack of proper food and clothing and shelter results in imperfect development. The small proportion of deaf, dumb, and blind persons in the United States is also in a measure due to the healthful nature of the foreign element; defective persons remain at home in Europe, and only the sound and vigorous emigrate. The potency of this factor is shown by the circumstance that while in the United States there is only one blind person in two thousand seven hundred and twenty inhabitants, and one deaf and dumb among two thousand and ninety-four, in Ireland the proportion is one blind in eight hundred and ninety-four, and one deaf and dumb in thirteen hundred and forty. Private charity does much to remove what trace of poverty and distress there is in America. Orphanages, industrial schools, blind asylums, institutions for the deaf and dumb, and other charities are very numerous and are increasing in number. The census returns show that there are about as many inmates in these as in the public institutions. Charitable institutions classed as miscellaneous number four hundred and thirty. Besides these there are fifty-six institutions for deaf and dumb persons, thirty institutions for the blind, and thirteen schools for feeble-minded children.

In the treatment of these three most important classes Democracy shows to much advantage. The reports of foreign writers seem to be unanimous in the opinion that in no other country is so much care and attention bestowed upon them as in America. Many of the prevailing improved modes of teaching have been first introduced in the American institutions.

Thus America exhibits not only the least poverty, but also the best system of alleviating it. More than half the distressed within her borders are relieved by voluntary charity; and this is ever encroaching on the fields of State charity. It is a decided gain to the world when compulsory charity, such as annually forces ten millions sterling from the pockets of the British taxpayer, is replaced by the charity which blesses equally him who gives and him who takes; and this is a change which is rapidly taking place in America. It may safely be predicted that with the growing self-dependence which republican institutions foster, State charities will be substantially restricted to such as have reached beggary through gross misconduct.

The close relation which exists between poverty and crime has received verification and repeated emphasis since Quetelet first published the results of his inquiries. In England it has been repeatedly shown that hard times bring increase of crime; and Dr. Mayr has shown that in Germany a rise in the price of flour is attended by an increase of robberies. Cheap food, on the other hand, is accompanied by diminution of crime. A scientific principle is thus added to sentiment in the song of "The English Roast Beef"—

> "The man that's well fed, sirs,
>   Can never do ill."

Accordingly we find that offences against property are fewer proportionately in the United States than in European countries.

The influence of free and universal education, together with that of political institutions which at every point inculcate self-respect and stimulate ambition, must be accorded much weight in keeping the Republic the freest of all civilized nations from pauperism and crime.

Humanitarian progress in the treatment of criminals in America is wholly the work of the last half century. The present generation will scarcely credit the inhuman treatment which the delinquent classes received during the preceding generation. Here are a few examples, taken from trustworthy sources, which give us the sad picture of the past:

"During more than fifty years (from 1773 to 1827) the enlightened State of Connecticut had an underground prison in an old mining pit in the hills near Simsbury, which surpassed in horrors all that is known of European or American prisons.

"The passage to the 'Newgate Prison,' as it was called, was down a shaft by means of a ladder to some caverns in the sides of the hill. Here rooms were built of boards for the convicts, and heaps of straw formed their beds. The horrid gloom of these dungeons can be realized only by those who pass along its solitary windings. The impenetrable vastness supporting the awful mass above, impending as if to crush one to atoms; the dripping waters trickling like tears from its sides; the unearthly echoes—all conspire to strike the beholders aghast with amazement and horror.

"Here from thirty to one hundred prisoners were crowded together at night, their feet fastened to bars of iron, and chains about their necks attached to the beams above. The caves reeked with filth, occasioning incessant contagious fevers. The prison was the scene of constant outbreaks, and the most cruel and degrading punishments failed to reform the convicts. 'The system,' says the writer quoted above, 'was very well suited to make men into devils.' The prisoners educated one another in crime. The midnight revels were often like the howling in a pandemonium of tigers, banishing sleep and forbidding rest!

"At Northampton, Massachusetts, a dungeon is described, only four feet high, without window or chimney, the only ventilation being through the privy-vault and two orifices in the wall. In Worcester, a similar cell was only three feet high and eleven feet square, without window or orifice, the air entering through the vault and through the cracks in the door. This was connected with a similar room for lunatics. At Concord was a cell of like construction; and in Schenectady, New York, it is related that three men confined a few hours in such a dungeon were found lifeless, though afterwards they were revived.

"Mr. Edward Livingstone, the great penal reformer of this country, mentions, in 1822, that from fifteen hundred to two thousand persons of both sexes were committed to prison in each year in New York City, all being presumed to be innocent, and the large proportion really so, and were forced into association with old criminals, eating, drinking and sleeping with them; then after having learned the lesson of crime they were turned out to practice it."

These were the good old times we often hear of but never read about. The barbarity of the punishments which characterized the period immediately succeeding the Revolution had been much mitigated before 1830, and the substitution of milder punishments has since gone on with the amelioration of the criminal's life in prison. Surer convictions and lighter sentences mark the progress of penal reform. In a century or two, the most potent deterrent to crime will probably be the simple notice in the press that "in the City Court yesterday the conduct of so-and-so was disapproved by the jury." A thoroughbred needs neither whip nor spur. An educated man born of educated parents is the human thorough-bred.

The progress made in the treatment of youthful crimi-nals is also to be credited to the half century we are con-sidering. Before 1830 little or nothing had been done to effect a distinction or even a separation in jail between children and adult criminals. The result of unrestricted intercourse between them may be imagined. The boy guilty of a first offence was lost; the veteran in crime be-came his hero, and he only longed for discharge that he might emulate his exploits. Young girls in like manner were confined with the most hardened women, with similar results. Strange as it may seem to my readers of to-day, it was not till 1824 that the first reformatory, the New York House of Refuge, was built. Its influence for good was felt at once; and others were soon established, and in 1874, just fifty years after the initiation of the movement, there were thirty-four reformatories in the country, valued at nearly eight million dollars. The aver-age number of inmates was eight thousand nine hundred and twenty-four; while up to that date no fewer than ninety-one thousand four hundred and two boys and girls had been received, and nearly seventy thousand were re-ported as permanently reformed—saved!

"These useful institutions are an immense advance on the prisons which preceded them. The youth is no longer confined with the mature criminal; the sexes also are separated; and at night, as a general practice, there is but one child in each cell, or, if in a large dormitory, the children are carefully watched to pre-vent evil communications. They are all taught useful trades, and have regular day instructions in schools besides religious teaching on Sunday. After their term of sentence has expired, or previously if their good conduct permit, they are indentured with worthy and respected farmers and mechanics."

Numerous societies exist in the large cities for the care of destitute children, the best known being the Children's Aid Society of New York, the growth and success of which have been remarkable. It began its labors in 1853 and has provided more than thirty thousand homeless children with homes and work in the country. Its lodging houses shelter an average of six hundred per night. Its industrial and night schools educate and partly feed and clothe more than ten thousand children per year. Its great aim is to save the vagrant, homeless, and semi-criminal children of the city by drawing them to places of shelter and instruction and finally transferring them to selected homes in the country, there being almost an unlimited demand for children's labor in this country. The result of these efforts is startling. The commitments for vagrancy in New York City fell from two thousand one hundred and sixty-one in 1861 to nine hundred and fourteen in 1871, and of young girls for petty stealing from one thousand one hundred and thirty-three in 1860 to five hundred and seventy-two in 1871, the population having increased in the interval seventeen per cent. Here is the true point at which to grapple with the difficulty, right in the beginning, before the innocent child learns the ways of its elder associates.

America has not been backward in applying modern ideas in the treatment of prisoners. Her penitentiaries now compare favorably with those of other nations, while no nation probably has gone so far in substituting mild for severe punishments. Repugnance to the death penalty is so strong that it has been abolished in several of the States. The large State prisons keep their prisoners steadily at work together during the day, and separate them in the cells at night. In some cases the labor is sold to contractors who pay so much per man, but it is said that this system does not work well, as it brings outside influence into contact with the prisoners. It is more desirable that State officials should superintend and dispose of the work. Many of the prisons are self-supporting or nearly so, while that of Ohio yields an annual profit to the State. None of the prisons rank higher than that of this State at Columbus. In it the convict may by good behavior diminish his sentence five days a month, and may receive an allowance not exceeding one-tenth of his earnings. At the end of his term, if he has gained the full commutation, he is restored to his rights of citizenship. No cruel or degrading punishments are employed, and no distinctive prison clothing is worn. The prison library is much used. Sunday school and prayer meeting are constantly attended, and there are two hundred well conducted members of the prison church. In the Massachusetts State prison the convicts established among themselves a society for mutual debate and improvement. Teachers and chaplains are appointed for prisons, libraries provided, and in short these institutions are conducted upon the idea that it is not so important to punish the offender for what he has done as to improve him, so that he will not be likely to break the laws again. In no department of human effort has a greater change been made for the better in America than in the treatment of the vagrant and criminal classes. How to punish the ignorant and misguided offender is not so eagerly discussed as how to prevent his growing up in ignorance and sin, and thus becoming an offender; nor does the question how to punish the criminal rank with the much more important query how he can be reformed. This is the first consideration, and he is surrounded with libraries, teachers, chaplains, to save him as much as possible from vile associates during his prison life, and save him if possible from himself.

In Du Boys' "History of Criminal Law" we are shocked to read that in the fourteenth century three swine were tried before a legal court and sentenced to death for murdering a shepherd. "The whole herd was also condemned as accomplices, and that part of the sentence was only remitted on appealing to the Duke of Burgundy, whose pardon was granted with all the forms of Chancery." And Berriat Saint-Prix enumerates more than eighty condemnations to death or excommunications pronounced from 1120 to 1741 against every kind of animal from the ass to the grasshopper. To us such grotesque proceedings in the name of Justice are incomprehensible. The next generation, or the next beyond, will probably read with horror of our inflicting the death punishment upon human beings. Two thousand years ago Confucius was asked by the king whether the unprincipled should not be killed for the sake of the principled. The sage replied by asking another question: "Sir, in carrying on your government why should you kill at all?" Surely it is time for us to ask that question now. It is not the least sign of the Republic's position among nations that in many States the death penalty is already a thing of the past.

The civilization of a people may be tested by the character of their punishments. The milder these are the more civilized the nation, as that home is to be rated highest in all the land in which the mildest system of parental government prevails, in which reproof takes its gentlest forms, and yet suffices. Judged by this standard the Democracy stands the test well.

Chapter IX

AGRICULTURE

And they shall beat their swords into plow-shares, and their spears into pruning-hooks: nation shall not lift up sword against nation, neither shall they learn war any more.—ISAIAH.

CERES is the prime divinity of the Republic. To her the American makes his most profound obeisance. Upon him her sweetest smiles are lavished in return.

In 1880 the principal nations stand thus in the value of their agricultural and pastoral products. At the head is the Republic, with $3,020,000,000 (£604,000,000), having marched in little more than a century from the foot to the head of the column. Russia, with her immense area and hundred millions of population, follows at a respectful distance with $2,545,000,000 (£509,000,-000). Imperial Germany with her $2,280,000,000 (£456,000,000) is so closely followed by La Belle France as to render the struggle for precedence quite interesting, for France shows $2,220,000,000 (£444,-000,000), $225,000,000 being the production of the juicy grape. Next comes Austria, with three hundred and twenty-two millions as the product of her extensive corn-lands and Hungarian plains. And then, sixth in the row, comes the beautiful Isle of the Sea, small but mighty, with $1,280,000,000 (£256,000,000)—a prodigious sum for her small area. Italy, Spain, Australia, and

144

Canada come last on the list, with a united product little
more than half that of the Great Republic. What will
the next decade show? Perhaps no change in the order
in which the nations stand, but it is certain that further
and further from her second, and more removed from
any, will stand the Republic—God bless her!

No victory of peace was so long deferred, or so complete when it came, as the conquest of the soil. A hundred years ago agriculture was in little better condition
all over the world than it was a thousand years before.
Indeed it has been boldly asserted that the Greeks, Ro-
mans, Egyptians, and Assyrians cultivated their soil better than any portion of the earth was tilled even a century ago. The alternation of crops was almost unknown;
and fields exhausted by frequent repetition of the same
crop were allowed to lie fallow, as in the time of Moses.
Drainage, where practiced, was of the rudest kind; and
in the sodden ground crops were thin and poor in quality,
and unhealthy as food. Farming implements were of the
most primitive type. The plough generally used was little
better than that of Virgil's time, and only scratched the
ground. The sower, with basket suspended by a cord
round the neck, walked over the field throwing handfuls
of grain on each side, as described in the parable, and as
shown even now by pictures in rural almanacs. The
reaping-hook, almost as old as the hills on which waved
the ripened corn, was the only means of cutting it, while
only the "thresher's weary flingin'-tree" of Burns enabled the farmer to separate the grain from the
straw.

In breeding and rearing cattle progress had been
equally insignificant. The quality of food given to cattle
was so bad that attention to breeding alone availed little
in improving stock. The average weight of oxen and
sheep sold in Smithfield market has more than doubled

since the middle of the last century, a result to be ascribed to improved feeding quite as much as to increased care in breeding.

The primitive condition of agriculture in America a century and a quarter ago is well illustrated in the following extract from a work by the Swedish traveller, Kalm. Speaking of the James River colonists, he says:

"They make scarce any manure for their corn fields, but when one piece of ground has been exhausted by continual cropping, clear and cultivate another piece of fresh land, and when that is exhausted proceed to a third. Their cattle are allowed to wander through the woods and uncultivated grounds, where they are half starved, having long ago extirpated almost all the annual grasses by cropping them too early in the spring, before they had time to form their flowers or to shed their seeds."

And the imperfect feeding caused the cattle to diminish in size generation by generation, till they grew so stunted and small, as to be appropriately called "runts."

The advance made in agriculture and cattle-raising during the last half century has been prodigious; and much of it is due either to the creation by American inventive genius of mechanical appliances, or to enforced European inventiveness resulting from American competition. From the earliest times American statesmen have directed their energies to the advancement of agricultural arts. Washington, with a burden of care such as has been the lot of few, found time to superintend agricultural operations and experiments. The importance of agriculture to civilization formed the text of his last annual message to Congress; and the last elaborate production of his pen, written only a week before his death,

was a long letter to the manager of his farms, containing thirty-two folio sheets of directions for their cultivation during several succeeding years. Most of Washington's successors to the Presidency gave personal attention to agriculture. One of the most distinguished of
them, Mr. Jefferson, invented the hill-side plough; and
Adams, Calhoun, Clay, and Webster forgot the anxieties
of statesmanship in the peaceful pursuits of the farm.
Beginning thus early, the advancement of agriculture
has continued to be the first care of American statesmen and the American people, with the result that the
Republic leads the world to-day not only in amount of
agricultural products but in excellence of agricultural
methods.

One-fourth of the total wealth of America is employed in the cultivation of the soil, and that is about
the proportion which agriculture contributes to the industrial product. Statistics for 1830 being untrustworthy,
comparisons cannot be made with so early a period; but
taking the figures of the census of 1850, which was very
complete, we find that in the short space of thirty years
the amount of improved land more than doubled. The
following table shows the extent and regularity of the
progress made:

	1850	1860	1870	1880
Total acres in farm	293,560,614	407,212,538	407,735,041	536,081,835
Acres improved	113,032,614	163,110,720	188,921,099	284,771,042
Number of farms	1,449,073	2,044,077	2,659,985	4,008,907
Average size of farms	203	199	153	134

It will be seen that the tendency is towards smaller
rather than larger farms, notwithstanding the gigantic

holdings which have been the fashion in recent years in some of the North-western States. The average farm has fallen in size from two hundred and three acres in 1850 to one hundred and thirty-five acres in 1880. As this result has been reached under a system of absolute freedom we are justified in assuming that the cultivation of holdings small enough to be worked by one family without employing help is found to be the condition best fitted for survival. When the writer was in the Northwest upon the huge estates there, sagacious agriculturists in the district predicted that the small farmer upon his eighty or at the most one hundred and sixty acres would eventually drive out the great capitalists who had undertaken to farm thousands of acres by means of others' labor. This is most cheering news, for it is manifestly better for the State that a race of citizens, each his own master and landlord, should inhabit the land and call a small portion of it his own, than that one man should be lord over thousands of acres and over hundreds of farm laborers. Political and economical ends fortunately unite in this the grandest of all branches of industry in the nation. The centralization which seems inseparable in manufacturing is not, we may console ourselves, to invade the realms of agriculture. The State is still to rest in security upon millions who possess and cultivate the soil divided into small farms. Such citizens are the very life-blood of the Republic.

The improved land in 1880 was but fifteen per cent. of the total area, but even then, according to Mulhall, it produced thirty per cent. of the grain of the world. The capital invested in farms and farming was $10,600,000,-000 (£2,120,000,000), being more than three times as much as that invested in manufacturing, the next largest industry. The difference between "acres in farms," and "acres improved" is that the former includes "woodland and forest," which although owned by the farmer has not yet been cleared for crops. This is on the average nearly one-half of the farm, so that the productive acreage of the country may be, and no doubt soon will be, largely increased by the present farmers without adding greatly to the number of farms. The total number of acres under crop is two hundred and eighty-four million seven hundred and seventy-one thousand and forty-two, of which permanent meadows, pastures, orchards and vineyards comprise sixty-one million seven hundred and three thousand eight hundred and ninety-eight acres, the remainder being tilled land and land sown with grass in rotation of crops.

It was a great survey at the beginning of the century to look back over sixty-five thousand square miles that had been brought under cultivation in the preceding decade. Between 1850 and 1860, however, two hundred and fifteen thousand square miles had been turned into farms, and between 1870 and 1880 two hundred and ninety-seven thousand square miles. Thus in ten years territory equal in extent to Great Britain and France combined was added to the cultivated area in America. Even yet the progress continues. During the last year the sales of public lands to settlers exceeded sixteen million acres—an area as great as Belgium and Denmark combined. In Dakota alone the new farms of 1883 exceeded six million acres—one-third of all Scotland. In the face of such facts it is clear that the Americans are the great agricultural people of the world, and that no other race has spread so diligently and so profitably over so great an area.

In 1880 an inquiry was made for the first time in the United States into the tenure of farms—whether cultivated by their owners, rented, or worked on shares, with the result shown in the following table:

ACRES IN FARMS		WORKED BY OWNERS		RENTED		WORKED ON SHARES	
		Number	Per Cent.	Number	Per Cent.	Number	Per Cent.
Under 3		2,601	60	875	20	876	20
3 and under	10	85,456	63	22,904	17	26,529	20
10 "	20	122,411	48	41,522	16	90,816	30
20 "	50	460,486	59	97,399	13	223,689	28
50 "	100	804,522	78	69,663	7	158,625	15
100 "	500	1,416,618	84	84,645	5	194,720	11
500 "	1,000	66,447	87	3,956	5	5,569	8
1,000 and over . .		25,765	90	1,393	5	1,420	5

This corroborates the current belief that the majority of farms in America are cultivated by their owners, nearly three million of the four million farms being of this class. Eight per cent. of the total were cultivated upon shares. The farms most frequently rented for money are the smallest farms, and their number steadily decreases. Only in the South does this system of renting, especially for a share in the proceeds, prevail to any great extent. The system has grown up since the war, in consequence of the subdivision of the great plantations, most of the lessees being colored people. It marks a temporary stage of development succeeding slavery, and is certain to pass away as the renters are able to buy the land from the former owners, their old masters. The free play of individual forces tends to make the cultivator of the soil its owner. There is no law of primogeniture or of entail in America, and the transfer of land is scarcely, if any, more difficult than the sale or purchase of a horse.

The reputed value of farm land is $19.21 per acre,

nearly £4, not much more than the rent per annum of some of the land in Britain. It ranges from $34 (nearly £7) in the North Atlantic group of States to $7.35 (£1.10) in the States of the Southern central group.

From 1850 to 1860 the value of farms more than doubled, while population increased only thirty-five per cent. On account of the Civil War the increase from 1860 to 1870 was less than that of population, but from 1870 to 1880 it rose thirty-seven per cent., which was seven per cent. greater than the increase of population, so that the tendency hitherto has been for land to increase in value even faster than the population. This has made the farmer of America highly prosperous during the past thirty years; for even if he has only made a living for himself and family from the produce and improved his land, he stands to-day with a property worth three and a half times its value thirty years ago. For every $500 (£100) invested in his farm he has $1,750 (£350) to-day. Had he rented his farm from some huge landlord this unearned increment would have gone to the landlord, and the work would have been left where he began except for the savings in money he might have been able to make. The rise of values going on around him, which he did so much to produce, would have been of no benefit to him. He would not have been half the man he is, nor worth half as much to the State. That State alone is absolutely secure from violent measures whose soil belongs to the mass of its well-doing citizens.

Improved implements and machinery have revolutionized agriculture in America. Their value in 1830 is estimated at but $150,000,000 (£30,000,000), in 1880 it exceeded $450,000,000 (£90,000,000). The widespread use of machinery is mainly due to three causes, the scarcity of labor, which has in turn stimulated the fertility of American invention, and the readiness,

amounting almost to anxiety, of the farmer to adopt the
latest and best devices. Then the greater portion of the
soil under cultivation is level and without obstructions,
and admirably adapted for the use of machinery. It is no
wonder that under such conditions America should be
the foremost agricultural country of the world. No other
country on earth has a chance in comparison. Even gigantic Russia grows not much more than half as much.
Here is the record as given by Mulhall:

COUNTRIES	ACRES UNDER GRAIN	PRODUCTION IN BUSHELS
United States . . .	118,000,000	2,698,000,000
Russia	158,000,000	1,585,000,000
Germany	43,000,000	990,000,000
France	40,000,000	840,000,000
Austro-Hungary . . .	35,000,000	520,000,000
United Kingdom. . .	12,500,000	445,000,000
Spain	15,000,000	300,000,000
Italy	18,000,000	270,000,000
Canada and Australia .	14,000,000	140,000,000

Just cast your eye over the march of the last thirty
years and satisfy yourself that the Republic has travelled
with its seven-league boots on. In 1850 only eight hundred and sixty-seven million bushels were produced; ten
years more, one thousand two hundred million; ten
more, one thousand four hundred million; and finally
ten more in 1880, two thousand seven hundred million
bushels from the generous bosom of good Mother
Earth. Of this aggregate one thousand seven hundred
and fifty millions were maize, four hundred and sixty
millions wheat, and four hundred and seven millions
oats. The maize or Indian corn crop is therefore double
that of wheat and oats. Maize, which is mostly consumed

at home, is the staff of life for the hog, and horses and
cattle are also fed upon it to a great extent throughout
the country; nevertheless the export trade has grown
year after year. Twenty years ago not $10,000,000 (£2,-
000,000) worth were sent abroad; in 1880 more than
five times that sum.

A grand sight is a field of corn on a hot day. I remember being upon a train in southern Illinois which, on account of obstructions on the line, had to lie upon a siding
for several hours. Nothing but corn was in sight over the
great level plain. I wandered among the immense stalks,
some at least fourteen feet high; a heavy dew had fallen
during the night, and the hot morning sun was now well
up in the heavens. Crack after crack resounded like pis-
tol shots. It was the corn bursting its coverings. I imagined I could actually see it grow; I know I *felt* it do so.
What would America do without its maize and cotton,
the two pillars upon which its agricultural supremacy so
largely depends! She is pretty sure of the future, however, for upon no other portion of the globe can these be
grown to such advantage.

England is more interested in the wheat than in the
maize crop. Well, the increase in this indispensable cereal
has been even greater than in any other crop. It is doubtful whether any agricultural growth was ever as rapid as
that of wheat in this country during the past thirty years.
Down to 1859 the Republic used to import wheat at intervals from Europe; now she is the purveyor of the staff
of life for mankind, producing one-fourth of the world's
crop. In 1850 only one hundred million bushels were
grown; in 1860 the crop was one hundred and seventy-
three millions, not bad, being an increase of seventy per
cent. in ten years; but in 1870 the amount was two hundred and eighty-seven millions, and in 1880 we find the

crop four hundred and fifty-nine millions. It exceeded five hundred millions of bushels last year.

Twenty-five years ago (1860) the export of wheat and flour averaged between six and eight millions sterling. In 1880 $190,000,000 (£38,000,000) worth were sent forth, of which Britain alone received $175,000,000 (£35,000,000).

The reported decrease in acreage under wheat this year (1885) on account of low prices will prove, in my opinion, to be only temporary, pending the adjustment to a standard of lower values. This great cereal will be grown, and delivered in British ports in constantly increasing quantities at prices even lower (if necessary) than those which have surprised so many eminent authorities. The British Commissioners who recently visited us and reported upon the agricultural situation did not allow for the shrinkage of the excessive margins of profit which the growth and transportation and merchandising of wheat have hitherto yielded at every stage of the operation. I differ from most of the foreign experts and believe that a continuance of the present depression throughout the world will send plenty of American wheat to the ports of Britain at lower prices than those of to-day. We shall see. The Republic has never yet had to show what it could do when put to it.

One is surprised to find that oats are so largely grown in America, for so little is heard of that modest grain compared with its much talked of neighbor. The Northwestern States are admirably adapted to its growth, and instead of Scotch and Irish oatmeal being imported for human food, as it was until recently, the native article is found fully equal to it in quality. Such was proved to be the case at the last Paris Exhibition. Indeed, nothing surprised me so much as to hear my Scotch visitors to America three years ago declare that American oatmeal

porridge surpassed the Dunfermline article. The other
indispensable commodity for a Scotchman, however, they
pronounced miserable; neither "Bourbon" nor "Old
Monongahela" found favor with them. The verdict was
that only by a stretch of politeness almost to bursting
was the stuff worthy to take the revered name of whiskey. This, however, is a matter of taste, for more topers
in the world prefer the republican to the queer Scotch
article.

The production of barley increases rapidly. The census of 1850 shows that only five million bushels were
grown then. In ten years it had increased to sixteen millions, in ten more (1870) to twenty-nine millions, while
1880 shows forty-four millions of bushels. So much for
bold John Barleycorn. The acreage under barley (1880)
was a little less than two millions; yield per acre twenty-
two bushels. The United Kingdom had then six hundred
and sixty thousand acres more devoted to this grain, so
the barley crop of America is not yet equal to that of the
old home, but its increase of growth here is extraordinary, for between 1850 and 1860 it was two hundred and
six per cent. It more than doubled in ten years. California is the leading State in barley and New York comes
next.

In the United States in 1880, one million eight hundred and forty thousand acres were sown with rye; product, twenty million bushels. Rye does not figure in the
returns for Britain, which are before me, the authorities
saying that very little is now grown there.

After all it is not maize, cotton, wheat, oats, barley,
or rye which is ruler in the agricultural kingdom, but
a more modest grass. Hay is the most valuable of all
American crops; the amount cut in 1880 exceeded thirty-
six millions of tons grown on more than thirty millions
of acres. It has kept pace with its rivals, for in 1850, not

quite fourteen million tons were grown. Even twenty years ago but nineteen millions were reported, so that it has nearly doubled in two decades.

Sorghum is the only important plant of recent introduction. Though a stranger, it seems to thrive in its new home, and its cultivation spreads rapidly. In 1880 more than twenty-eight million gallons of molasses were made from it, more than half a gallon for every man, woman, and child in the country.

We now come to the great Southern staple, King Cotton. An ancient and honorable potentate truly, for does not Herodotus tell us four hundred and fifty years B. C. that the Indians were then weaving it into cloth, and did not Cæsar cover the Forum and the Sacred Way, too, with awnings of cotton to shade the dignitaries of the Imperial City from the rays of the sun? In 1621 the first cotton was planted in America. It did not take kindly to the climate. Many experiments failed, although repeated at different times and at various places; and more than a hundred and fifty-seven years elapsed before a pound of cotton was exported. "In 1784, a small quantity of cotton was imported into Liverpool, where it was at first considered as an illegal transaction, as it was not supposed possible for it to have been the growth of any of the States of the Union; and when, about the same period, a duty was proposed in the United States Congress on the import of foreign cotton, it was declared by one of the representatives from South Carolina, that the cultivation of cotton was in contemplation by the planters of South Carolina and Georgia, 'and that if good seed could be procured it might succeed.'"

We ought never to give up readily a new thing, whether plant or idea, for success often lies just beyond the last failure. For the six years following the exports to England were respectively one hundred and nine, three hundred and eighty-nine, and then eight hundred and forty-two bags. After Independence (1776) cotton began to attract special attention. Whitney's gin for separating the seeds from the fibre removed the only obstacle to its almost unlimited production. A tariff upon the importation of cotton goods led to the manufacture of cloth at home, and cotton cultivation receiving a further impetus, America soon became the leading source of supply for the world. Not to go back further than half a century we find that in 1830, nine hundred and seventy-six thousand eight hundred and forty-five bales were grown; in 1880, the crop was five million seven hundred and fifty-seven thousand three hundred and ninety-seven bales, valued at $275,000,000 (£55,000,000). Of the 1830 crop, $30,000,000 (£6,000,000) worth was exported; of the 1880 crop, $220,000,000 (£44,000,000), of which England took nearly two-thirds. The latter, however, included manufactured cotton, of which in 1830 there was none. So that the value of the cotton exported exceeded that of wheat by $30,000,000 (£6,000,000).

Tobacco-growing still continues to prosper in America, although surely the coming man is not to smoke. Chewing is already a thing of the past, and the pipe and cigar are doomed. Before many generations the smoker will be considered as disgusting as the chewer is to-day. America increased her crop eighty per cent. from 1870 to 1880, and six hundred and thirty-eight thousand acres are now devoted to the weed. Its value in 1880 was three and a half millions sterling. Brother Jonathan makes a fair division of his tobacco with the rest of mankind, for he sends just about half of it abroad and smokes the other half himself. "Take a cigar," he says, and hands one to less favored nations, reserving only one for himself. Generous fellow, Jonathan!

We must not ignore the so-called fruit of old Ireland,

the potato, which however is a native, true American, in origin. America does her share in growing potatoes, those apples of the earth. In 1880 she produced two hundred and three millions of bushels, a little more than four bushels to every man, woman, and child. I do not believe I had my fair proportion, which for every adult must be six bushels, nor do I think any one in America will admit having devoured his share. He will rather dispute the census returns. As none were exported, we must pass as a potato-eating people, or suspect our fellow-citizens of Irish descent of having eaten much more than their share, which they probably did.

The enormous quantity of fruit grown and consumed in America surprises the visitor. Notwithstanding its cheapness, the orchard products in 1880 were valued at $52,500,000 (£10,500,000), and there was imported an average of six pounds of fruit to each person, worth altogether about $20,000,000 (£4,000,000).

The total value of the year's product of Uncle Sam's farm in 1880 was $2,225,000,000 (£445,000,000), and it was not a good year for prices either. He has netted much more than that since—more than $2,500,000,000 (£500,000,000). Indeed, Mulhall values the total agricultural products for 1884 at no less than $2,721,500,000 (£544,300,000).

Let us now glance at the live stock upon his gigantic farm and their products, and see what he has to show us there.

He first asks us to review his hogs, a motley mass ranging from the patrician Howard (he of Bedford, M. P.) down to the plebeian, long-snouted grunter, which must "root or die." Fifty-six and three-quarter millions march past. Imagine their salute. Every man, woman, and child in the land owns one hog and a little more. Now comes his cattle with their glowering eyes, and the line stretches till nearly forty-six millions are counted. Eighteen and a half millions of them are milch cows, the most widely scattered and most equally diffused of all his beasts. Throughout America every family of three persons have one milch cow and a fraction of another one. He exhibits his sheep next, forty-five millions of them, and enough left over to stock an ordinary country. Not quite a sheep to every inhabitant, but pretty near it.

Will it please you now to look at Uncle Sam's horses? Trot them out. Twelve millions and a half of these useful, noble animals, ranging from the fastest trotters in the world, from "Maud S" with her record of a mile in two minutes, eight and three-quarter seconds, to the half-wild "tackey" of Florida. There they are, followed by more than two millions of mules and asses, which close the long procession. The census proves that on the average every family in the country really owns a horse, a cow, four pigs, and three sheep, not a bad start for a young farmer.

Were the live stock upon Uncle Sam's estate ranged five abreast, each animal estimated to occupy a space five feet long, and marched round the world, the head and tail of the procession would overlap. This was the host of 1880; that of 1885 would be ever so much greater, and still it grows day by day, and the end of its growth no man can foretell.

Having reviewed the live stock, let me now conduct you to the dairy to see the butter and cheese departments. Four hundred thousand tons of butter were made in 1880, an average of nearly sixteen pounds for every man, woman, and child in the country. Ah! the Yankee's bread is buttered in more ways than one. In 1870, eighty thousand tons of cheese were made; in 1880, one hundred and twenty thousand tons. Since the introduction of the factory system, cheese manufacturing has increased enormously. The American does not care for cheese as his progenitor does. What he makes he sends largely abroad to figure as Stilton, Cheshire, or Cheddar in Britain, for he manufactures all brands, and you cannot tell the republican article from its monarchical prototype. The cheese exported in 1881 was worth more than three and a quarter millions sterling. The statistics laid before the National Butter, Cheese, and Egg Association at its late meeting in Chicago represent that the annual value of dairy products in this country is $100,-000,000 (£20,000,000) while the amount of capital invested in cows is said to be greater by $40,000,000 (£8,000,000) than that invested in bank stocks.

What does the American do with all the products of this live stock and dairy? First, he supplies his own wants —and these are great, for fifty-six millions of the most prosperous people in the world, every one of them determined to have the best he can afford, and accustomed to the most expensive food, consume an enormous amount. The surplus he exports, and Britain is by far the largest recipient, taking of many articles half of all he has to spare.

In 1870 began a new traffic—the exportation of living cattle—of which $400,000 (£80,000) worth were sent to Britain; in 1880 this trade exceeded $12,500,000 (£2,500,000). The exportation of fresh beef was tried in 1875, and in 1880 the value of this article exported was $7,500,000 (£1,500,000).

The American hog has been a prime favorite in Europe during the past twenty years. In 1860 the amount of hams and bacon exported was only $2,050,000 (£410,000); in 1880 the demand was for more than $50,000,000 (£10,000,000) worth. Britain takes the greater part. What a prejudice against American hams and bacon formerly existed there! I remember walking one day

through a curer's establishment in an English town where
the pigs of the district were killed and who was supposed
to deal only in the genuine home article. He furnished,
no doubt, the much praised ham and sweet bacon of
which my friends boasted as so different from the foreign article. A pile of half hidden boxes, marked Chicago, caught my eye. I called the proprietor aside and
asked whether the contents were superior or inferior to
the domestic. He smiled and said: "Sometimes the one
and sometimes the other," adding, "We are queer folk!"
The American article now stands upon its merits, but
many a ton of it is still sold as genuine English. $85,000,-
000 (£17,000,000) is the annual revenue of Uncle Sam
from his pigs.

But little mutton is sent abroad. The value of the exports in 1884 was less than $300,000 (£60,000). But
with the steady and rapid improvement in the breed of
sheep which is taking place in America, we may anticipate at no distant date a large trade in this article, which
Australia has found so profitable.

Twenty years ago the mutton of America was not
worth eating. It is still inferior to that of Britain, but
it is growing better every year. Whether it can ever
reach the grade of the best Scotch is doubtful, but the
improvement in the sheep here is shown by the increase
of wool, which is beyond the increase in the number of
sheep. Between 1850 and 1860 the increase of wool production was fourteen per cent.; during the next decade it
was sixty-six per cent., and between 1870 and 1880 no
less than one hundred and forty-seven per cent. The
average fleece in 1850 was but two three-tenths pounds;
in 1880 it had nearly doubled (four four-tenths pounds).
The fleece of a sheep in the North averages more than
five pounds, but in the genial South the animal does not
need so warm a coat. If God tempers the wind to the

shorn lamb, He also adapts the fleece to the climate, and
sees that the Southern sheep is not over-burdened. In this
matter of sheep's covering one agrees with the sage who
said that, "Although the Lord does temper the wind to
the shorn lamb, the Lord considers it man's business *not
to shear too close.*"

Wool-growing in America shows the usual increase.
In 1830 the fleece was but eighteen millions of pounds;
in 1850, fifty-two million; in 1860, sixty million, and in
1870, one hundred million. In the last ten years it has
much more than doubled, for in 1880 the fleece weighed
two hundred and forty millions of pounds. Could any
one believe that America grows more than double the
amount of wool grown in the United Kingdom! It surprised me to find that such was indeed the case, for the
fleece of the latter in 1880 was but one hundred and
twelve millions of pounds. As one travels through Britain, go where he will, he is scarcely ever out of sight or
out of hearing of the omnipresent sheep. In English
meadows and on heather hills the white specks dot the
ground. In our coaching tour we seemed to pass through
endless herds of sheep on both sides of the road, while
upon this side of the Atlantic we scarcely see the innocent creatures, and indeed what can be called a flock is
the rarest sight. Yet the stragglers counted upon the
three million square miles exceed the crowded flocks of
Britain, whose pastoral beauties they so much enhance.
Mulhall gives the average of wool per sheep in the
United Kingdom as four pounds, and that of America
as five pounds; which is correct if the Southern sheep be
not included. This is another surprise to me. I should
have said the average amount of wool upon the British
sheep far exceeded that of its seemingly less prosperous
transatlantic fellow. It is evident that America is more
favorably placed for sheep growing than is generally sup-

posed. Is there anything, I wonder, in the agricultural or live stock line in which she cannot excel!

Let me call the attention of my readers to the significant fact that no articles of general consumption have increased in price in America during recent years except beef, mutton, and pork, which have advanced inordinately, the opening of European markets to American producers having naturally reduced the supply at home. With these exceptions the cost of living has been much lessened. The growth of this export trade is seen by the following figures. In 1870 the total value of exports of meat in the hoof, fresh or preserved, was only $17,500,-000 (£3,500,000); in five years it had run up to nearly $70,000,000 (£14,000,000), and in 1880 no less than $117,500,000 (£23,500,000) worth were taken from the home market. America was not prepared to undergo this unexpected drain, hence the change in values. The export value of beef in 1870 was less than $20 (£4) per head, in 1880 it was not far from $75 (£15). Three and a half beeves were thus supplied ten years ago for the cost of one in 1880. A similar appreciation has taken place in the value of sheep, the price of which, $2 (8s) per head in 1871, rose to $4.25 (17s) nine years later. In live hogs we have the same result, though these obtained their maximum value in 1874, when each hog exported cost more than $10 (£2). Restrictive legislation in various countries having interrupted the trade, prices during 1880 averaged only $5 (£1) per head. But even had no hostile legislation been passed, the capacity of this country to supply in a short time any number of hogs required must have occasioned a rapid fall in prices. What has happened with hogs must happen soon with cattle and sheep. Look out for a great fall in these from the figures of 1880. The Republic was taken unawares.

Let us see what will be her response after a few years to the demands upon her ever growing herds.

To conclude with a summary. The farms of America comprise eight hundred and thirty-seven thousand six hundred and twenty-eight square miles, an area nearly equal to one-fourth of Europe, and larger than the four greatest European countries put together (Russia excepted), namely, France, Germany, Austria and Hungary, and Spain. The capital invested in agriculture would suffice to buy up the whole of Italy, with its rich olive-groves and vineyards, its old historic cities, cathedrals, and palaces, its king and aristocracy, its pope and cardinals, and every other feudal appurtenance. Or, if the American farmers were to sell out, they could buy the entire peninsula of Spain, with all its traditions of medieval grandeur, and the flat lands which the Hollanders at vast cost have wrested from the sea and the quaint old towns they have built there. If he chose to put by his savings for three years, the Yankee farmer could purchase the fee-simple of pretty Switzerland as a summer resort, and not touch his capital at all, for each year's earnings exceed $550,000,000 (£110,000,000). The cereal crop for 1880 was more than two billions and a half of bushels. If placed in one mass this would make a pile of three and a half billion cubic feet. Built into a solid mass as high as the dome of St. Paul's (three hundred and sixty-five feet), and as wide as the cathedral across the transepts (two hundred and eighty-five feet), it would extend, a solid mass of grain, down Fleet Street and the length of the Strand to Piccadilly, thence on through Knightsbridge, Hammersmith and South Kensington, to a distance of over six miles. Or it would make a pyramid three times as great as that of Cheops. If loaded on carts, it would require all the horses in Europe and a million more (thirty-three and a half millions) to remove it, though each horse drew a load of two tons. Were the entire crop of cereals loaded on a continuous train of cars, the train would reach one and a half times round the globe. Its value is half as great as all the gold mined in California in the thirty-five years since gold was found there. The corn and cotton fields of America form kingdoms in themselves surpassing in size some of those of Europe.

In 1884 more than half a million animals were sent to Europe alive, while nearly a billion pounds of meat was sent over. And four years before the total value of meat on the hoof, fresh or preserved, sent to Europe, was $1,175,000,000 (£235,000,000). It is hard to realize just what this muster really means. If the Atlantic could be crossed as the Red Sea was by Moses' host, and these animals were placed ten abreast, each averaging five feet in length, the procession would be fifty miles long. Such a line the Republic sends every year to Europe; "the dead meats" being far beyond this, however, in value, for, as usual, here we find the dead as compared to the living in "the great majority." Of cheese one hundred and thirteen million pounds were exported last year (1884), while one-fifth that quantity of butter was sent to lay upon the bread which the Republic had sent to Europe. She is no niggard, this Greater Britain; she scatters her bounties not only profusely but in palatable proportions. May her capacity for good works never grow less!

These enormous food exports suggest serious thoughts concerning the future. The populations of the Old World are fast increasing without any extension of soil or corresponding increase of productiveness. Since the beginning of the century one hundred and seventy-two millions of Europeans have grown to three hundred and twelve millions. This is an advance unprecedented in the history of the Old World. Without the enormous shipments of food from America and other places such an increase would probably have been impossible. The present consumption of food by Europe is vastly greater than its production. The deficit per year of grain is three hundred and eighty million bushels, more than a bushel for every man, woman, and child in Europe; while that of meat amounts to eight hundred and fifty-three thousand tons, six pounds for every man, woman, and child. The future growth of Europe, therefore, seems chiefly dependent upon supplies of food from abroad—mainly from America: every addition to the population must be fed for the most part from without. The United Kingdom is particularly thus dependent. Mr. Giffen estimates that twelve millions, one-third of the whole population, already live on imported food.

It would be difficult to exaggerate the consequences of this fact, ever growing in importance. The social and economic changes involved may be of the most radical character. No doubt, as Mr. Caird and other eminent authorities state, that by better and more thorough cultivation the soil of Europe and especially that of Britain can be made to yield an increase, but we assume that this can be obtained only at greater cost and to a small extent. The proportion of Europeans dependent for food upon the New World will probably increase from year to year. Happily there is no question as to its undeveloped resources, which are capable of extension quite sufficient to meet any possible demand for a period if not quite as far as we are tempted to look ahead, certainly quite as far as we can see ahead, which is a very different matter. When we think over the changes produced during fifty years' march of this Republic we must surely hesitate to speculate beyond what the next fifty years are to bring, and for fifty years ahead at least we can see that

America can give Europe all the food it will require.
Beyond that let posterity manage for itself. The man
who is always telling you what he would have done "if
he had been there" in any given emergency is he who
never gets there. And none of my readers will ever "get
there" to the day when the Republic cannot respond to
any call made upon her for agricultural products. Millions and millions of fertile acres, under sunny skies and
watered with refreshing showers, still lie before us only
awaiting the plough, to respond with food for man.

It is in the cultivation of this heritage and the building up of the cities and of the roads and railways and
telegraphs which must accompany this work and the
erection of school-houses and churches throughout the
land that the American people will find their proper development, not in chasing the fiction of the carrying of
merchandise upon the high seas for which they must
contend at a disadvantage. Much less should they call
for the building of war ships. The present lack of a navy
ensures the nation a dignified position. It is one of the
chief glories of the Republic, that she spends her money
for better ends and has nothing worthy to rank as a ship
of war. To build a few small ships and call them a navy
will invite comparison, and the "rascally comparative"
must only make the Republic ridiculous, for she either
wants the strongest navy in the world or none. If she
builds the weakest she builds her ships for the stronger
enemy to sink or capture, if she ever has an enemy, which
is to be doubted unless she flaunts before the other powers great monster ships expressly designed to work them
injury. There is an effort to produce a scare just now in
regard to her defenceless sea coast; any small power
could attack her ports and levy contributions, it is said.
So any man who walks down Broadway may be attacked
by a disorderly fellow, but no one suggests that we walk

about, therefore, in coats of mail. There is not a port of
America which could not be efficiently closed, if necessary, against an assailant before he had time to reach it;
fortunately there is little prospect that the Republic will
ever have an assailant if she remain unarmed. When nations provide themselves with arms ostensibly for defence, *offence* travels not far in the rear, accompanies it
as shadow does substance. Shakespeare tells us

> "How oft the means to do ill deeds
> Make ill deeds done."

I beseech my fellow Republicans to leave to the monarchies of the Old World the folly and the crime of
building and maintaining these vast engines of destruction, the mere possession of which tends to make war
between nations which would otherwise have remained at
peace.

Of all the lessons which the Democracy has given,
or is capable of giving, to people in less advanced stages
of political development, this ranks supreme, that peace
has its victories still more renowned than war. So far,
the Democracy can congratulate itself that its country's
reputation rests not upon conquest nor wars of aggression, but upon the nobler foundation of peaceful, orderly,
industrial development. Men and brethren, let us see to
it that our Representatives do not tarnish this record by
stripping the Republic of the majestic robes of golden
Peace to array her in the panoply of barbarous War!

Chapter X
MANUFACTURES

"In a general way, it may safely be predicted that the nation which has the most varied industry is likely, all other things being equal, to be the most prosperous, powerful, and contented. Agriculture, though the first and most essential of all callings, is still far from yielding the best results from a commercial and industrial point of view." "ENGLAND'S SUPREMACY."—JEANS.

LABOR is discovered to be the grand conqueror, enriching and building up nations more surely than the greatest battles," says Channing.

Of this truth the Republic is proof conclusive, for she has become the greatest manufacturing nation of the world by labor, not by luck.

"What men call luck,
Is the prerogative of valiant souls."

Since the earliest period in their history the American people have devoted great attention to and manifested unusual aptitude for manufactures. The first colonists fully realized their importance; and so energetically did they devote themselves to their development that by 1670, when the population numbered less than two hundred thousand, their progress had already begun to excite the jealousy of the mother country. Despite the restrictions which Great Britain placed upon the colonial trade, the manufacture and commerce of America grew rapidly. The moral cost at which the advance was made,

169

however, was very great. It may be gauged by the fact, certified by the Hon. David A. Wells, that the colonists were "a nation of law-breakers: nine-tenths of the colonial merchants were smugglers. One-quarter of the whole number of the signers of the Declaration of Independence were bred to the contraband trade. John Hancock was the prince of contraband traders, and, with John Adams as his counsel, was on trial before the Admiralty Court in Boston at the exact hour of the shedding of blood at Lexington, to answer for half a million dollars' penalties alleged to have been by him incurred as a smuggler." The evils and sufferings caused by the narrow policy of the home government can be but vaguely conceived even in view of this wholesale demoralization of a generous and otherwise law-abiding people. The efforts of the British to cripple the industries of America did not end, as might be supposed, with the success of the Revolution. Transatlantic manufacturers sought to continue their repressive measures long after Independence was achieved, and their methods of procedure took many a curious turn. Bishop, the historian of American industry, says:

"It was supposed to be an object worth large sacrifices on the part of the English manufacturers to break down the formidable rivalship of growing but immature manufactures in America, by means of heavy consignments of goods to be disposed of at auction, and upon the most liberal credits, to the merchants. That this policy had the approval of eminent British statesmen, is shown by the remarkable language of Mr. Brougham in Parliament, soon after the peace (1815), when he declared in reference to the losses sustained by English manufacturers in these transactions, that it was 'even worth while to incur a loss upon the first exportation, in order by the glut to stifle in the cradle these rising manufactures in the United States, which the war had forced into existence contrary to the natural course of things.'"

All this is of the past, and is only referred to as essential to a proper understanding of the subject under review. Britain did what she did because in those days nobody knew any better, as explained in the chapter upon occupations.

The steady nature of the progress of American manufactures is indicated by the ever increasing ratio of manufactures to population. This is shown by Mulhall as follows:

PRODUCT PER INHABITANT

| 1830 | . . . | £1.8 | 1850 | . . . | £9.1 | 1870 | . . | £21.2 |
| 1840 | . . . | 5.7 | 1860 | . . . | 12.2 | 1880 | . . | 22.0 |

An increase of more than ten times the products per inhabitant in fifty years.

It is interesting to note that as the country became more densely settled, the importance of manufactures relative to agriculture increased. In 1850 the capital invested in manufactures was only eight per cent. of that in agriculture. In 1860 it was thirteen per cent.; in 1870 nineteen per cent.; and in 1880 it reached twenty-three per cent., or nearly one-fourth that of agriculture. In 1870 the value of the products of manufacture less that of raw materials was seventy-one per cent. of the value of agricultural products, while in 1880 the proportion had risen to eighty-nine per cent. So that great as the growth of agriculture in America has been, and the world has never before seen the like, that of manufactures has been even greater. No statement in this book will probably cause so much surprise as that the young Republic and not Great Britain is to-day the greatest manufacturing nation of the world, for she is generally credited with being great only in agriculture.

The annual product of each operative has advanced

in value from $1,100 (£220) in 1850 to $2,015 (£403) in 1880; a result largely due to improvements in methods and machinery. This cause, joined to the increase in number of workers, resulted in an advance of total manufactures from $1,060,000,000 (£212,000,000) in 1850 to $5,560,000,000 (£1,112,000,000) in 1880—an increase of nearly six hundred per cent. in thirty years. During the same period the increase of British manufactures was little more than a hundred per cent. Their total in 1880 was but $4,055,000,000 (£811,000,000).

An industry which has attained gigantic proportions during the fifty years under review, is that of flouring and grist-mills. Indeed if we judge by value of products, this is the foremost industry of the United States; for the product of 1880 exceeded $500,000,000 (£100,000,000). The capital invested in this industry was $177,400,000 (nearly £36,000,000), there being in operation no fewer than twenty-four thousand flouring and grist-mills with a daily capacity of five million bushels—sufficient if need be to grind flour for not only the fifty millions of Americans, but for three hundred million Europeans, who annually consume one billion three hundred and forty-seven million bushels.

The value added to the food by milling was thirteen per cent. of the cost of the grain. During the decade ending 1880 the capital employed in this industry increased forty-six per cent.; the grain dealt with increased forty-seven per cent.; wages increased forty-nine per cent. The number of hands employed however diminished slightly—a circumstance due to improvements in machinery. This is a growing characteristic of all American industries: the drudgery is ever being delegated to dumb machines while the brain and muscle of men are directed into higher channels.

The industry next in importance, judged by value of

product, is slaughtering and meat packing. Though of comparatively recent origin, this industry has attained enormous proportions. The capital employed in 1880 was about ten millions sterling, furnishing employment to more than twenty-seven thousand hands, whose wages amounted to $10,500,000 (£2,100,000), an average of nearly $400 (£80) each. The beeves slaughtered numbered one million seven hundred thousand; sheep, two million two hundred thousand; hogs, sixteen millions. This was enough to give every man, woman, and child in America and Great Britain half a pound of meat thrice a week for a year. That this industry is to undergo vast developments is shown by the attention paid to the pastoral interests: farming stock increased thirty-three per cent. all round during the ten years ending in 1880. There were in that year nearly a hundred and fifty million cows, sheep, and hogs in the United States.

It is at Chicago that the traveller sees the murderous work going on upon the grandest scale, for in 1880 five and three-quarter million pigs were turned into pork, and half a million cattle "packed." So rapidly is this industry increasing that in Chicago alone one million one hundred and eighty thousand and nine hundred cattle were killed last year. The perfection of the machinery employed is illustrated by the claim Chicagoans make for it, viz., that you can see a living hog driven into the machine at one end, and the hams from it safely delivered at the other end before the squeal of the animal is out of your ears. But, as Matthew Arnold said, when asked to see this verified, or at least the foundation upon which the story rests, "Why should I see pigs killed! Why should I hear pigs squeal!" He declared. My readers can therefore see, if so inclined, one of the sights which a distinguished traveller missed, which is ever a great advantage.

The iron and steel industries rank next in importance,

the product for 1883 being valued at $400,000,000 (£80,000,000). The production of pig-iron has increased at a prodigious rate. The output for 1883 was five and a quarter million tons, more than thirteen times the quantity produced in 1840. With this unparalleled increase in quantity, there has gone a corresponding improvement in quality which has placed American iron and steel on a par with the best produced by the iron-king, Great Britain.

In 1870 the United States was much below France or Germany as regards the manufacture of steel; ten years later it produced more than these countries together. America now makes one-fifth of the iron, and one-fourth of the steel of the world, and is second only to Great Britain. In steel, America will probably lead the world in 1890, as may be seen from the following summary:

	1850	1870	1881
	Tons	*Tons*	*Tons*
Great Britain, . .	49,000	245,000	1,780,000
United States, . .		64,000	1,374,000
Germany, . . .	22,000	170,000	865,000
France, ...		94,000	418,000

Probably the most rapid development of an industry that the world has ever seen is that of Bessemer steel in America. As the foregoing table shows, there were only sixty-four thousand tons of all kinds of steel made in 1870. Of this only forty thousand tons was Bessemer; twelve years later, 1882, the product was one million two hundred and fifty thousand tons. This is advancing not by leaps and bounds, it is one grand rush—a rush without pause, which has made America the greatest manufacturer of Bessemer steel in the world. Last year the Republic made one million three hundred and seventy-three thousand five hundred and thirteen tons, which was seventy-four thousand tons more than Great Britain made. In steel rails her superiority is even more marked. The output of Britain was six hundred and forty-seven thousand tons against nine hundred and fifty-four thousand made in the United States.

Pennsylvania wears the iron crown, nearly one-half the capital invested being there, while forty-six per cent. of the total product is contributed by it. Ohio ranks second, New York follows, with Illinois closely treading on her heels.

The future outlook for the iron and steel industries of America is highly encouraging; for iron-stone in greater or less quantities has been discovered in most of the newly-opened States of the West. The production of iron was commenced between 1870 and 1880 in no less than six States, Colorado, Kansas, Nebraska, Oregon, and Texas, and in New Hampshire in the East. These infant industries are rapidly developing, but a great increase of population must take place near them before the aggregate product can reach a high figure. Pennsylvania will probably increase her iron and steel product in the future as fast as these new districts.

Closely following the iron and steel manufactures comes the lumber trade, an industry peculiarly American. Since 1850 the value of annual product has increased fourfold, the capital employed having advanced in nearly the same ratio. In 1880 this industry gave employment to one hundred and forty-eight thousand hands, who received wages to the amount of nearly \$32,000,000 (£6,400,000). The product was worth \$233,268,729 (£46,653,745). The principal seat of this industry is Michigan, a region which fifty years ago had not been invaded by the wood-cutter. The capital invested in the lumber trade in that State was nearly forty million dollars in 1880, or more than one-fifth of the total lumber investment of the country. The amount of superior timber cut in 1880 in the three principal lumbering States, Michigan, Wisconsin, and Minnesota, was seven billion five hundred million feet. This is exclusive of many millions of railroad ties, staves, and sets of headings out of inferior wood. In the Southern States more than one billion five hundred million feet of pine were cut in 1880; while it was estimated that there remained standing not less than two hundred and sixteen billion feet. But full statistics of the enormous quantities of wood available in the various States are unattainable. Texas is said to have twenty-one billion feet of loblolly pine, of which sixty-one and a half million feet were cut during 1880. At the present rate of cutting, the timber area of Michigan, Wisconsin, and Minnesota will last, allowing for growth, from twenty to twenty-five years; but that of the South, which is four times as great, is said to be ample for an indefinite period. Enormous forests are being opened in Washington Territory, Oregon, and Northern California. The cutting of trees may be conducted more methodically in the future than in the past, but there is little danger of the supply diminishing. There are vast regions in America where the raising of timber is the only cultivation possible, and other places where trees can be more profitably grown than anything else. This will always remain so, so that there need be no apprehension either that the forests will be totally destroyed, or that the supply of merchantable lumber will fail. The quality and variety of American woods are almost too well known to need emphasis. The ash, cherry, maple, mahogany, walnut, and many other valuable varieties are exported to Europe, frequently cut and shaped, ready to be put together as finished work. The wealth of America's forests is illustrated by the collection of native woods in the

New York Museum of Natural History, which comprises more than four hundred different varieties. The wealth of the Republic would be but partially estimated if, upon Uncle Sam's great estate, we omitted the "growing timber," from the live oak of Southern Florida up to "the huge pine, hewn on, not Norwegian, but North-western hills."

Foundry and machine shop products rank next in value. The value placed on these is more than $214,000,000 (£42,800,000); so that the value of the iron industries of America, as indicated above, ought to be increased by this sum.

Cotton manufactures have increased at a great rate in many lands, but nowhere so rapidly as in America. Those of England in 1880 were nearly six times greater than in 1830; those of America were eighteen and a half times greater. The competition of mother and child lands in this important industry is briefly shown by the following table, which also shows the small amount consumed by other countries:

CONSUMPTION OF COTTON IN MILLION POUNDS

	1830	1840	1860	1870	1880
Great Britain, . .	250	454	1,140	1,101	1,404
United States, . .	52	135	410	530	961
Germany, . . .	56	120	220	260	390
France, ...	87	110	215	250	340
Various, . . .	162	231	286	239	649
	607	1,050	2,271	2,380	3,744

It appears from the above that the cotton industries of America have increased nearly three times as fast as those of the rest of the world. The mother land still leads

finely in the race however. Grand, plucky little racer!
One dislikes to see a big, overgrown giant chasing you
with his seven-league boots on; but do not be too much
discouraged. He is your own son and bodes no harm.
You taught him of what his strain is capable. The prize
will still remain in the family. You who love primogeniture so dearly (every one to his taste) surely cannot
grudge your eldest boy anything.

At the beginning of the century, although the cotton
crop was only one seventy-seventh what it was in 1880,
only two per cent. of it was manufactured at home, as
against thirty-one per cent. in 1881. In this, as in many
other industries, we see the parent and child land in
friendly rivalry absorbing the great bulk, and leaving the
rest of the world nowhere in the race. Thus the two
Nations combined take two-thirds of the whole, and leave
but one-third for the rest of the world. The capital invested in cotton manufacture in the United States in
1880 was $208,000,000 (£41,600,000), the number of
operatives was one hundred and seventy-two thousand
five hundred and fifty-four, who received in wages
$42,000,000 (£8,400,000). The value of the product ex-
ceeded $192,000,000, (nearly £40,000,000). Compared
with the figures of the previous decade, the capital shows
forty-seven per cent. increase, number of looms forty-
nine per cent. increase, number of operatives twenty-
eight per cent., and cotton consumed fifty-eight per cent.
It is a noteworthy fact that the American method of cotton manufacture is the most economical of labor in the
world. An American operative deals with one-sixth more
material than the British operative; one-third more than
the German, two and a half times as much as the French
or Austrian, and five times as much as the Russian. This
may be in part explained by the fact that the proportion
of men is greater in American than in European fac-

tories; though the superior nature of American machinery is the main cause of difference. The native American,
and even the acclimatized European, is not content to remain in any position which he thinks can be as well or
better filled by a machine. If there is no such machine in
existence, he sets his wits to work and invents one, and
the patent laws of the country give him ample protection
at a merely nominal cost. This is the chief reason why
America produces more per head than any other country.

The American woollen industry also has expanded
greatly during recent years. Since 1860 it has increased
threefold, an increase six times as great as that of
Britain, which, during the same period, was only fifty
per cent. In 1880 the United States were hardly behind
Britain in product, the total manufactures being as follows:

	MILLION POUNDS	POUNDS PER INHABITANT	VALUE
United Kingdom, . .	338	9.8	£46,100,000
United States, . . .	320	6.6	43,000,000

Since 1880 the Republic has no doubt left her parent
far in the rear. In 1883–4 about three hundred and
ninety-six million pounds of wool was consumed in the
United States, and three hundred and twenty million
pounds of this was grown at home. The wool production
is now about six times greater than it was twenty-five
years ago; and already exportations are assuming important figures. Uncle Sam may be destined soon to
clothe, as well as to feed, his European brother.

The capital invested in woollen manufacture in 1880
was about nineteen million sterling. The hands employed
exceeded eighty-six thousand, who received wages to the
amount of $26,000,000 (more than £5,000,000), an

average of nearly $300 (£60) each. Although between
1870 and 1880 the capital invested increased to twenty-
one and one-half per cent., the number of establishments
decreased thirty-one per cent. As machinery is improved
and elaborated, its cost tends to put small capitalists out
of the competition and to increase the average size of the
manufacturing establishments. That great improvement
in machinery took place during the decade is shown by
the fact that the value per hand added to the materials
by manufacture increased seventeen and one-fourth per
cent.; and that concentration of labor into larger establishments occurred, is shown by an increase of seventy-
six and one-half per cent. in the average capital per establishment, and an increase of fifty-eight per cent. in number of hands per establishment.

The manufacture of mixed textiles for 1880 reached
a value of $66,250,000 (£13,250,000). Silk manufac-
tures employed capital to the amount of $19,000,000
(£3,800,000), and labor to the amount of thirty-one
thousand hands who received $9,146,705 (£1,829,341)
in wages. The net value of materials used was $18,500,-
000 (£3,700,000) and value of the products $34,500,-
000 (£6,900,000). Worsted goods were valued the same
year at $33,000,000 (£6,600,000) while hosiery and knit
goods reached $29,000,000 (£5,800,000).

In the carpet trade, which is of recent origin, we have
another example of the concentration of capital and
labor in large establishments. Since 1870 the decrease in
the number of establishments has been marked. Yet has
the capital nearly doubled, and the product increased
eighty-three per cent. in the decade. For 1880 the product was worth $21,750,000 (£4,350,000), and consisted
of twenty-two million yards of two-ply ingrains, nine and
one-half million yards of tapestry, four million yards of
Brussels, and half that quantity of Venetian carpets.

One is startled to find that more yards of carpet are manufactured in and around the city of Philadelphia alone than in the whole of Great Britain. It is not twenty years since the American imported his carpets, and now he makes more at one point than the greatest European manufacturing nation does in all its territory. Truly the old lands are fast becoming petty little communities; their populations so small, their products so trifling, in comparison with those of the Giant of the West!

The manufacture of boots and shoes is one of the oldest and most important industries of America. It is also one of the best developed—developed not simply in regard to size, but in perfection of methods. Here machinery seems to have reached its culmination. The human hand does little but guide the material from machine to machine, and the hammering, the stamping, and sewing are all done by the tireless energy of steam. It is no fiction to say that men put leather into the machine at one end, and it comes out a perfect fitting boot at the other. By means of such a machine, a man can make three hundred pairs of boots in a day, and a single factory in Massachusetts turns out as many pairs yearly as thirty-two thousand bootmakers in Paris. In 1880 America had three thousand one hundred of these mechanical St. Crispins, making new pedal coverings every four months for fifty million people. The old fashioned cobbler with last and "taching-end" is as surely doomed to extinction as the New Zealand Maori. Even the small capitalist who is willing to adopt the most approved methods when able, finds himself placed *hors de combat* by his stronger rivals. In 1870 America had three thousand one hundred and fifty-one bootmaking establishments, employing ninety-one thousand seven hundred and two men. Ten years later the workmen had increased to one hundred and eleven thousand one hundred and fifty-two, but the number of establishments had fallen to one thousand nine hundred and fifty-nine, a decrease of nearly thirty-eight per cent. Even yet machinery continues to be improved. In the decade ending 1880 the increased number of hands was but twenty-one and one-quarter per cent., but the increased value of products was forty-one and a half per cent. The increase of capital was forty-three and one-quarter per cent. How far the concentration of capital is destined to go, no one can foretell. The survival of the fittest means here the survival of the most economical; and that large establishments are more economical than small ones is proved by the non-survival of the latter. It is probable that the only limit to the concentration of labor is that imposed by the capacity of the directing mind which presides over it.

There are many other industries which claim by their importance some mention here; but lest details should become tiresome to the reader there is appended, in tabular form, a few particulars of the most important industries hitherto unnamed. But even the most conscientious reader is hereby specially permitted—and advised—to skip this table. The author did not make it, you know, and he is only solicitous for the text.

In this table the two items which will probably most excite surprise are those which seem to tell us that the sober-suited male spends six times as much for his clothes as the more gaudily dressed branch of the race. The explanation of this is found in the enormous development of ready-made clothing in the country. Let any one stop for a moment at the windows of one of these establishments, which generally occupy entire squares in most of the cities, and notice at what extremely low prices quite respectable clothing is offered, and if he be a British visitor few sights will more surprise him. Prices are not above those in Britain, and the clothing is better made;

the material may however not be quite so good, for a mixture of inferior stuff is suspected in the home product. Still it is excellent and serviceable, and is constantly improving in quality. There is seen in this branch another

Manufacture	Estab-lish-ments	Capital	Hands	Wages	Value of Product
Leather Currying,	2,319	$16,878,520	11,053	$4,845,413	$71,351,297
Tanning, . . .	3,105	50,222,054	23,821	9,204,243	113,348,336
Ship Building, .	2,188	20,979,874	21,345	12,713,830	36,800,327
Paper, ...	692	46,421,202	24,422	8,525,355	55,109,914
Glass, ...	211	19,844,699	24,177	9,144,100	21,154,571
Dyeing & Finishing,	191	26,223,981	.....	....	32,297,420
Sugar & Molasses,	....	....	.....	....	155,484,915
Printing & Publishing, . . .	....	....	.....	....	90,789,442
Agricultural Implements, . .	....	....	.....	....	68,640,486
Furniture, . .	....	....	.....	....	68,037,902
Carriages & Wagons, . . .	....	....	.....	....	64,951,617
Drugs & Chemicals,	....	....	.....	....	38,173,658
Clothing (Men's) Ready Made, .	....	....	.....	....	209,548,460
Clothing (Women's) Ready Made, .	....	....	.....	....	32,004,794
Railroad & Street Cars, . . .	....	....	.....	....	27,997,591
Hardware, . .	....	....	.....	....	22,653,693
Sewing Machines,	....	....	.....	....	13,863,188

development of the wholesale idea, which gives America its good and cheap watches and many other things. In the manufacture of men's clothing men are divided into classes and a thousand suits are cut and sewed by machinery for each class from the same material. Only the misshapen man is now compelled to be measured and fitted by himself. The garments adapted for boys' wear offered by these wholesale manufacturers are so much more varied in style, and so much cheaper than can be obtained from smaller tailors, that this branch may be said to be entirely monopolized by the manufacturers. Prices are lower than those prevailing in Britain for similar garments. Not only the working classes but all except the few rich are fast becoming patrons of these ready-made establishments which, it may be mentioned, do a strictly cash business. This in itself is one reason for their low prices, and it exerts a decided influence for good upon the habits of the poorer people. Here again we have that law of concentration which seems inseparable from manufacturing, the smaller being constantly merged into the greater factories.

When we come to the dress of delightful, vain woman, however, we have a total arrest of this concentration. Her tastes or whims are so numerous, so diverse, that she must express herself in her dress, and sometimes very loudly too; still in this we can at least ask the world to judge between the monarchy and the Democracy without fear of the verdict. The American woman of all classes sets an example to her monarchical sister in dress. The full-blown wife of the local magnate from the provinces decked out in all the colors of the rainbow, and apparently with a ram-rod down her back, which extends high through her neck too, and probably divides into two prongs midway, one going down each leg to her feet,— that spectacle has no compeer upon this side of the water. Even the wife of the California miner who has "made his pile," or of the Pennsylvania speculator who has "struck oil," seems to submit herself to a tolerable dress-maker before she appears in public in New York or Washington. Still there is no possibility of success if the attempt were made to manufacture a thousand bonnets or dresses of any one pattern; that any other woman had one of these would render the next hideous, positively offensive to the æsthetic sense of the second purchaser. The guarantee required by the purchaser of a fashionable bonnet apparently is that it can be worshipped without breaking the commandment. There must be nothing like it in the heavens above nor in the earth beneath nor in the waters under the earth; and in many cases there is not. For this reason, if it be a reason at all, we find the census reporting that men spend six times the sum that women do upon clothing. Were the receipts known and reported of the thousands of small retail dressmakers who supply the principal parts of women's dress we should no doubt find these figures more than reversed.

The power used in manufactures in the United States is equal to three million four hundred and ten thousand eight hundred and thirty-seven horse power—a force capable of raising a weight of seventeen billion tons one foot high. Of this force sixty-four per cent. is steam power and thirty-six per cent. water power. The increase of total power between 1870 and 1880 was forty-five per cent. In the same time the increase in product of manufactures was fifty-eight per cent., another sign of improved machinery. The increase of power per hand in all branches of manufacture amounted to ten per cent., which indicates the extent of the transfer from manual to mechanical power during that period.

The transfer is still going on, and man is ever getting Nature to work more and more for him. A hundred years ago she did little but grow his corn, meat, and wool. Now she cuts the corn, gathers, binds, threshes, grinds, bakes it into bread, and carries it to his door. The wool she spins, weaves, and sews into garments, and then stops not until she has placed it within the future wearer's reach, be he ever so far away. Or she will carry him wheresoever his lordly desire may lead him. Across continents and under seas she flies with his messages. Ever obedient, ever untiring, ever ready, she grows more responsive and willing in proportion as her lord makes more demands upon her. Already she has taken to herself the drudgery which long burdened man; and under triumphant Democracy she is ever seizing on other work to relieve him, and leave his life freer for happiness. In other lands men are not so happy. Instead of making conquests over nature, they strive for conquests over each other, incited thereto by selfish and conceited kings and self-styled noblemen. But the end is near. It is probable that it is by an industrial conquest feudalism and standing armies in Europe are to be overcome; and that has already begun. America, blessed land of peace, is inundating the world not only with her products, but with her gospel of the equality of man as man, and the old-time nations will soon be forced to divert their energies from war to peaceful work.

The position America has acquired not only as a manufacturer of the coarser products but of more artistic articles is remarkable. In all articles of silverware, for instance, no nation competes successfully with her. A New York establishment, which dwarfs all other similar establishments in the world, carried off the gold medal for artistic work in silver at the Paris Exhibition of 1855, and also of 1878; also the gold medal from the Emperor of Russia. Twenty per cent. of all its enormous manufacture of silverware is now sold abroad. In this branch, as in engraving, the republican workman has achieved pre-eminence. This is but the beginning of his triumphs in the higher branches of art. Others are as certain to follow as the sun is to shine, for the manhood and intelligence of the workman, his position of equality in the State, must find expression in his work.

We have an interesting example of republican success in another branch of manufacture—that of watches.
It is not very long since every watch carried by the American was imported. To-day America exports watches
largely to most foreign countries and especially to
Europe. These indispensable articles were formerly made
by hand in small factories. Switzerland, that land of
cheap labor, was the principal seat of the manufacture.
Thirty-five years ago the American conceived the idea of
making watches by machinery upon a gigantic scale. The
principal establishment made only five watches per day
as late as 1854. Now thirteen hundred per day is the
daily task, and six thousand watches per month are sent
to the London agency. Three other similar establishments, conducted upon the same general plan, are kept
busily employed. In short the Republic is now the world's
watchmaker. Notwithstanding the fact that labor is paid
more than double that of Europe, the immense product,
the superior skill of the workman, and the numerous
American inventions connected with the business, enable
the republican to outstrip all his rivals. It will soon be
so in all articles which can be made of one pattern in
great numbers, for in such cases the enormous home market of the American takes so much more of any article
than the home market of any other manufacturer that he
is enabled to carry on the business upon a gigantic scale,
and dispose of his surplus abroad. In confirmation of this
view let us take the manufacture of thread, for which the
two great firms at Paisley, Scotland, are so justly celebrated the world over.

The pioneer firm began operations in Paisley in 1798,
the other followed in 1820. They began to manufacture
in the United States in 1866 and 1869—*not twenty years
ago*. Yet their combined capital in works upon this side
already about equals their capital in Paisley, the product

of sixty years' growth. In other words, twenty years in the Republic has equalled sixty in Scotland. In twenty years more Clark & Coates will in all probability consider their original home works in dear old monarchical Paisley as but a branch of the main stem in the great Republic.

Another illustration of the same character is seen in the manufacture of pig-iron. The writer well remembers raising a laugh not twenty years ago at the table of one of the Scotch iron kings, the Bairds, by prophesying that even their enormous product would soon be reached by a manufacturing concern in America. Where would the laugh be now? The Bairds do not produce nearly as much to-day as the American concern, and next year the difference in favor of the republican manufacturer will be much greater, as his capacity is constantly being increased to meet the swelling demands of the new country. So it is in every branch of manufacture, so rapidly is the child land dwarfing her illustrious mother. One has only to have faith in the Republic. She never yet betrayed the head that trusted, or the heart that loved her.

In Mr. Pidgeon's clever book, "Old World Questions and New World Answers," which is, upon the whole, the best book of its kind that I know of, we find the author unerringly placing his finger upon the one secret of the Republic's success, viz.: the respect in which labor is held. If I wished to indicate one of the sharpest contrasts between men in the world, and few will deny my right to judge here, I should say that which exists between the artisan in monarchical Britain and republican America. I echo every word Mr. Pidgeon says:

"Gloze it over as we may, there is a great gulf fixed between the ideas of Old and New England on this radical question of the dignity of work. Our industrial occupations consist, speaking generally, of mere money-spinning. The places where, and the people by whom, we carry them on, are cared for economically, and that is all. It is not in our business, but by our 'position,' that we shine in the eyes of ourselves and our neighbors. The social code of this country drives, yearly, numbers of young men, issuing from our public schools and universities, either into the over-crowded learned professions or into government clerkships, whose narrow round of irresponsible duties benumbs originality, and weakens self-reliance. Capable, educated girls are pining for a 'career' in England, while posts, even the most important, are filled in New England by 'young ladies,' the equals of ours in everything which that phrase denotes, and their superiors in all the qualities that are born of effort and self-help. It is no one's fault, and I am not going to rail at the inevitable. We were originally a feudal country, and cannot escape the influence of our traditions. The man who does service for another was a 'villein' in the feudal times, and is an 'inferior' now; just as a man of no occupation is a 'gentleman,' and a governess a 'person.' Use has made us unconscious of the fact that the 'dignity of work' is a mere phrase in our mouths, while it blinds us to the loss of national energy, which avenges outraged labor.

.   .   .   .

"Let us look to it, while the battle of free trade rages across the Atlantic, as rage it soon will, that we import some American readiness and grip into our board-rooms and offices, some sense of the dignity of labor into our workshops."

This writer truthfully gives the facts, but into the causes of this sense of the dignity of labor in the Republic, and its absence in the Monarchy, he has not ventured to seek. Let me supply this lack. If you found a State upon the monarchical idea which necessarily carries with it an aristocracy, by so much more as you exalt this royal family and aristocracy you inevitably degrade all who are not of these classes. That is clear. If at the pinnacle you place people who are exempt from honest labor and despise it, whether such labor be that rendered by ministers, physicians, lawyers, teachers, or other professional men, or tradesmen or mechanics; if you create a court from which people in trade, and artisans, are excluded; if you support a monarch who declines to have one in trade or a wage receiving man presented to her, thus entailing upon honest labor the grossest insult, what can be the result of the system but a community in which the dignity of labor has not only no place but one in which, as in Britain, labor is actually looked down upon! This is the very essence of the monarchical idea.

The Queen of Great Britain grossly insults labor every moment of her life by declining to recognize it. And all her *entourage*, from the Duke who walks backwards before "the Lord's anointed" for four thousand a year, down or up to the groom of the stole—whatever that may be—necessarily cherish the same contempt for those who lead useful lives of labor.

Mr. Pidgeon would cure this evil of his country by giving a better education to the people. So far, so good, but until this educated people goes to the root of the evil and sweeps away the present foundation upon which their government rests and founds in its place a government resting upon the equality of the citizen, he may legislate from June to January, year after year, and labor will still hold no honored place in the State. How can it ever be even respected so long as a monarch and a court and an aristocracy despise and insult it.

> "Nature rejects the monarch, not the man;
> The *subject* not the *citizen;* for kings
> And subjects, mutual foes, for ever play
> A losing game into each other's hand,
> Whose stakes are vice and misery."

Never will the British artisan rival the American until from his system are expelled the remains of serfdom and into his veins is instilled the pure blood of exalted manhood. Ah, Mr. Pidgeon! you should know that before you can have an intelligent, self-respecting, inventive artisan, like the American, the State must first make him a *man*.

Of course we hear the response to all this from the ostrich class: Britons have done pretty well, have they not? So far they have managed not only to hold their own in the world, but to successfully invade many provinces naturally belonging to others. Have not the British race come out ahead? Granted, and why? Because until recently they have had as competing races those less free, and therefore less *men* than themselves. Compare a Briton and his political liberties with a German, or with any Continental race and the law I indicate receives confirmation. The freer the citizen, the grander the national triumphs. Who questions that the overthrow of the doctrine of the divine right of kings and the supreme authority of Parliament have not exerted a powerful influence upon the national character. And when a new race appears which enjoys political equality, shall the law not hold good, and the prize fall to the freest and therefore to the best man? And this is precisely what is going on before our eyes. Will any competent judge of the two countries upon this vital point dispute the immense superiority of the republican workman? Will not Mr. Howard of Bedford, for instance, or Mr. Lowthian Bell, or Mr. Windsor Richards, or Mr. Edward Martin— all of whom have investigated the subject—will they not tell their fellow-countrymen as I tell them, and as Mr. Pidgeon tells them, that the *Citizen* leads the *subject*. The theory of the equal status of the workingman in the State here lies at the root of his superiority, both as a citizen and as a skilled workman. We find that in handling a shovel (which few native Americans do), the

British man in his cool climate can do more work than his fellow-countryman can do, or at least than he does here; but when we come to educated skilled labor, the average Briton is not in the race. Nor will he be until he too is subject to no man, but the proud citizen of a commonwealth founded upon political equality. The stuff is in him, but the laws of his country stifle it at his birth, and prevent its proper development all the years of his life.

The struggle for existence has already begun afresh, this time other weapons than the spear and sword. European nations must rid themselves of the weight they now carry if they would not fall further and further behind in the race. The people must first take their political rights, and secure perfect equality under the laws. This obtained, the rest is easy, for the people of all countries are pacific and bear nothing but good will to each other. Where ill will has grown it is the work of hereditary rulers and military classes, not responsible to the masses. From the jealousies and personal ambitions of these, the people are happily free, and hence from their advent to power there must come a rapid diversion of force from international war into the peaceful channels of industrial development. The reign of the Democracy means ultimately no less than the reign of peace on earth, among men good will.

Chapter XI
MINING

"Deep in unfathomable mines
Of never-failing skill,
He treasures up his vast designs
And works his sovereign will."

In PRECEDING chapters the superlative form of adjectives has been so often applied to America when contrasted with other lands, that many a foreign reader, who now for the first time realizes the magnitude and greatness of the Republic, may not unnaturally begin to feel dubious about it all. He may be inclined to believe that it is not a veritable nation to which such magnificent attributes are ascribed, but some fabled land of Atlantis. Nevertheless it is all real and true. The Republic is surely, as we have already seen, the largest, most populous, wealthiest civilized nation in the world, and also the greatest agricultural, pastoral, and manufacturing nation. And now we have one more claim to make—it is the greatest mining nation as well. Greatest on the surface of the soil, as she undoubtedly is, her supremacy below the surface is yet more incontestable. Over every part of the vast continent Nature has lavished her bounties in a profusion almost wasteful. Beneath fields of waving corn, ripening in a perfect climate, are layers upon layers of mineral wealth. Deposits of gold, silver, coal, iron, copper are found in quantities unknown elsewhere, and the rocks yield every year rivers of oil. To crown her bounty and aid in its utilization, and, as if in pursuance of the law "To him that hath shall be given," Nature has lately blessed her with a gift as remarkable as it is rare—an agent rich in beneficial influences, and helpful to a degree which renders every other natural gift prosaic in comparison—natural gas, a fluid distilled by Nature deep in the earth and stored in her own vast gasometers, requiring only to be led into workshops and under boilers to do there the work of a thousand giants.

Let me describe this new wonder first. Seven years ago a company was drilling for petroleum at Murraysville, near Pittsburgh. A depth of one thousand three hundred and twenty feet had been reached when the drills were thrown high into the air, and the derrick broken to pieces and scattered around by a tremendous explosion of gas, which rushed with hoarse shriekings into the air, alarming the population for miles around. A light was applied, and immediately there leaped into life a fierce, dancing demon of fire, hissing and swirling around with the wind, and scorching the earth in a wide circle around it. Thinking it was but a temporary outburst preceding the oil, men allowed this valuable fuel to waste for five years. Coal in that region cost only two or three shillings per ton, and there was little inducement to sink capital in attempts to supersede it with a fuel which, though cheaper, might fail as suddenly as it had arisen. But as the years passed, and the giant leaped and danced as madly as at first, a company was formed to provide for the utilization of the gas. It was conducted in pipes under the boilers of iron works, where it burned without a particle of smoke. Stokers and firemen, and all the laborers who had been required to load and unload coal, became superfluous. Boring began in other districts, and soon around Pittsburgh were twenty gas wells, one yielding thirty million cubic feet a day. A single well has furnished gas equal to twelve hundred tons of coal a day. Numerous lines of pipes, aggregating six hundred miles, now convey the gas from the wells to the manufacturing centres of Pittsburgh and Alleghany City and their suburbs. The empty coal bunkers are being whitewashed; and where in some works one hundred and twenty coal-begrimed stokers worked like black demons in Hades feeding the fires, one man now walks about in cleanly idleness, his sole care that of watching the steam and water-gauges. The erstwhile "Smoky City" is now getting a pure atmosphere; and one would little suspect that the view from the cliffs above the Monongahela River included the thousand hitherto smoky furnaces of the Iron City. Private residences in Pittsburgh are supplied with natural gas, and all heating and cooking are done with this cheap fuel. Already ten thousand tons of coal per day are displaced by it, and slack, which even before the application of natural gas was worth only three shillings per ton in Pittsburgh, is now almost worthless. At present gas wells in and around Pittsburgh are so numerous as to be counted by hundreds. The number of companies chartered to supply natural gas in Pennsylvania up to February 5, 1884, was one hundred and fifty, representing a capital stock of many millions. Since that date numerous other charters have been granted. More than sixty wells have been drilled at Erie, Penn. Gas has also been found in small quantities in the States of Ohio, West Virginia, Kentucky, Indiana, Illinois, Alabama, Kansas, Dakota, and California. It is used for manufacturing purposes upon a small scale in eight towns in New York, in twenty-four towns in Pennsylvania, and in five in Ohio, but so far the region around Pittsburgh is the only one in which the much-desired fuel has been found in abundance. New uses are constantly being discovered. Glass is made purer by means of the gas, the covered pots formerly used in the furnaces being found unnecessary. Iron and steel plates are cleaned and prepared for tinning by passing a current of gas over them while red-hot. The old process of pickling in acid solutions caused partial corrosion of the plates, which required to be carefully cleaned from the acid. It is also useful in cleansing delicate fabrics. The dephosphorization of iron through the agency of natural gas is being attempted, with partial success. The attempts, however, have resulted in the formation of carbon, which has been found suitable for electric light carbons. In every department of industry discoveries are constantly being made which, if not so important as those named, are yet of great value. The gas at present running to waste within piping distance of Pittsburgh is estimated at *seventy million cubic feet per day!*

Closely allied to natural gas is natural oil or petroleum, for gas is probably the distilled product of the oil, forced by subterranean heat and pressure out of the carbonaceous deposits which abound throughout Pennsylvania. Though rock-oil was known to the early Chaldeans, and is referred to by Herodotus, Pliny, and other ancient writers, it was not utilized for manufacturing purposes until 1847, when Young, of Glasgow, made lubricating oil from petroleum obtained from Derbyshire, England. Then began in England and America the distillation of oil from coal; and in 1860 there were in the United States not less than forty factories producing about five hundred barrels per day. But these were doomed to speedy extinction; for in the preceding year a company had been formed in Pennsylvania to drill for the oil which was seen oozing in various places, from the river banks and floating on the water. The Indians, by spreading blankets over the surface, used to collect small quantities of this oil to mix with their war-paint and for medicinal purposes. Crude petroleum, under the name of Seneca oil, had, so late as thirty years ago, the reputation of a universal curative. The quack advertisements which set forth the virtues of this medicine began:

> "The healthful balm, from nature's secret spring,
>   The bloom of health and life to man will bring;
> As from her depths the magic liquid flows,
>   To calm our sufferings and assuage our woes."

It sold then for $2 (8*s*) per bottle. Alas for human credulity! Since the oil, which once cured everything, brings but one dollar per barrel it has lost all virtue, and cures nothing.

The first drilling in Pennsylvania resulted in a flow of ten barrels a day, which was sold for fifty cents a gallon. A period of wild excitement followed. Wells were sunk all over the country. Some were failures, but oil was often reached. Of one well it is recorded that it yielded four hundred and fifty thousand barrels of oil in a little more than two years, while another is said to have given not less than half a million barrels in a twelve-month. An oil property, Storey Farm, Oil Creek, with which I was intimately connected, has a remarkable history. When, about twenty-two years ago, in company with some friends I first visited this famous well, the oil was running into the creek, where a few flat-bottomed scows lay filled with it, ready to be floated down to the Alleghany River upon an agreed-upon day each week, when the creek was flooded by means of a temporary dam. This was the beginning of the natural oil business. We purchased the farm for $40,000 (£8,000), and so small was our faith in the ability of the earth to yield for any considerable time the hundred barrels per day which the property was then producing, that we decided to make a pond capable of holding one hundred thousand barrels of oil, which we estimated would be worth, when the supply ceased, $1,000,000 (£200,000). Unfortunately for us the pond leaked fearfully; evaporation also caused much loss, but we continued to run oil in to make the losses good day after day until several hundred thousand barrels had gone in this fashion. Our experience with the farm may be worth reciting. Its value rose to $5,000,000 (£1,000,000); that is, the shares of the company sold in the market upon this basis; and one year it paid in cash dividends $1,000,000 (£200,000)—rather a good return upon an investment of eight thousand pounds. So great was the yield in the district that in two years oil became almost valueless, often selling in bulk as low as thirty cents per barrel, and not unfrequently it was suffered to run to waste as utterly worthless. But as new uses were found for the oil, prices rose again, and to remove the difficulty of high freights, pipes were laid, first for short distances, and then to the seaboard, a distance of about three hundred miles. Through these pipes, of which six thousand two hundred miles have been laid, the oil is now pumped from two thousand one hundred wells. It costs only ten cents to pump a barrel of oil to the Atlantic. The present daily yield of the oil-producing district is about seventy thousand barrels, and the supply, instead of diminishing, goes on increasing yearly. More than thirty-eight million barrels of thirty-three gallons each were in store one day in November, 1884. The value of petroleum and its products *exported* up to January, 1884, exceeds in value $625,000,000 (£125,000,-000).

In the Pittsburgh district we find another mineral deposit of immense value, a remarkable coal seam of great thickness, which makes a coke of such quality as to render it famous throughout the continent. It is so easily mined that a man and a boy can dig and load nearly thirty tons in ten hours. In Chicago, and in St. Louis, in the blast furnaces of Pittsburgh and in the silver and lead mines of Utah, this coke, "compact, silvery and lustrous," is an important factor in the metallic industries of the Republic. It gives Pittsburgh advantages which cause it to rank as an iron producer in advance of towns situated on the very beds of iron-stone. Well may the Iron City burst into song:

> "I am monarch of all the forges,
>   I have solved the riddle of fire;
> The amen of nature to need of man
>   Echoes at my desire.
> I search with the subtle soul of flame
>   The heart of the rocky earth,
> And hot from my anvils the prophecies
>   Of the miracle years blaze forth.
>
> "I am swart with the soot of my chimneys,
>   I drip with the sweat of toil;
> I quell and scepter the savage wastes
>   And charm the curse from the soil.
> I fling the bridges across the gulfs
>   That hold us from the To Be,
> And build the roads for the bannered march
>   Of crowned Humanity."

In the same lucky State of Pennsylvania are deposits of valuable anthracite coal, which, though including in all an area of only four hundred and seventy square miles, are of immense thickness. These deposits, which in parts vary from fifty to seven hundred feet thick, and average about seventy feet, make this wonderful region of greater value than many coal fields of ten times the area. Near Pottsville there is a thickness of three thousand three hundred feet of coal measures. The cubic contents of the anthracite coal field, allowing fifty per cent.

for loss in working, is estimated at thirteen billion one hundred and eighty million five hundred and thirty-five thousand tons of merchantable coal—a store capable of furnishing the present consumption, or thirty million tons per year, for four hundred and thirty-nine years. By that time men will probably be burning the hydrogen of water, or be fully utilizing the solar rays, or the tidal energy, or using some undiscovered means of profitably getting heat and power by diverting natural phenomena. They will probably not feel the want of anthracite coal. At present, however, this fuel is especially precious on account of its hardness, density, and purity, which render it available for iron smelting without coking, while to its freedom from smoke is due the pure atmosphere of Eastern American cities. The view from Brooklyn Bridge would delight a Londoner, used to the murky atmosphere of the English metropolis. He would see the roofs and chimneys of two great cities for miles, but hardly a particle of smoke to mar the purity of the bright air, or sully a sky which rivals that of Italy in clearness.

In twenty-five States and Territories, distributed all over the continent, north, south, east, and west, from Alabama to Rhode Island and thence to California and Oregon, coal is now being mined, while it is known to exist in several others. The future value of this extensive distribution of coal can be but vaguely estimated; but taken in connection with the fact that iron ore is found in nearly every State of the Union and is mined in twenty-nine of them, it is clear that its value in the near future will be enormous. A vast expansion is taking place in the coal industry: in 1850 the total product was but seven and a quarter million tons; in 1880 it was seventy-one million tons, and in 1884 it reached ninety-seven and a half million tons. Including the local and colliery consumption the figures for 1884 approximate one hundred and seven million tons. That of Great Britain for the same year was one hundred and sixty million tons. The rest of the world produced only one hundred and thirty million tons; so that mother and child lands together produced more than twice as much coal as all the world beside.

To the world's stock of gold America has contributed, according to Mulhall, more than fifty per cent. In 1880 he estimated the amount of gold in the world at ten thousand three hundred and fifty-five tons, worth $7,240,-000,000 (£1,448,000,000). Of this the New World contributed five thousand three hundred and two tons, or more than half. Australia and the United States have competed keenly during the last thirty years for precedence, but it remains with the Republic. The struggle is thus indicated:

	MILLIONS STERLING			
	1851–60	1861–70	1871–80	THIRTY YEARS
United States, ...	102	98	70	270
Australia, ...	104	82	72	258

In 1881–2–3 the Republic was leading by $4,000,000 (£800,000) per year. The world's production of gold during the above thirty years was worth $3,930,000,000 (£786,000,000); so that Australia and America produced together about five-sevenths of the whole. The yearly production of gold in the United States since 1880 has averaged $31,250,000 (£6,250,000), being one-third of the total product of the world.

Of silver America has contributed to the world's supply even in larger ratio than of gold. Of the one hundred and ninety-three thousand tons estimated to have been produced during the last five hundred years, the

Americas contributed one hundred and sixty-two thousand two hundred tons, or eighty-four per cent. Though this was mainly the product of Mexico and Peru, the United States of late years have come to the front. The following table gives the world's production since 1850:

	MILLIONS STERLING			
	1851–60	1861–70	1871–80	THIRTY YEARS
Spanish America, . . .	49	64	70	183
United States, ...	10	16	68	94
Germany and Austria, . .	15	18	20	53
Various, ...	7	12	22	41
	81	110	180	371

The difference between sixteen and sixty-eight marks the increase of silver-mining in the Republic which has taken place in ten years—an increase almost incredible. One of the most remarkable veins of metal known is the Comstock Lode in Nevada. This lode, to which Mark Twain has given a European celebrity by his description in "Roughing It," is of great width, and extends over five miles. It is as if Oxford Street and Uxbridge Road were filled to the house-tops with rich gold and silver ore from Holborn Viaduct to Acton. In fourteen years this single vein yielded $180,000,000 (£36,000,-000). In one year, 1876, the product of the lode was $18,000,000 (£3,600,000) in gold and $20,500,000 (£4,100,000) in silver—a total of $38,500,000 (£7,-700,000). Here, again, is something which the world never saw before! Since 1880 the annual product of silver in the United States has averaged $46,200,000 (£9,-240,000). If the present rate of increase is maintained until 1890, the next decade will show a hundred million sterling as the Republic's addition to the silver of the world. The increase from sixteen to sixty-eight in ten years is remarkable; but it is more wonderful that the rate should be maintained.

America also leads the world in copper, the United States and Chili contributing nearly one-half the world's supply. The product of the Republic has increased six-fold since 1860. In that year the total product was five thousand three hundred and eighty-eight tons; in 1870 twelve thousand six hundred tons; in 1880 twenty-seven thousand tons, and the yield for 1884 was no less than sixty-three thousand five hundred and fifty-five tons! There's revolution for you! From six hundred and fifty tons in 1850 to sixty-three thousand! On the south shore of Lake Superior this metal is found almost pure in masses of all sizes up to many tons in weight. It was used by the native Indians, and traces of their rude mining operations are still visible. One mine in this district, known as the Calumet and Hecla, produces nearly thirty per cent. of the whole copper output of the United States —about eighteen thousand tons in 1884. It paid its owners $4,000,000 (£800,000) for two years' dividends. Copper mining is carried on in twenty-one States and Territories, and ore has been found in several others. This industry is rapidly developing, and doubtless before the next census the annual output will be double what it is now.

In 1870 the importation of lead into the United States amounted to forty-two thousand tons. In ten years this had fallen to four thousand tons. Then the tables were turned and the United States, instead of importing lead, began to send it abroad, although in small quantities. In 1884 it was exported to the amount of twenty-six thousand pounds. This implies a rapid development of lead mining in the Republic. Indeed, in 1880, America was the first lead producing country in the world, though Mulhall places her slightly behind Spain. The progress of the industry is shown in the following table, which also indicates the stages of the competition:

	METRIC TONS			
	1830	1850	1880	1883
Great Britain, ...	48,000	55,000	51,000	39,817
Spain, ...	23,000	27,000	92,000	127,000
United States (Mulhall), ...	3,700	36,000	89,000	
United States (Whitney & Caswell), .	8,000	22,000	97,825	140,000

The difference in the two American estimates for 1880 is probably due to the fact that the census statistics of the production of lead are only partial. In Utah, for example, which is not reported as producing any, lead is mined and smelted in connection with silver. Its product in 1880 was fifteen thousand net tons, and that of Nevada sixteen thousand six hundred and fifty-nine. The product of Colorado alone was thirty-five thousand six hundred and seventy-eight tons. The lead district of the upper Mississippi and of eastern Missouri jointly produced twenty-seven thousand six hundred and ninety tons, while another district of southwestern Missouri and southeastern Kansas is reported to have produced twenty-two thousand six hundred and twenty-five tons the previous year. So that even the larger estimate would probably have to be increased, were accurate figures at hand. Caswell's estimate for 1884 is one hundred and forty thousand tons, of which one hundred and twenty thousand tons are de-silverized lead. Lead is produced in thirteen States, mainly in the West. Colorado wears a leaden rim to her silver crown, she alone producing twice as much as the lead mines of Great Britain. Indeed, a single mine at Leadville produces two-thirds as much as all Great Britain, although lead is here only a by-product of silver mining. The Horn Silver Mine in Utah produced, in 1884, forty thousand tons of ore, averaging thirty and nine one-hundredths per cent. of lead and thirty-nine ounces of silver, the latter alone nearly paying all the expenses of extraction, treatment, and marketing. Here again the owners got a million dollars for a year's dividends. The world's production of lead for 1883 was four hundred and fifty-four thousand tons. Of this more than half was produced by two countries—the Republic and Spain.

Zinc is now produced in America in large quantities. Previous to 1873 the amount obtained was very small; but in 1880 the year's product greatly exceeded that of Great Britain, being twenty-three thousand two hundred and thirty-nine tons, against fifteen thousand nine hundred and forty-seven. In 1884 the domestic product had increased to thirty-five thousand tons. The import of zinc into the Republic has fallen off in a corresponding degree, being but one-fifth what it was in 1873, while prices have been reduced about eighty per cent. The Republic already ranks third among the zinc producers of the world.

The mineral resources of the United States comprise also quicksilver, the ores of chrome and nickel, cobalt, platinum, iridium, antimony, arsenic, etc., etc. Salt deposits are worked in various States, and sulphur, graphite, and gypsum abound. Mineral phosphates are found in South Carolina, where they are worked into fertilizers for domestic consumption. Granite, marble, sandstone, and other fine building stones and roofing slates are abundant, and form the objects of large and profitable industries.

The treasures of earth have been among the most important elements in the growth and prosperity of the

Republic. Besides great and direct gains, there have been many indirect benefits resulting from the opening up and settlement of extensive regions. Large towns have sprung up with magic growth in the wilderness. Where miners settled, agriculturists and mechanics soon came to minister to their wants. In this way some of the richest and largest towns of the West originated. San Francisco is the most notable instance. A later example is furnished by Leadville, which ten years ago was the centre of a barren, uninhabited region, the haunt of the catamount and grizzly bear. Now it is a town of wide streets and handsome stone buildings, court-house, hospitals, churches, schools, and all the attributes of a large civilized city. The surrounding district is populated by agriculturists. In ten short years the discovery of a rich lead vein has transformed the wilderness into an Arcadia. Where, a few years ago, the only sounds heard were the growl of the coyote or the occasional whoop of the savage, the busy hum of a city, the lowing of cattle, or the beat of a steam crusher now wake the echoes of the hills.

The Republic seems to stand like the variety shopkeeper in Colorado, who put up in his shop in a flaming placard, "If you don't see what you want just ask for it." We have only to want a mineral and seek for it, when nature places it before us. A few years ago there was not a pound of speigel (so essential for the Bessemer steel process) made in the United States. We had not the proper ores, we said. A hundred thousand tons were used every year and every ton was imported. To-day we have the ores from Lake Superior, from Virginia, from Arkansas, and all the speigel we need can be made at home. So too with ferro-manganese. This is a metallic substance as essential for the manufacture of mild steel as speigel is for steel rails. Eighty dollars a ton was paid by our manufacturers up to last year, and every ton came across the sea. We needed the precious ore, and, *presto,* a rich mine appears in Virginia and another in Arkansas. It has been tested and the former is pronounced to be the richest and purest in the world. "It will make ferro-manganese," said our manager. "Sure?" "Yes, sure." "Try it." Result: the Republic may be shut off to-morrow from foreign speigel and ferro-manganese and scarcely know it. Within her own broad bosom she has all the requisites for the manufacture of any kind of steel.

Tin is the only metal she now lacks. But let no one be surprised to read some day the announcement that all other deposits of tin in the world sink into insignificance compared to those just discovered in America. But even without this one precious mineral my readers will surely conclude from the story of the mineral treasures of the Republic which I have attempted to tell that this is indeed the favored land.

That the reader may the better be enabled to estimate the extent of the enormous mineral treasures of the Republic, I will summarize in order the several principal deposits and contrast them with those of each country which ranks next to America in mineral wealth. We begin with the black diamond, coal, as the mineral which perhaps lies closest to the root of industrial success. How then is the Democracy provided with this indispensable treasure?

Well,—the coal area of the United States comprises three hundred thousand square miles; Great Britain's coal field twelve thousand. The whole of the world has but four hundred thousand square miles. The Republic therefore has twenty-five times the field of the parent land; and, I am almost ashamed to confess it, she has three-quarters of all the coal area of the earth. For shame! to leave only one-quarter for all the rest of the world! In good round Scotch I say to her: "The deil's greedy but ye're misleard." So it is, my readers—but "as sure 's death we canna help it."

Let us see about the precious metals. Gold and silver have I none, was not written of this giant. She has contributed to the stock of gold in the world, estimated at ten thousand three hundred tons, more than one-half the whole. Australia has given her a close race during the past thirty years, but the Republic remains ahead.

In silver the Republic begins to challenge even the fabulous mines of Mexico and Bolivia, still classed as Spanish America, from which most of the silver supply of the world has hitherto been drawn. In the ten years between 1850 and 1860, these mines furnished more than half of all the silver produced. In the next decade, 1860 to 1870, it was still the same, $320,000,000 (£64,-000,000) being their product, while the total was but $550,000,000 (£110,000,000). In these two decades the infant Republic produced only $50,000,000 (£10,000-000) and $80,000,000 (£16,000,000) respectively. But with the discovery of the silver mines of Nevada and Colorado, which lay till then in the untrodden wilderness, the United States came rapidly to the front, and in the last decade, 1870 to 1880, she shows $340,000,000 (£68,000,000) as against the $350,000,000 (£70,000,-000) of all the Spanish-America mines together. Germany and Austria produced about $100,000,000 (£20,-000,000), and various countries as much more. Since 1880, the race is more and more to the Republic, for the average product of her silver mines since then exceeds $46,250,000 (£9,250,000) per annum, one-third of the silver production of the world.

Leaving the "yellow geordie" and the "white monie," as Bassanio did, let us see how it fares with the humbler, dingy, dull copper—the bawbee. The world's production of copper in 1883 was exactly two hundred thousand tons. Of this, America supplied more than one-fourth, fifty-two thousand tons; the whole of Europe gave only seventy-one thousand tons; Chili but forty-one thousand tons.

Is it not amazing that one nation should in itself have each of the three metals in such abundance! Australia has gold, and the Republic says to her, "So have I in value greater than yours." Mexico and Bolivia call, "Here stand we with the dazzling mines of Peru," and the Republic answers, "Our silver mines exceed those treasures." Chili has been the main source of the copper supply, and now the Republic leads her in her own special field.

It was not copper after all that Bassanio preferred, but the dull leaden casket. Let us see then about this valuable article. The world produced in 1883 four hundred and fifty-four thousand metric tons, and of this the Republic contributed one hundred and forty thousand, more than a fourth. Spain comes next to her with one hundred and twenty-seven thousand, followed by Germany with ninety-five thousand. Britain figures here for forty thousand tons, not a bad showing for so small an area.

In zinc, the Republic is making fast strides. Its manufacture may be said to have begun about 1870, when only seven thousand tons were produced. The product in 1884 reached thirty-eight thousand tons; the British product in 1883 was twenty-three thousand tons, but either of these is insignificant compared with Germany's contribution, one hundred and sixteen thousand tons. We shall see how long it will take the young giant to forge alongside of his great German competitor in this branch of manufactures; twenty years may do it, or even less.

Thus the Republic supplies one-fourth of the lead,

one-fourth of the copper, one-third of the silver, one-half of the gold of the world. Monster of the Pactolean stream, must everything you possess and everything you touch turn to gold, that you may dominate the earth?

Thank God, these treasures are in the hands of an intelligent people, the Democracy, to be used for the general good of the masses, and not made the spoils of monarchs, courts, and aristocracy, to be turned to the base and selfish ends of a privileged hereditary class. The weakest nation may rest secure, Canada on the north, and Chili on the south, for the nature of a government of the people is to abjure conquest, to protect the weak neighbor from foreign aggression if need be; never to molest, but to dwell in peace and loving neighborliness with all. The Republic is, indeed, the child of covetous, grasping, ever-warring Britain, but being relieved of monarchical institutions and the militarism which is their necessary following, she has thrown away the rude sword and scorns to conquer except through love. It is a proud record for the Democracy that the giant of the Western Continent is not feared by the pigmies which surround him, but is regarded with affection and admiration in the day of prosperity, and as a sure and potent defender, upon whom they can safely call in the day of trouble.

Had the monarchy retained possession of the country how different must have been the result. Added to the inevitable wars of an aristocratic and military system, there would have been the hate of republics as republics, for no royalist ever would let a republic live if he could help it; for though not generally wise, they are not quite so devoid of reasoning self-interest as to court self-extinction. Every weak nation upon the continent would have lived in fear. No neighbor ever liked the British. No neighbor ever can until the masses are known to

them and make the government of England in its deal-
ings with other nations a true expression of themselves.
The people of Britain are most lovable; its ruling classes
are just what monarchy and privilege make of men and
women—selfish, narrow, conceited, and tyrannical, and
wholly unmindful of others. For this reason, while the
British have always been feared, they have never been
loved by other races.

All this will change, however, when the Democracy
rules their country. The parent land will become in Europe what the Republic is upon the American continent
—the unselfish counsellor, the guide, the true and trusted
friend, of its less powerful, less advanced nations. It is
not by wicked conquest over other States, but by honest,
peaceful labor within its own bounds and with the good
will of all its neighbors that the Democracy builds up the
State.

Chapter XII

TRADE AND COMMERCE

"The great ships which pass between the old and the new lands are shuttles weaving a glorious web. Already 'Arbitration' has been fully spelled out upon the pattern, and now comes the motto—'Peace and Good Will Forever.'"

THE United States of America furnish the only example in the world's history of a community purely industrial in origin and development. Every other nation has passed through its military stage. In Europe and in Asia, in ancient times as well as in modern, social development has been mainly the result of war. Nearly every modern dynasty in Europe has been established by conquest, and every nation there has acquired and held its territory by force of arms. Men have been as wild beasts slaughtering each other at the command of the small privileged classes. The colonies of America, on the other hand, were established for commercial purposes, and generally the land they acquired was obtained by purchase or agreement, and not by conquest. Devoted to industry, the American people have never taken up the sword, except in self-defence or in defence of their institutions. Never has the plough, the hammer, or the loom, been deserted for the sword of conquest. Never has the profession of arms been honored above or even equally with other professions. Indeed, before the Civil War, soldiers were objects of popular ridicule; and even now, when almost every American above forty years of age has either himself shouldered a musket, or has relations who have fought for the unity of the country, the soldier of fortune—a type common among other peoples—is unknown. Such a man as the sanguinary author of "Under Fourteen Flags," a book descriptive of his butchering of fellow-men under fourteen different flags, would provoke among Americans feelings of repugnance and disgust. American regiments are regiments of workers. Emblazoned on their banners are not the names of cities sacked or of thousands slaughtered, but the names of inventors, civilizing influences, labor-saving machines. "By this sign shall ye conquer" was also the divine prediction for them; but the symbol was the plough, not the cross-shaped hilt of a sword.

The two armies are those which the poet Holmes has so well contrasted:

"One marches to the drum-beat's roll,
    The wide-mouthed clarion's bray,
And bears upon a crimson scroll,
    'Our glory is to slay.'

One moves in silence by the stream,
    With sad, yet watchful eyes,
Calm as the patient planet's gleam
    That walks the clouded skies.

Along its front no sabres shine,
    No blood-red pennons wave;
Its banner bears the single line,
    'Our duty is to save.'"

While the millions of Europe have been struggling in the thralls of military despotism, the American people have been for one hundred years peacefully working out a career of usefulness. The result is that their industrial successes have placed them at the head of the world in wealth and power. While practically independent herself, America has become indispensable to Europe. Without her bountiful supplies of cotton, grain, and meat, millions of Europeans would lack food and clothing.

The commercial history of the United States may be set forth in a few words. The net imports including coin and bullion, $22,500,000 (£4,500,000) in 1790, were $75,000,000 (£15,000,000) in 1830. And in the next term of fifty years, we find them bounding from this figure to $740,000,000 (£148,000,000). The exports show even a more rapid advance, for these began in 1790 at $20,000,000 (£4,000,000) reached $60,000,000 (£12,-000,000) in the forty years to 1830, and during the past half-century, we find them $725,000,000 (£145,000,-000), so that in fifty short years, the foreign commerce of the Republic has increased elevenfold. The amounts of imports *per capita* of the population have increased during the last fifty years from $6.25 (£1 5s) to about $15 (£3), while exports increased from $5 (£1) to $16.60 (£3 6s). Let us see what the few leading articles are which go to make up this commerce. What did the Republic buy from the world in 1883? Sugar and molasses to the extent of $100,000,000 (£19,875,000). Surely Brother Jonathan has a sweet tooth, for he spent more for sweet things than for anything else. For wool and woollen goods he spent $55,000,000 (£11,000,000), for chemicals $45,000,000 (£9,000,000). Even cotton goods, although he exports them himself, he wanted from others, to the tune of $35,000,000 (£7,000,000), some curious things in cotton, I suppose, which pleased his fancy, or *her* fancy, more likely. Silks he paid just a little more for, or $37,000,000 (£7,400,000) went for these. The Scotch say "She never bode for a silk goon that didna gat the sleeve o't." The American woman goes for the full goon and gets it, although now it is generally of domestic manufacture, no matter what may be the label. Raw silk to be manufactured is imported to about one-half the value of imported silks, which proves how very much more is made at home than is bought abroad, the value of the raw silk being many times less than the finished goods. His cup of coffee costs the American $42,000,000 (£8,400,000) per year, and tea, $17,000,000 (£3,400,000). These are the principal purchases he makes from others.

Now what does he sell to these good friends whom he honors with his patronage? He does a thriving business truly in this department. First comes his cotton exports. The world bought from him in 1883, $250,000,000 (£50,000,000). Then his wheat department disposed of $120,000,000 worth (£24,000,000), and in the form of flour $55,000,000 more (£11,000,000). Meat, eggs, butter, and other provisions kept not a few of his hands busy, for no less than $107,000,000 (£21,400,000) had to be sent forward to satisfy the world's wants. Even petroleum to the extent of $45,000,000 (£9,000,000) he sent forth to light the world; and nasty tobacco to end in smoke cost his customers that year no less than $22,000,000 (£4,400,000). Wood and its manufactures to the extent of $26,500,000 (£5,300,000) was taken, a great deal of it, no doubt, in the shape of furniture. Iron and steel manufactures make a much better showing than expected, for he really exported these, such as sewing machines, agricultural machinery and a thousand and one Yankee notions, to the sum of $22,500,000 (£4,500,000). And finally Uncle Sam sends from his big farm some of his millions of live cattle and sheep, and gets $8,500,000 (£1,700,000) for them.

These products are drawn from several departments, which may be classed under the general heads of agriculture, manufactures, mines, forest, etc., and tabulated as follows, with the amounts contributed by each:

Agriculture, ...	$550,000,000	£110,000,000
Manufactures, ...	20,500,000	4,100,000
Mining, ...	56,250,000	11,250,000
The Forest, ...	7,050,000	1,410,000
The Fisheries, ...	7,250,000	1,250,000
All others, ...	7,250,000	1,250,000

Thus does he, the young hopeful, lay under contribution all wealth-producing sources to swell his prosperous and rapidly increasing business with the world.

We see that, notwithstanding the almost incredible expansion of home manufactures, the American citizen imports more and more from other lands. See him only fifty years ago patronizing other people to the extent of $6.25 (£1 5s) per year, and now every man, woman, and child spends $15 (£3) for foreign goods. His tariff may be very high and quite outrageous in the opinion of many, yet he buys about three times as much per head under it as he did fifty years ago. It cannot be so very bad after all, although it is none the less true that year after year America gains firmer control of her own markets for manufactured articles. Every year sees a decrease of these relatively to the total imports. In crude and partially manufactured articles imports are increasing; in 1860, for instance, the proportion of these was only twenty-six per cent., but by uninterrupted advances every decade it rose in 1885 to forty per cent. of the total importations, while manufactured articles fell from seventy-four to sixty per cent. of the whole.

The balance of trade, to which, despite the teaching of economists, Americans still attach great importance, has during the last ten or eleven years been continually and greatly in favor of the Republic. In the space of fifty years foreign commerce has increased fivefold. It has nearly doubled since 1860, in spite of the check it received during the war. It increased greatly in 1880, and reached its maximum in 1883; since that time there has been a falling off of fourteen per cent., due to the protracted period of depression. Up to the year 1876, with a few exceptions, the imports were in excess of the exports of merchandise, the maximum difference being reached in 1872, when the excess was $182,000,000 (£36,400,000). Since then the balance has been the other way, the highest figure being reached in 1879, viz.: $264,000,000 (£52,800,000). Taking the period from 1860 to 1885, imports increased sixty-three per cent., while the increase in exports was one hundred and twenty-nine per cent.

It is usual to speak of the Republic as without commerce. Much dire prophesying of coming decay is indulged in because the sea-going commerce is now chiefly carried in foreign ships. The tendency is to limit the term "commerce" to the carriage of merchandise to and from other countries. So limited, America has indeed little to boast of. The change from wooden to iron and steel ships cut her out of a large part of the carrying trade which no fiscal regulations or lack of regulations can possibly restore. For the same reason that water will not run up hill, ships cannot be sailed by dearer to cheaper countries. Had America ten thousand large ships, their crews from chief engineer to cabin-boy would be foreigners, because these can be secured cheaper in Liverpool or Antwerp than in New York. Americans can do better than sail the seas for the pittances earned by the men of the older lands. The first cost of ships must necessarily for the same reason be much more here than upon the Clyde. If the navigation laws were repealed to-morrow no American capital would purchase foreign-built ships for trade abroad; and if they did the flag might indeed be the Stars and Stripes, but ship and crew would be British. The voice might be the voice of Jacob, but the hand would be the hand of Esau. In no sense would the commercial marine thus created be American or add to American wealth. For generations yet to come the attempt to become the chief carriers of merchandise, if made, must result in failure and render the Republic ridiculous.

Here is the fable which meets the case:

"Ah, ha!" said the turtle to the lion, as the latter proudly walked the shore, "any kind of a beast can walk on the land as well as you do, but let us see you do this," and then it turned a somersault in the sea. The lion tried. Result, the turtle fed upon the lion for many days.

America has no business with ocean navigation till her continent is filled, and prices of labor and material are down to the European basis. Let her leave the stormy sea to the motherland, whose "home is on the ocean wave," and stick to land as her natural heritage. Columbia's home is on the fertile prairie.

Notwithstanding all this, America still manages to do some of the carrying trade in her wooden ships, in the construction of which she has her rivals at a disadvantage, because the timber is here. She carried in 1880 about $280,000,000 (£56,000,000), or more than one-sixth of her whole foreign commerce. The coasting trade of America, from which foreigners are excluded, presents a fairer showing, being thirty-four million tons. The total sea-going tonnage of the nation in 1884 was three million one hundred and eighty-one thousand eight hundred and four tons, which places her next in rank to Britain, and far ahead of any other nation.

From the unique position of Britain as the carrier of the world, it follows that her people have unconsciously been led to attach far too much importance to the foreign trade as it concerns nations in general. Even in her own case it is trifling compared to her internal commerce. Her railways alone carry three times as much as all her ships, foreign, sea-going, and domestic traffic combined. "The milkman who brings the daily portion of milk to him who dwells in city or town," says Edward Atkinson, the American Adam Smith, "represents a commerce of vast proportions, almost equal in this country, in its aggregate value, to the whole sum of our foreign importations."

The home commerce of America as compared to her foreign is as twenty-one to one; and even Britain's gigantic foreign commerce is only one-sixth as great as the home commerce of America.

The shipping engaged in this internal commerce has an aggregate tonnage of one million tons, which, added to the sea-going, gives as the total American tonnage engaged in commerce four million two hundred and fifty thousand tons, as against the seven million tons of Britain. The total American traffic with foreign nations is sixteen millions of tons. If every ton carried in foreign ships were carried in American ships, the additional trade would not be as great as the natural increase of her home commerce for a single year. Truly a paltry prize to contend for and make such a fuss about. The American coasting tonnage alone more than doubles the entire foreign traffic (thirty-four as against sixteen million tons), while the domestic commerce by rail is reported as two hundred and ninety-one, and by steamers on lakes and rivers as twenty-five and a half millions of tons. Thus it appears that our internal commerce, of which so little is heard, is more than twenty times greater than the foreign trade. One ton of foreign to twenty tons of domestic commerce! Really there is no greater impostor than the distinguished stranger known as "Foreign Commerce."

The inter-dependence of our States, and hence the commerce between them, is shown in an interesting way by an illustration borrowed from my friend Mr. Edward Atkinson—"a homely illustration in a subject not fitted for poetic treatment, nor likely to appeal to the imagination, *commerce in hogs*. The great prairies of the West grow corn in such abundance that even now, with all our means of inter-communication, it cannot be all used as food, and some of it is consumed as fuel. It often happens that the farmer upon new land, remote from railroads, can get only fifteen to twenty cents per bushel for Indian corn, at which price, while it is the best, it is also the cheapest fuel that he can have, and its use is an evidence of good economy, and not of waste. Upon the fat prairie lands of the West, the hog is wholesomely fed only upon corn in the milk or corn in the ear; thence he is carried to the colder climate of Massachusetts, where by the use of that one crop in which New England excels all others—ice—the meat can be packed at all seasons of the year; there it is prepared to serve as food for the workmen of the North, the freemen of the South, or the artisan of Europe; while the blood, dried in a few hours to a fine powder, and sent to the cotton fields of South Carolina and Georgia to be mixed with the phosphate rocks that underlie their coast land, serves to produce the cotton fibre which furnishes the cheapest and fittest clothing for the larger portion of the inhabitants of the world.

Here, then, is commerce, or men serving each other on a grand scale, all developed within the century, and undreamed of by our ancestors. The vast plains of the

West, enriched by countless myriads of buffalo, can spare for years to come a portion of their productive force. Commerce sets in motion her thousand wheels, food is borne to those who need it, and they are saved the effort to obtain it on the more sterile soil of the cold North. Commerce turns that very cold to use. The refuse is saved, and commerce has discovered that its use is to clothe the naked in distant lands. Borne to the sandy but healthy soils of Georgia and South Carolina, it renovates them with the fertility thus transferred from the prairies of Illinois and Indiana, and presently there comes back to Massachusetts the cotton of the farmers, the well saved, clean, strong, and even staple, which commerce again has discovered to be worth identifying as the *farmer's,* not as the planter's crop, made by his own labor, and picked by his wife and children.

Much is said in Britain about the tariff policy of the Republic, but the results of that policy I fear are but little understood. The general impression is that the duties charged are so exorbitant as seriously to cripple trade between the old and new lands. So far from this being true, Britain has no customer to whom she sends so much of her manufactures, nor any with whom her trade increases so rapidly. This so-called highly protective and heavily taxed Republic imports more British goods than any other people. Here are the figures for 1883, which was a poor year for American business: Britain sent goods to India in that year valued at twenty-four millions sterling, to Germany nineteen millions, to France eighteen millions, and to the Republic twenty-seven millions sterling.

The total importations of America that year were $725,000,000 (£145,000,000), and of this vast sum more than a full one-third, or $250,000,000 (£50,000,-000) came from Britain and British possessions; $185,-

000,000 (£37,000,000) came from Great Britain and Ireland proper.*

To show how overwhelmingly the Republic buys from Britain, we have but to contrast its purchases from other lands. France, in 1882, supplied only $90,000,000 (£18,-000,000) worth of goods, and Germany but $56,000,-000 (£11,200,000) worth. The combined trade of these two principal sources of supply after Britain, exceeds but little more than one-half of Britain's sum including British possessions, nor do they combined come near equalling the purchases from Britain proper, for together France and Germany sent but $146,000,000 (£29,200,000), while Britain sent $196,000,000 (£39,-200,000).

Britain could lose either France or Germany, and almost both combined as purchasers, and her trade would not suffer as much as from the withdrawal of the much abused American. Is it not time for the Monarchy to be just a little mindful of this fact, and to behave itself accordingly towards its dutiful offspring, who year after year increases his patronage, and takes of her manufactures more than he takes from all the rest of the world? The question of Free Trade in America is one which will not be within the reach of practical politics in the lives of those now living. To bring it about, one of two courses is necessary: either the revenue must be raised by increased internal taxation, or the duty must be enormously raised upon the only necessaries of life which America imports largely, sugar, coffee, etc.; neither of these seems probable. A new duty upon the food of the people of Britain is just as probable as one in America; even democratic President Cleveland in his first message to Con-

*The difference in value between this thirty-seven million pounds and the twenty-seven million pounds reported as exports that year from Britain to the United States may be found in the differing values at the place of manufacture in Britain and value in America duty paid.

gress, states that any reduction in the tariff should be made in the duties now imposed upon the necessaries of life. The tendency is all in this direction. The second course would be to raise revenue by direct taxation; this is the ideal standard, and the Republic in its march may some day work up to it, and give another advanced political lesson to others; so far no nation has ever tried even to approach it; evidently it is not for our day or generation.

What then is the possible and consequently the only probable outcome of tariff discussion? Nothing beyond a possible gradual reduction of duties at intervals of some years, say five or six per cent. each decade, but these reductions speaking generally will be made only upon such articles as can be manufactured profitably here, with lower than the existing duties, nor will the duties be lowered to a point which will cripple the home manufacture. The question is not now which policy is the better for a new nation, Free Trade or Protection, but how is the huge fabric of manufactures to be dealt with, the greatest in the world, as we have seen. It has been called into existence upon certain conditions and has accommodated itself thereto. The conservatism of the Democracy is so ingrained as to justify one in prophesying that great care will be taken not to disturb it unduly. I often hear surprise expressed in Europe that the vast body of consumers should bear so contentedly the extra cost upon what they purchase, the result of heavy duties. The explanation is two-fold; first, manufacturers are spreading rapidly over most of the States; the Southern States of Alabama, Tennessee, Missouri and others for instance are really protective States now from this cause, as are Minnesota and Michigan in the North-west; but the second cause lies much deeper. Prices of articles are no longer generally fixed by the foreign but by the home competition.

One instance may illustrate many other branches in which the consumers buy what they need very cheap, in many cases about as cheap as the European does, wholly irrespective of duty. The duty upon steel rails is say $17.50 (£3 11s) per ton, market price in Britain, £5 ship's side Liverpool, total in New York, provided they were transported and laid down there for nothing would still be $42.50 or £8 10s. The railroads of America have had no difficulty in purchasing hundreds of thousands of tons at $28 (£5 12s), and they know well that if any considerable portion of their requirements had to come from abroad the cost would very greatly exceed this.

In clothing, which was formerly the article upon which the greatest difference in price existed between the two countries, the case is much the same. Some competent friends visiting us from England assure me that prices generally are as cheap as at home and in some cases even cheaper. Foreign competition has been recommended as the necessary and certain cure against exorbitant profits being exacted by the home manufacturer to the detriment of the consumer; very good, but precisely the same cure is found, from vigorous home competition. As far as the foreigner was concerned, as we have seen in the case of steel rails, the American manufacturer might have had forty-two dollars and fifty cents per ton for rails which he was forced to sell for twenty-eight dollars, which was only the British price, twenty-five dollars, with a fair rate of transportation to New York and expenses incident thereto, without a penny added for duty. What forced him to do so and give the consumer rails for twenty-eight dollars? Home competition.

Even our monarchical friends in Canada bought steel rails from American mills last year, because the cost was less than was demanded for those of British manufacture, although both were alike as to duty.

I merely venture to give the facts bearing upon the present aspect of the question as far as the Republic is concerned, that those in Europe who bewail the hard fate of the consumer here may be comforted, for truly he is not paying the fair cost of his supplies plus the duty, but only the unprecedentedly low prices established by the close and unremitting competition of home manufacturers, and these prices, as has been shown in the chapter on manufactures, are with rare exceptions not much above those of Britain. It is for these reasons that the consumer is not troubling himself, and cannot be made to trouble himself, very greatly with the question of the tariff.

Far be it from me to retard the march of the world towards the free and unrestricted interchange of commodities. When the Democracy obtains sway throughout the earth the nations will become friends and brothers, instead of being as now the prey of the monarchical and aristocratic ruling classes, and always warring with each other; standing armies and war ships will be of the past, and men will then begin to destroy custom-houses as relics of a barbarous monarchical age, not altogether from the low plane of economic gain or loss, but strongly impelled thereto from the higher standpoint of the brotherhood of man; all restriction upon the products of other lands will then seem unworthy of any member of the race, and the dawn of that day will have come when

"Man to man the world o'er
Shall brothers be and a' that."

Chapter XIII
RAILWAYS AND WATERWAYS

"And you will then (when the Colonies achieve independence) see how the earth will be beautified! What culture! What new arts and new sciences! What safety for commerce! Navigation will precipitate all the peoples toward each other. A day will come when we will go into a populous and regulated city of California as one goes in the stagecoach of Meaux."
—Marquis D'Argenson. (1745.)

THE inhabitants of the tight little island of Britain or of the miniature States of Europe can have no conception of distance as understood by the American. The vastness of the American continent gives a corresponding width to the conceptions of space formed by its inhabitants. The State of New York is almost as large as England, while Texas is larger than France, or England and Germany combined. California has a greater area than Austria; and some other States and Territories, known only by name in England, like Nevada, Colorado, Oregon, and Nebraska, have areas greater than several European kingdoms.

The distance from New York to Chicago exceeds that from London to Rome, while San Francisco is farther from the Atlantic coast than Quebec is from London. The journey from Philadelphia to New Orleans is nearly twice as great as that from London to St. Petersburg; while Jerusalem, Cairo, Cyprus, Constantinople, Astrakan, and Teneriffe are all nearer to Hyde Park corner than Salt Lake City is to Boston, and Salt Lake City is only two-thirds of the way across the continent. During the Civil War the frontier defended by General Grant exceeded in length a line drawn from London across the Channel and Continent to Constantinople, thence through Asia Minor and Palestine to the great pyramid at Cairo, and thence still on up the Nile as far as the first cataract. And this line, if drawn, would be many miles shorter than the journey from New York to the city of Portland, Oregon.

These comparisons will help the British reader to conceptions which are as familiar to the American as the star-spangled emblem of his nationality. It will also help the European to form a slight estimate of the labor and cost by which there has been spread over this vast continent a net-work of railways which ramify it in every part. One hundred years ago America was almost as much a dark continent as Africa is now. A few adventurous pioneers and explorers had forced their way to the Father of Waters, and descended by it to the Gulf of Mexico, but a transcontinental journey was unthought of until 1803, when, at the recommendation of President Jefferson, an exploring expedition was sent to the Pacific under command of Captain William Clarke and Meriwether Lewis. It was considered a wonderful feat when the little party under their charge penetrated the wilderness across the mountains and down the westward slope to the mouth of the Columbia River on the Pacific, two years and four months being required for the journey and return. Even in 1830 there were no facilities for internal travel. The States along the coast had constructed rough turnpike roads, and railways were just introduced; but the heart of the continent was practically closed to all but the most adventurous.

Two-thirds of all the mails were carried in lumbering

stage-coaches, with bodies hung upon leather straps that they might swing freely in any direction without being knocked to pieces as they struggled over the corduroy roads. A trip in one of these vehicles tossed the traveller as if he were in a fishing smack upon the Channel in a storm. The other third was carried upon the backs of horses and in sulkies. Steamboats were carriers over only a few small short routes, and there were only twenty-three miles of railway laid in all the land. All this was as late as 1830, just over fifty years ago.

The discomforts of stage-coach travelling in America cannot even be guessed at in these days of palace-cars and forty miles per hour express trains. The books of early visitors are full of invective and complaints at the horrors of an American stage. The Norwegian, Arfedson, wrote in 1832:

"A traveller intending to proceed thence (from Augusta, S. C.) by land to New Orleans is earnestly recommended to bid adieu to all comforts on leaving Augusta, and make the necessary preparations for a hard and rough campaign. If he has a wife and children unprovided for, and to whom he has not the means of leaving a suitable legacy, let him by all means be careful to insure his life to the highest amount the office will take; for the chances of his perishing on the road are ten to one, calculated according to the following table of casualties:

1 by horses running away,	3 by murder,
2 by drowning,	4 by explosion."

Miss Martineau in 1834–5 thus describes her experiences:

"The mail roads are still extremely bad. I found in travelling through the Carolinas and Georgia, that the drivers consider themselves entitled to get on by any means they can devise: that nobody helps and nobody hinders them. It was constantly happening that the stage came to a stop on the brink of a wide and a deep puddle, extending all across the road. The driver helped himself, without scruple, to as many rails of the nearest fence as might serve to fill up the bottom of the hole, or break our descent into it. On inquiry, I found it was not probable that either fence or road would be mended till both had gone to absolute destruction.

"The traffic on these roads is so small, that the stranger feels himself almost lost in the wilderness. In the course of several days' journey, we saw (with the exception of the wagons of a few encampments) only one vehicle besides our own. It was a stage returning from Charleston. Our meeting in the forest was like the meeting of ships at sea. We asked the passengers from the South of news from Charleston and Europe; and they questioned us about the state of politics at Washington. The eager vociferation of drivers and passengers was like such as is unusual, out of exile. We were desired to give up all thoughts of going by the eastern road to Charleston. The road might be called impassable; and there was nothing to eat by the way."

Even as late as 1850 Sir Charles Lyell says:

"After comparing the risks it seems to be more dangerous to travel by land, in a new country, than by river steamers, and some who have survived repeated journeyings in stage-coaches show us many scars. The judge who escorted my wife to Natchez informed her that he had been upset no less than thirteen times."

To the inconvenience of stage travelling, described in these extracts, must be added that of being jolted over corduroy roads, made of logs placed longitudinally across the road, with nothing to fill up the inequalities of surface. On roads where there was no competition the slowness of the stages was very exasperating. One writer says: "We scarcely averaged more than three and a half miles an hour; and in urging the drivers even to this speed, had to submit to no little insolence into the bargain." The insolence of drivers is complained of by nearly all the English travellers at this period. Passengers had also to look after their own baggage, and to get out into the mud and rain to fasten it to the coach when the jolting had loosened the straps.

The *Democratic Review* for September, 1839, says that in 1835 the "speed of communication achieved by the express mail was deemed almost the acme of mail improvement"; and as examples it mentions the following:

		Days	Hours
From New York to	Washington, ...	1	8
" "	Richmond, Va., . . .	2	13
" "	Columbia, S. C., . . .	6	3
" "	Milledgeville, Ga., . . .	7	15
" "	Mobile, Ala., ...	12	12
" "	New Orleans, ...	14	0
" "	Columbus, O., ...	4	16
" "	Indianapolis, Ind., . . .	7	14
" "	St. Louis, Mo., ...	13	10
" "	Huntsville, Ala., . . .	11	22
" New Orleans to	Montgomery, Ala., . . .	3	21
" "	Nashville, Tenn., . . .	10	0
" "	Louisville, Ky., . . .	13	0
" "	Cincinnati, O., ...	14	11
" "	Columbus, O., ...	16	9
" "	Pittsburg, Pa., ...	15	5

How diverse were the means of travel in those days is well illustrated by a journey from Troy to Chicago made in 1832 by Mr. Philo Carpenter. He took the Erie Canal to Buffalo, and thence went by lake steamer to Detroit. Four and a half days was then the usual time for this passage. From Detroit Mr. Carpenter went by weekly mail-coach to Niles, and then took passage from Niles to the mouth of the St. Joseph River on a flatboat. Thence he was conveyed by two Indians in a bark canoe which they improvised, as far as the mouth of the

Calumet, where one of the Indians was seized with a colic and they refused to proceed further. Our traveller then bargained with a settler for the use of a lumber wagon drawn by oxen; and with this he eventually reached Fort Dearborn, as Chicago was then called. The limited express now does this journey in twenty-four hours, and the traveller never has to leave his peripatetic hotel.

After 1830 came the transition period, when primitive railways began to compete with canal-boats and stage-coaches. In the Philadelphia *Public Ledger* for May 22, 1836, appeared the following advertisement, headed by a primitive looking engine and cars:

"FARE REDUCED TO $12.—NEW EXPRESS FAST PACKET LINE, *from Philadelphia to Pittsburgh*—the only line exclusively for passengers, *via* Lancaster and Harrisburgh Railroads and Pennsylvania Canals. Leaves daily at 6 o'clock A.M.—*through in three days.* For passage apply to, at the office 51 Chestnut Street, below Third Street, John Cameron, Agent."

And two years later in the same journal appears the following:

"FARE REDUCED! Leech & Co.'s packet line to Pittsburgh, *via* Railroads and Canals. *Through in four and a half days.*"

Upon one of these canal-boats I saw arrive in Pittsburg the first locomotive that ever came west of the Ohio River.

The early railroads seem very rude judged by modern standards:

"Passenger cars were small vehicles, holding no more than from eighteen to twenty-four passengers, and not much, if any, heavier than the large stage-coaches. The iron (used for rails) was flat-bar iron, from half to three-fourths of an inch thick, spiked on wooden sleepers which were lightly tied, and on tracks not perfectly graded or heavily ballasted. The locomotives weighed from two to six or seven tons, and drew corresponding loads. Great weight and high speed would have destroyed the tracks. One of the dangers of travel was from 'snake-heads,' caused by the loosening of the ends of the thin rails, which, bending up, were caught between the wheels and driven through the bottom of the cars, wounding or impaling any one who sat over the point of entrance. Instead of grading up or down steep declivities, cars were passed over the incline by counter-weights of box-cars, loaded with stone, which balanced them like window-weights, and made it easy to pass up one as the other went down. . . . Twenty miles a year were in those days rapid railroad building."

The first railway trains were drawn by horses or mules, though locomotives were early introduced from England and duplicated in America. An account of the Mohawk and Hudson Railroad, printed in William's *Register* for 1833, concludes with the words:

"Passengers are carried upon this road in coaches, drawn by horses, and by the locomotive-engines, whose powers are not yet conclusively tried."

And from a passage in the *Charleston Patriot* for April, 1830, it would appear that other means of propulsion had been tried.

"Yesterday afternoon, a sail was set on a car on the railroad, before a large assembly of persons. It went at the rate of twelve to fifteen miles per hour, with fifteen persons on board. Afterwards thirteen persons and three tons of iron were carried at the rate of ten miles per hour. Considering the haste, and imperfect manner, in which the sail was got up, the result was highly gratifying."

But the most curious of propelling machines was one invented by Detmold. This was an engine run by a horse walking on an endless platform like the early horse-ferries. This curious machine carried passengers at the rate of twelve miles an hour.

Observe how the interior of the continent has been thrown open to civilization. A Santa Fé merchant wrote in 1830, "on the day of our departure (with wagon-trains drawn by mules) from Independence we passed the last human abode upon our route; therefore, from the borders of Missouri to those of New Mexico, not even an Indian settlement greeted our eyes." And when wagons instead of pack-mules were first used for internal transportation, the extraordinary nature of the change was sufficient to justify the following in Nile's *Register* for May 8, 1850:

"A party of seventy men, with *ten wagons,* was recently fitting out at St. Louis, for an expedition to the Rocky Mountains! What next?"

Nearly thirty years later a regular stage line was established, by the Pike's Peak Express Company, between the Missouri River and the Rocky Mountains. Transportation was effected by wagon-trains, and ox and mule-trains; and so perfectly did this line work, that a distance of seven hundred miles was made in six days and nights. Then in the spring of 1860 the owners of the Pike's Peak stage line established what was known as the Pony Express, which served as a daily fast-mail line between the cities of the Atlantic and Pacific coasts. The scheme was a marvel of American enterprise. Previous to that time, over three weeks were required to convey mails by steamer from New York to San Francisco. This Pony Express made the distance between the railway terminus on the Missouri River and the Pacific in eight or nine days. Brave men and first-class stock were required, for Indians and highwaymen were often encountered, and the relay stations were sometimes burned, and the stock run off. Almost the entire distance of nearly two thousand miles to be traversed was one vast solitude. No delays were permitted, the mail-bags were kept constantly on the move during these long and lonely trips. Horses were changed at every station, and riders at intervals of from fifty to seventy miles. The rapid time made caused the government to send the mails overland.

From such small beginnings has grown the magnificent railroad system of America. When the success of the first road had been proved, others quickly sprang into existence; and presently all over the inhabited portions of the continent men were digging, grading, blasting, tunnelling at a rate which has hardly suffered diminution, and has never ceased. The development of the resources of the country by means of these artificial highways has gone on with marvellous rapidity.

Finally the idea of stretching a railway line across the entire continent began to take possession of the public mind. As early as 1846 the feasibility of such an undertaking had been discussed in Congress, and in 1849 the idea took tangible shape in the form of a bill introduced by Senator Benton. In 1851 surveying parties were sent out to decide upon a route; but delays afterwards resulted from differences between the Northern and Southern States. When the war removed this obstacle acts of Congress were passed providing subsidies in gold and land to the corporations authorized to build the road. Work was commenced in 1863, but only in a dilatory way. In 1865 the work progressed at a rate unheard of before. The rails were laid at the rate of two and three miles a day, and in one instance eight miles of track were laid. The line was completed and thrown open to traffic throughout its entire length in 1869. Since then three other transcontinental lines have been constructed; and now every part of the great Republic is the neighbor of the other part. The Bostonian does not think of his fellow-citizens of New Orleans as one thousand six hundred miles away, but as distant only forty-odd hours. The New Yorker does not speak of the thousand miles intervening between him and Chicago, but only of the twenty-four hours required to get there. In one sense space has been annihilated in America, and time is now the only measure of men's separation from each other.

American railways were built under charters for short distances, but as population increased these were consolidated and managed as great through-lines between termini hundreds of miles apart. In time these main lines absorbed branch and connecting lines, and now there are several systems, each serving extensive districts. Of these the most important, the Pennsylvania, is a good example. Its net-work of lines aggregates five thousand four hundred and ninety-one miles, with more than a thousand miles of second, third, and fourth tracks: gross earnings in 1884 were $80,000,000 (£16,000,000). The tonnage was sixty-three million tons, and the cost of moving perhaps the lowest in the world, being about four mills (less than a half-penny) per ton per mile. Certainly no rates for traffic in Europe are so low as the average received by the Pennsylvania Railroad. This line is solidly built, stone ballasted, and in every respect compares favorably with the trunk lines of Europe, if we except numerous road crossings at grade which would not be tolerated abroad. From its depot opposite New York four times per day through trains start for the great West, with sleeping-coaches which run through without change to Chicago, St. Louis, and Cincinnati; in special cases when desired, the travelling party may pass on to San Francisco or to New Orleans without change. A "dining" or "hotel-car" is attached at proper intervals and every luxury supplied upon these peripatetic Delmonicos. The

New York Central, Erie, and Baltimore and Ohio are systems of similar character between the East and West.

Chicago, the Western metropolis, has also its corresponding railway systems some of which are of great magnitude. The Chicago, Burlington and Quincy has three thousand three hundred and seventy-three miles, the Chicago and North-western three thousand two hundred and seventy-one miles, and the Chicago, Milwaukee and St. Paul, the work of that man of Aberdeen, Alexander Mitchell, no less than four thousand eight hundred and four miles under its sway.

It is with railways as with manufacturers; consolidation into the hands of a few organizations seems the inevitable tendency. The saving and efficiency thus effected over the hundred former disjointed petty corporations, each with its officers and staffs, are so manifestly great that nothing can prevent these consolidations. What the outcome of this massing of forces is to be is difficult to foretell, but that it is in accordance with economic laws is certain; therefore we can proceed without fear. We are on sure ground, hence the final result must be beneficial. If corporations grow to gigantic size and attempt to use their powers like giants, forgetting that they are the creatures and servants of the State, we may safely trust the Democracy to deal with them. There is no problem which an educated people cannot and will not solve in the interests of the people when solution is demanded.

The American railway system, starting fifty-five years ago at nothing, has reached, in 1885, one hundred and twenty-eight thousand miles of line. The whole of Europe has not so many, for in 1883 it had only one hundred and fourteen thousand three hundred miles, and the entire world but two hundred and seventy-nine thousand eight hundred and fifty miles. The record for the past ten years shows with what strides the iron road is girding the continent, for during that period no less than fifty-four thousand two hundred and eighty miles were built. When we read that in 1880 India, with its two hundred and fifty millions of people, added to its railways only two hundred and seventy-three miles, and the Republic, with its fifty millions, added in 1881 eleven thousand five hundred miles, we get some idea of the speed at which she rushes on. *The whole of Europe has not built as many miles of railway as the Republic has during some recent years, and in* 1880 *the whole world did not build as many.* It will be only a few years, probably not ten, ere the railway lines of America exceed in length those of all the rest of the world. The Republic in one scale, and "The World" in the other, and "The World" kicking the beam! Monster, you were called into existence only to redress the balance of the Old World, and within one short century we find you threatening to weigh it down! The Republic against "the field" and no takers!

In no other country is travel so comfortable and luxurious. For this we are chiefly indebted to a remarkable American invention, the sleeping-car, without which such extended lines would have remained an imperfect instrument for the consolidation of the people. Journeys between the oceans, requiring seven days and nights to perform, or even that between Chicago and other Western cities to New York and the East, which occupy but twenty-four to forty-eight hours' consecutive travel, could have been undertaken only in extreme cases, had the unfortunate traveller been required to sit up, as in the old-fashioned cars. Well do I remember that, when a clerk in the service of the Pennsylvania Railroad Company, a tall, spare, farmer-looking kind of man came to me once when I was sitting on the end seat of the rear car looking over the line. He said he had been told by the conductor that I was connected with the railway company, and he wished me to look at an invention he had made. With that he drew from a green bag (as if it were for lawyers' briefs), a small model of a sleeping berth for railway cars. He had not spoken a minute, before, like a flash, the whole range of the discovery burst upon me. "Yes," I said, "that is something which this continent must have." I promised to address him upon the subject as soon as I had talked over the matter with my superior, Thomas A. Scott.

I could not get that blessed sleeping-car out of my head. Upon my return I laid it before Mr. Scott, declaring that it was one of the inventions of the age. He remarked: "You are enthusiastic, young man, but you may ask the inventor to come and let me see it." I did so, and arrangements were made to build two trial cars, and run them on the Pennsylvania Railroad. I was offered an interest in the venture, which, of course, I gladly accepted. Payments were to be made ten per cent. per month after the cars were delivered, the Pennsylvania Railroad Company guaranteeing to the builders that the cars should be kept upon its line and under its control.

This was all very satisfactory until the notice came that my share of the first payment was $217.50 (£43). How well I remember the exact sum; but two hundred and seventeen dollars and a half were as far beyond my means as if it had been millions. I was earning $50 (£10) per month, however, and had prospects, or at least I always felt that I had. What was to be done? I decided to call on the local banker, Mr. Lloyd, state the case, and boldly ask him to advance the sum upon my interest in the affair. He put his hand on my shoulder and said: "Why, of course, Andie, you are all right. Go ahead. Here is the money." It is a proud day for a man when he pays his last note, but not to be named in comparison with the day in which he makes his first one, and *gets a banker to take it.* I have tried both and I know. The cars paid the subsequent payments from their earnings. I paid my first note from my savings so much per month, and thus did I get my foot upon fortune's ladder. It is easy to climb after that. A triumphant success was scored. And thus came sleeping-cars into the world. "Blessed be the man who invented sleep," says Sancho Panza. Thousands upon thousands will echo the sentiment, Blessed be the man who invented sleeping-cars. Let me record his name and testify my gratitude to him, my dear, quiet, modest, truthful, farmer-looking friend, T. T. Woodruff, one of the benefactors of the age.

This brings us to another remarkable man, George M. Pullman, as great a genius in organization and administration as Woodruff was in his peculiar line. It did not take this typical American of Chicago very long to see what part sleeping-cars were bound to play upon the American continent; and while a few cautious old gentlemen in Philadelphia were managing the original cars, in that dawdling temporizing way which is so amusing, making ten bites of even the smallest cherry, this young man laid his daring plans. He would contract for twenty or thirty cars, while the Philadelphia people hesitated to engage for one. The result was that Mr. Pullman completely eclipsed them. I soon saw that we had a genius to deal with, and advised the old concern to capture Mr. Pullman. There was a capture, but it did not quite take that form. They found themselves swallowed by this ogre, and Pullman monopolized everything. It was well that it should be so. The man had arisen who could manage, and the tools belonged to him. To-day his company has a paid-up capital of about thirty millions of dollars, and its ramifications extend everywhere. Mr. Pullman is a remarkable man, for he not only manages this business, he has created it. Before he appeared upon the scene a sleeping-car company had no rights which a railway company was bound to respect. Mr. Pullman has made the business respectable, and the travelling public are very much his debtors. Should Mr. Pullman's life be spared, I prophesy that the young contractor for elevating buildings in Chicago will leave a monument for himself in his new industrial town of Pullman which will place his name with those of Salt of Saltaire and Godin of Guise. A short roll of honor this, which contains the list of those who, springing from honest poverty, have made fortunes through honest toil, and then—ah, here comes the secret of the shortness of the list—and then turning back to look upon the poor workers where they started, have thereafter devoted their fortune and abilities so to improve the industrial system as to give to that class a better chance in life than it was possible for themselves to obtain. Mr. Pullman has made a start upon this toilsome path. His future deserves to be carefully watched.

If ever aerial navigation becomes practicable it will like railways attain its highest development in America; for here men's lives are too full of activity to permit lounging in parlor-cars drawn wearily by a locomotive at only forty miles an hour when it is possible for men to soar through the air and outstrip their own symbolic eagle in its flight.

Nature has done much for America as regards facilities for transportation. Her inland seas, containing one-third of all the fresh water in the world, and her great rivers lay ready at hand awaiting only the application of steam to vessels to render them magnificent highways. A vessel sailing round the edges of these American lakes traverses a greater distance than from New York to Liverpool.

The rivers of America are also the largest in the world. After the Amazon and the La Plata comes the

Mississippi, with an outflow of over two million cubic feet per hour. This mighty river, which the Indians called in their picturesque language Father of Waters, is equal in bulk to all the rivers of Europe combined, exclusive of the Volga. It is equal to three Ganges, nine Rhones, twenty-seven Seines, or eighty Tibers. "The mighty Tiber chafing with its flood," says the Master. How would he have described the Mississippi on the rampage after a spring flood, when it pours down its mighty volume of water and overflows the adjacent lowlands! Eighty Tibers in one! Burns' picture of the pretty little Ayr in flood has been extolled, where the foaming waters came down "an acre braid." What think you of a tumbling sea twenty miles "braid" instead of your "acre," dear Robin? The length of the Mississippi is two thousand two hundred and fifty miles, while its navigable tributaries exceed twenty thousand miles. The Father of Waters collects his substance from water-sheds covering an area of more than two and a half million square miles.

The Hudson is navigable by large steamers as far as Albany, one hundred and fifty miles inland from the Atlantic. There are quite a dozen other rivers in which the like is possible. Many well-known sea-ports are considerable distances from the coast properly speaking. Such are Philadelphia, Baltimore, New Orleans, and on the Pacific coast, Portland. The presence of inland ports, with extensive docks, piers, and large craft, is a constant source of astonishment to the European traveller. The sight of ships of three thousand tons burden, fifteen hundred miles from salt water, is sufficient to surprise one in whom the sight of rigged ships has always been associated with the sea. Walking along the quays of the lake cities, Buffalo, Toledo, Chicago, or Duluth, one might well imagine himself at the sea-coast.

These great natural waterways have been supplemented, and connected with each other by artificial canals. There were in the United States in 1880, four thousand four hundred and sixty-eight miles of canals, which had cost $265,000,000 (£53,000,000). Nearly two thousand miles of canal had, however, been abandoned, having been rendered valueless by the superior facilities offered by railroads. Many of the canals still worked were reported not to be paying expenses, and part of these also will no doubt soon be abandoned. The freight traffic on canals in 1880 amounted to twenty-one million forty-four thousand two hundred and ninety-two tons, yielding a gross income of $45,000,000 (£9,000,-000).

The early history of navigation in America presents as many curious contrasts and interesting facts as do other divisions of the history of American progress. From beginnings which to us seem ludicrously small and crude, the greatest results have come. At the beginning of the century a successful steamboat had not been built. For twenty or thirty years inventors in France, Scotland, England, and America had been working and planning to apply a principle which they saw was perfectly applicable; but lacking knowledge of one or two little essentials, they only passed from failure to failure, yet constantly getting nearer and nearer to success. John Fitch and Oliver Evans are the names of the earliest representatives of America in this great struggle.

After each experimenter had contributed some new light, an American engineer, Robert Fulton by name, gathered, in 1807, the multiplicity of lights into one great flame, and made practicable by the help of all what each had tried in vain to achieve by himself. Fulton's "Clermont" was the first commercially successful steamboat ever built. A boat of one hundred and sixty tons burden, she was launched on the Hudson in 1807, and

ran over a year as a passenger boat between New York
and Albany. The first steamboat of the Mississippi Valley was built by Fulton in 1811, and was called the
"Orleans." She had a stern wheel, and went from Pittsburg to New Orleans, more than two thousand miles, in
fourteen days. The next year Henry Bell, of Scotland,
built the "Comet," of thirty tons, which plied between
Glasgow and Greenoch, and in 1813 sailed around the
coasts of the British Isles. In 1819 the "Savannah," three
hundred and eighty tons burden, crossed the Atlantic
from America, visited Liverpool, St. Petersburg, and
Copenhagen, and returned. Nineteen years later, the
"Great Western," one thousand three hundred and forty
tons, and the "Sirius," steamed across the Atlantic from
England, and only two years afterwards, namely 1840,
the present justly celebrated Cunard line was established,
inaugurating an era of ocean travel which has revolutionized human life, and brought the old and new worlds
within six days of each other. On a Sunday afternoon in
August last, I sailed from Queenstown upon the Cunarder "Etruria," and on Saturday afternoon the noble
ship was moving up New York Bay. Just six days from
harbor to harbor. That was my last trip across the ferry;
contrast it with my first, seven weeks upon a sailing vessel!

Internal navigation has an equally interesting history.
The earliest transportation by water was effected by
means of keel-boats. These drifted down well enough
with the current, but had to be forced up stream with setting poles. The keel-boat was long and narrow, sharp at
the bow and stern, and of light draft. From fifteen to
twenty hands were required to propel it. The crew,
divided equally on each side, took their places upon the
running boards extending along the whole length of the
craft; and each man, setting one end of a long pole in the

bottom of the river, brought the other to his shoulder, and bending over it, with his face nearly to the plank, exerted all his force against the boat, treading it from under him. While those on one side were thus passing down in line to the stern, those on the other, facing about, were passing towards the bow, drawing their poles floating on the water. The keel-boatmen kept their rifles constantly within reach in case Indians should attempt to surprise them. Their journeys often lasted several months. These keel-boatmen, living a semi-barbarous life, developed traits more befitting the aboriginal savage than the descendants of Europeans. Human life with them appears to have had little more sanctity than the lives of the animals they shot on the river-banks. The descriptions of the now extinct keel-boatmen left by contemporary writers surpass in horrible detail anything ever written of Western cowboys or miners. They have now disappeared before steamboats and civilization as completely as the wildernesses amongst which their lives were mostly spent. With other barbarisms of "the good old times," they have sunk into oblivion. R. I. P.

One of the earliest packet lines we read about is the following:

> "On the 11th of January, 1794, a line of two keel-boats with bullet-proof covers and port-holes, and provided with cannon and small arms, was established between Cincinnati and Pittsburgh, each making a trip once in four weeks."

The defensive equipment of these keel-boats is very suggestive. Nothing enables one better to contrast "now" and "then."

It is interesting to read how our fathers occasionally compared the comforts of their days with the discomforts of our grandfathers; how proudly they spoke of improvements, and how delighted and content they were with accommodations which seem to us comfortless and mean. Here is a characteristic sample, written about 1845, when steamboats, uncomfortable and slow, were everywhere replacing lines of stages or horse-packets.

"In leaving Bangor, Maine, in a steamboat, though only for a short trip, I am thereby reminded of the difference which has taken place in our city, and throughout the country, in the mode of travelling between the present time and only twenty years since. I say twenty years, because it is about twenty years since I left the paternal home, and in the good sloop 'Betsy' took passage for Bangor, where we arrived in safety after eight days' toil. The usual mode of travelling then, from Bangor, was by the lumber coasters; in which passengers, male and female, were stowed away in the few berths in the cabin, or sprawled around upon the uncarpeted floor. There was indeed a semi-packet with a few extra berths hung round with a narrow and rather scanty red bombazette frill. But mean as these accommodations may now (1845) be considered, they afforded the best means of conveyance between Bangor and Massachusetts, and during the rainy seasons in the spring and fall—the only conveyance; for instead of three daily stages west, as now, the mail was carried once a week only, and then on horseback between Bangor and Augusta. During the winter, to be sure, Moses Burley conveyed the mail, and occasionally a passenger or two in a sleigh with a tandem team; and during the summer in a rickety covered wagon. . . . Then there was no small mail route to any of the towns above Bangor, and the old register in the monthly advertisement of the postmaster, of two fingers' long, enumerated letters for the whole region round about. These reminiscences have brought vividly to mind the appearance of the village as it was then. There were but five brick buildings erected, including the old distil house, that has since been removed to give place to the City Point Block. There were but eighteen stores—a few mechanics' shops—one bridge, and that the Kenduskeay, where toll was required—the court-house, now city hall— a wooden gaol—three taverns, and a few dwellings."

How delightfully confidential this old writer is! He has long since been gathered to his fathers, and even his name is forgotten, but he must have been a good man, who took an intelligent interest in what he saw.

Though steamboats offered greater facilities and comfort to travellers than sloops or stages, yet they were miserably conducted, and often dangerous. Indeed, the frequency of collision and explosions was appalling. It became common to have "safety-barges" towed by the steamboat; and an illustration of a boat of this character appended to an advertisement in the *Commercial Advertiser* for June 16, 1830, shows that the engine and boiler (and apparently the paddle-wheel) were placed right at the bow, as far away as possible from the passengers on the "safety-barge." In 1834–5 Miss Martineau found steamboat travelling in the West proverbially dangerous. She says:

"I was rather surprised at the cautions I received throughout the South about choosing wisely among the Mississippi steamboats; and at the question gravely asked, as I was going on board, whether I had a life-preserver with me. I found that all my acquaintances on board had furnished themselves with life-preservers, and my surprise ceased when we passed boat after boat on the river delayed or deserted on account of some accident."

Since that day the stringent regulations which provide for governmental inspection of all boats, have made steamboat travel upon the rivers as safe as it is delightful. An excursion from St. Louis or Cincinnati to New Orleans upon one of the floating palaces which now traverse the lower Ohio and Mississippi ranks as one of the most enjoyable modes in which a holiday can be spent.

The traffic floated upon these Western rivers will surprise many. Take the Ohio, for instance; a competent authority has stated that the total of its trade from its

head at Pittsburg to its mouth at New Cairo, about a
thousand miles, exceeded in 1874 $800,000,000, or
£160,000,000, a sum greater than the total exports of
the nation about which we hear so much. It is upon the
Ohio that the cheapest transportation in the world exists.
Coal, coke, and other bulky articles are transported at
the rate of one-twentieth of a cent, one-fortieth of a
penny per ton per mile. This is made possible by means
of barges, many of which are lashed together and pushed
ahead by a steam tug. The current, of course, carries
along the floating mass. The steamer has little to do but
to guide while descending and to tow the empty barges
back. The records of 1884 show that there were owned
in the city of Pittsburg for use on the river four thousand three hundred and twenty-three vessels, including
barges, with a tonnage of one million seven hundred
thousand tons. One hundred and sixty-three of these were
steamboats. Twenty thousand miles of navigable waterways lie before these Pittsburg craft, and many thousand
miles more are ready to be opened by easily-constructed
improvements in the lesser streams. This work the general government is steadily performing year after year,
as well as improving the existing navigation. Even to-
day a boat can start from Pittsburg for a port four thousand three hundred miles distant, as far as from New
York to Queenstown and half-way back, or as far away
as the Baltic ports are from New York. Said I not truly,
that Nature made Britain only as a small model and the
Republic full working size?

From what a small acorn has the mighty oak of river
navigation grown! Here is the very first prophecy of the
coming events connected with the use of these great
streams, and from whom, of all men, should such a
prophecy more fittingly come than from a minister? Here
are the words of the Rev. Manasseh Cutter, D.D.,

LL.D., of Ipswich, Massachusetts, who was at once minister, scientist, statesman, and the agent of the New England and Ohio Company, which started at Marietta, Ohio. Blessed man, he it was who succeeded in getting passed the famous ordinance of 1787, which prohibited slavery in the old North-west Territory, and secured that fair domain forever to freedom. Here is the prediction he made in a pamphlet published in 1787:

"The current down the Mississippi and Ohio, for heavy articles that suit the Florida (Mississippi) and West Indian markets, such as Indian corn, flour, beef, timber, etc., *will be more loaded than any stream on earth.* ! ! ! ! It was found by late experiments that sails are used to great advantage against the current of the Ohio; *and it is worthy of observation that, in all probability, steamboats will be found to be of infinite service in all our river navigation.*"

That was written twenty years before Fulton's practically successful application of steam to navigation, and a quarter of a century before the first steamboat which ever ploughed the Western rivers was built at Pittsburg. Six years after the prediction about steamboats the country hailed, as a wonderful evidence of progress, the inauguration of a regular line of sail and oar boats between Cincinnati and Pittsburg. Two boats were built for the line. They made the round journey every four weeks, so that every two weeks a traveller had a chance to start, and take a two weeks' journey on the beautiful river. I wish, as I write, that we could do so now. This was our Nile in a dahabeah right here at home. Why do not we try it now? What could be more delightful than the Ohio in a small boat moved by oar and sail? We have not the time, we say. Ah, ladies and gentlemen, we have not the sense.

But just listen to the precautions deemed essential, as

late as the beginning of the century, which the advertisement sets forth:

"No danger need be apprehended from the enemy, as every person on board will be under cover made proof against rifle or musket balls, *with convenient portholes for firing out.* Each of the boats is armed with six pieces carrying a pound ball, also a number of good muskets amply supplied with ammunition."

So the tedium of the journey, you see, was likely to be relieved by a skirmish now and then with the noble savage, and our travellers were not expected not to shoot back from under their ironclad cover. The first steamboat troubled the waters in 1811. In 1810 we find *Cramer's Magazine Almanac* making the startling announcement:

"A company has been formed for the purpose of navigating the river Ohio, in large boats, to be propelled by the power of steam-engines. The boat now on the stocks is one hundred and thirty-eight feet keel, and calculated for a freight, as well as a passenger boat, between Pittsburgh and the falls of the Ohio."

It is gratifying to learn that in one year the "New Orleans," for such was the name, actually cleared $20,000 (£4,000). No wonder the building of steamboats rapidly increased. There is nothing so creative as a good dividend.

The steamboats plying between New York and Boston, and also upon the Hudson between New York and Albany, have always impressed the foreign traveller as unequalled. The dimensions of some of the floating palaces are noteworthy. The tonnage of the "Pilgrim," for instance, is three thousand five hundred registered tons, making her the largest inland steamboat in the world; speed, twenty knots per hour. She carries one thousand four hundred passengers, and is lighted by nine hundred and twelve electric lamps.

Miss Martineau has left a description of boat travelling on the Erie Canal in New York State. Compare the following with our floating palaces and Pullman cars!

"On fine days," she writes, "it is pleasant enough sitting outside (except for having to duck under the bridges, every quarter of an hour, under penalty of having one's head crushed to atoms) and in dark evenings the approach of the boat-lights on the water is a pretty sight; but the horrors of night and wet days more than compensate for all the advantages these vehicles can boast. The heat and noise, the known vicinity of a compressed crowd, laying packed like herrings in a barrel, the bumping against the sides of the locks, and the hissing of water therein like an inundation, startling one from sleep—these things are very disagreeable.

"The appearance of the berths in the ladies' cabin was so repulsive that we were seriously contemplating sitting out all night when it began to rain so as to leave us no choice."

This journey from Utica to Schenectady, a distance of eighty miles, took twenty-two hours, while the packet to Rochester, one hundred and sixty miles, took forty-six hours; much longer than is now required to go from New York to St. Paul, Minnesota, one thousand three hundred and twenty-two miles.

In the short fifty years under review, we have displaced the stuffy, slow canal boat as a mode of travel for the limited express; the small steamer with its safety barge for the floating palaces.

If there is anything calculated to make man thankful for the blessings which he enjoys in this last quarter of the nineteenth century, it is the study of the conditions of life under which our ancestors lived. Not that we can form even an estimate of them. Discomforts which would make life unendurable to us were unnoticed by them, and probably they suffered in many ways at which we cannot even guess. If the record of their miserable mode of life were complete, the picture would without doubt be even more repulsive than it is. Auguste Comte has gravely propounded a religion of humanity which he says is worshipful because of its victories over nature, and over the discomforts by which the life of primitive man was surrounded. There have been religions founded on less worthy grounds than these. Man has indeed played a wonderful part in the world; and nothing can be more marvellous than the way in which he has subjugated the forces of nature, and yoked them to his chariot and his boat.

But let us be modest, for as sure as fate those of the next generation, looking back upon this, our present life, are to contrast their happier condition with ours and pity us as we have ventured to pity our forefathers. The march of humanity is upward and onward, for all the countless ages to come. Improved physical conditions react upon mental conditions and some day man is to read with surprise that once there was upon earth a state of warfare between divisions called nations, that Europe once continually taught nine millions of men how best to butcher their fellows, and called this vile work a profession. The coming man will marvel that intemperance prevailed in these barbarous days, that there were paupers and criminals without number, and that even in Britain the many were kept down by the few, that the soil there was held and used by a class, and that a million sterling was taken from the public revenues every year by one family and spent in vulgar ostentation or riotous dissipation, a family which was an insult to every other family in the land, since it involved the born inferiority of all others. He is to read of all this as we now read of the armored keel-boat and the horse locomotive, and thank his stars he was not born as we have been before the dawn of civilization. "As one man's meat is another man's poison," so one age's civilization is the next age's barbarism. We shall all be barbarians to our great, great grandchildren.

We have not travelled far yet, with all our progress upon the upward path, but we still go marching on. That which is, is better than that which has been. It is the mission of Democracy to lead in this triumphant march and improve step by step the conditions under which the masses live; to ring out the Old, and to ring in the New; and in this great work the Republic rightly leads the van.

Chapter XIV
ART AND MUSIC

"The study of art possesses this great and peculiar charm, that it is absolutely unconnected with the struggles and contests of ordinary life. . . . It is a taste at once engrossing and unselfish, which may be indulged without effort, and yet has the power of exciting and to gratify both the nobler and softer parts of our nature, the imagination and the judgment, love of emotion and power of reflection, the enthusiasm and the critical faculty, the senses and the reason."—GUIZOT.

"Of all the liberal arts, music has the greatest influence over the passions and is that to which the legislator ought to give the greatest encouragement. A well composed song strikes and softens the mind, and produces a greater effect than a moral work, which convinces our reason, but does not warm our feelings, nor effect the slightest alteration in our habits."
                            —NAPOLEON AT ST. HELENA.

H ALF a century ago, it was the fashion in Europe to decry anything American, and to sneer at even the suggestion of culture in the United States. A country without historical or poetical associations, devoid of all the sources from which the genius of the Old World had derived its inspirations—in short, a new country whose energies must for generations be directed in practical channels cannot hope to compete, it was argued, in the fine arts with nations whose traditions and culture reach back for centuries. In 1824 a contributor to *Blackwood's Magazine* wrote:

"The fine arts, generally, are neglected by the Americans. By this I mean, that they, the Americans, do not themselves cultivate them. They have foreign musical composers and sculptors, among them, most of whom are indigent or starving, but none of their own. Architecture is hardly in a better state. I know of no capital American architect."

The writer then makes one exception to his sweeping declaration—painting.

"In this the Americans have made a surprising proficiency; surprising, not only by comparison with what they have done in every other department; but surprising (if we consider their numbers, infancy, and want of encouragement), when compared with what we ourselves have done, or any other people, during the same period."

He then cites, in support of this assertion, the names of Copley, West, Trumbull, Rembrandt Peale, Allston, Morse, Sully, Stuart, Leslie, Newton, and Chester Harding, but ends by qualifying his praise with the remark that the most celebrated of these men were educated in Great Britain, and some of them born there.

Another class of critics went still further and asserted that a genius for art was incompatible with a republican form of government. "It would seem," says a writer of about the same time, in the London *Quarterly Review,* "that a high and refined genius for art is indigenous to monarchies, and under such a form of government alone can it flourish, either vigorously or securely. The United States of North America can never expect to possess a fine school of art, so long as they retain their present system."

Art indigenous to monarchies! Did any one ever hear such an absurdity? The great law is that each shall produce fruit after its kind, but this genius makes a monarchy produce the greatest of all republics, the republic of art. In art, the source of that which gives the finer

touches to human life, all is republican; there is no trace
of hereditary privileges within its bounds; it is as free, as
unstained of these injustices as the American Republic
itself. Art asks not,

> "Wast thou cottager or king,
> Peer or peasant; no such thing."

Who knows or cares who Michelangelo's father was;
or what was Beethoven's birth, or whether Raphael was
an aristocrat, or Wagner the son of a poor actuary of
police? Just imagine monarchy in art—a hereditary
painter, for instance, or a sculptor who only was his
father's son, or a musician, because born in the profession! What claims from birth have Liszt, Rubenstein,
Glück, or the Scotch laddies from their heather hills, the
sons of shepherds and tradesmen; the Millaises, Orch-
ardsons, Petties, Hunters, and Blacks, but from the republicanism of art. Our rulers these, in art, by virtue of
the universal suffrage of their fellows. The royal violin-
ist's parentage gives him no place in art which he has
not earned, nor do the creditable etchings or sculptures
of the royal princesses advance them one iota beyond the
merit of their work. Nor is it in the power of Victoria,
nor can it be her wish, to advance them one step in the
republic of art, were she twenty times their mother.

> "A king can make a belted knight
> A marquis, duke, and a' that,"

but let him try his hand upon creating ranks in the commonwealth of art, of music, and of literature, and where
is he! The aristocrats there are better born than he himself because heaven-born; "nobles by the right of an
earlier creation, priests by the imposition of a mightier
hand." Millais and Leighton, Benedict and Sullivan were

knighted by the monarch, but these rulers in art and music have not yet recognized Her Majesty or any of her family in their republics beyond the stage of "Honorable Mention." The Queen dispenses her degrees, even to a peerage, for brewing beer or playing court lackey. In the republics of art and letters, as Her Majesty finds, our rulers are much more fastidious. The standard is different. If Art be, as she is, a most jealous mistress, she is as just as she is exacting and no respecter of persons. There is nothing monarchical about her. Nay, when the monarch leaves the tinsel of official life and rises to real work in the higher domain of art, her drawings are pronounced good, and by so much she is an artist. Her books —for letters, too, like art, are republican—are most creditable in this, that a queen should have thought about making a book at all; for it is true all the same that "a book's a book although there's nothing in't," and the effort to write a book is in itself praiseworthy. Whatever a person of high rank achieves in the higher realms of art deserves handsome acknowledgment. The royal family of England to-day should receive, and I pay them the compliment to believe they do receive, more genuine satisfaction from their literary and artistic labors than from their rank, and would value distinction in the republics of art, music, and letters, if acquired, beyond rank in society—which can confer no honor, because purely accidental; for such, my readers, is the effect of this republican atmosphere in letters and art upon all who once enter its charmed circle and breathe its sweet influences, that even these royal people, exalted by a fiction in political life, would be the first to repel with proud indignation the slightest intimation that their works were to be judged by any lower standard than the republican test—by the suffrage of the people, in comparison with the performances of the sons of shepherds, delvers, weavers, and ditchers, their equals in the Republic. This is highly creditable to them. Such as have contributed, however humbly, to art, music, or literature—beginning with Her Majesty herself—are to be held in special honor. They have their places in the republic of art. Were the Prince of Wales animated, like them, with the true spirit of art and letters, it might extend to his ideas about position, and then he could not accept the throne except by a vote of his fellows calling him to it, as the person best fitted to serve the State. He would scorn place granted for any reason but for his ability to serve. His motto can only in this way be lived up to.

Death levels all ranks; the republics of art and of letters do no less. Contestants for place in these gracious commonwealths are stripped of all distinctions and start upon equal terms. The equality of the citizen is the fundamental law upon which is founded all that brings sweetness and light to human life. Thus, my friends, art is republican, literature is republican, religion is republican. (No hereditary privilege in the church.) Every good is republican. That alone which is valueless, hurtful, and unjust is monarchical; but fortunately, as we have seen, the poison of hereditary rank is confined to very narrow limits, beyond which it is not recognized.

This curious writer, who would have monarchy allied with art, built his theory upon the exploded idea that only monarchs and the aristocracy, which flutters around courts, could or would patronize the beautiful. That theory is unfortunate, in view of the fact that the best patrons of art are the Americans, and the monarchy, at least, is not conspicuous for its treatment of art or artists. Music and art, like literature, flourish in our day, not by the patronage of a class, but from popular support. Nothing flourishes in our day but through the support of the people—monarchy itself must play to them and please them for its daily bread. One breath of popular displeasure and it becomes a thing of the past.

It seems strange, in the light of the present, that any one could read history so awry as to lead him to the conclusion that monarchy favors art or literature. But it is too late to render necessary any refutation of such assertions. Time has proved its falsity, and we may now safely relegate it to the curiosities of literature. But there is a modicum of truth in the assertion of the writer in *Blackwood* of sixty years ago, that the Americans did not then cultivate the fine arts. A few painters, whose names are still pointed to with pride by their countrymen, had enlivened the drear monotony of our art horizon, but they were Americans in little more than the accident of birth. Most of them were born under the British flag, and the art of all was but a reflection of foreign schools and methods. Nor does this militate against their skill as artists, nor against the right of Americans to include them among their countrymen. It is well to remember that France had no art till Da Vinci and Primaticcio showed the way; and that in England Holbein, Lely, and Van Dyck made possible a Reynolds and a Gainsborough. It is perhaps a little remarkable that these early American painters, who won as much credit abroad as at home, should have left little inspiration behind them, for it is certain that those who immediately succeeded them did not attain to a similar reputation. Perhaps this is to be accounted for in the fact that the energies of the people were directed by the exigencies of their surroundings into more practical channels than the pursuit of the beautiful. In the building up of a new country there is little time for art cultivation; the establishment of a political and social system and the development of industrial resources must precede and furnish the foundation on which the superstructure of art may rise. Nature must be conquered before she can be admired. Men must be fed and clothed ere they can moralize.

About the beginning of the period to which we have constantly referred—of fifty years ago—American art began to rise from its dark age, as we may characterize the period immediately succeeding that of the colonial painters. Up to that time there had been no training schools, no public galleries of any consequence, and but a small audience capable of appreciating good work. In 1826 the National Academy of Design was organized in New York, under the presidency of Samuel F. B. Morse, as the successor of the American Academy of Fine Arts, which died after the fire of the same year had destroyed its art collection. Similar institutions had been founded early in Philadelphia and in Boston, but the National Academy has always exercised a paramount influence in the development of American art.

About ten years later the American Art Union, an incorporated institution for the distribution, by lot, of works of art, came into existence, and during more than a decade aided much in educating the people, and in bringing into notice many artists who might otherwise have found it difficult to win recognition. But this gain was loss; the influence of the lottery system must have transcended a hundred-fold any possible advantage gained through it by art. Happily the day for such gambling is over, but we meet with the evil still, where one would least expect it. There is a moral in the story of the poor parishioner, who regretted to his minister that he could not pay his quarter's pew rent.

"Been gambling in stocks, I suppose," said the minister, testily. "No, sir, not that." "Well, speculating in oil, then." "No, sir; I went to your church fair, sir, and was roped into so many lotteries." Tableau.

Several small public galleries like those of the Athenæum in Boston, and of the Historical Society in New York, and a few private collections were found in different parts of the country, which all exercised a considerable influence in raising the standard of popular taste. People began to buy pictures, and, as was natural, began by buying very poor pictures. European dealers, taking advantage of the comparative ignorance of the country in art matters, flooded the principal cities with alleged examples of the old masters, which found a ready sale thirty or forty years ago, but which gradually disappeared as their worthlessness was understood, and now it would be difficult to find one of these early art treasures of America in any respectable house unless it may have been preserved among the rubbish of the garret. The experience thus gained was of the utmost value. The American, with his quick perception, soon learned to distinguish between the good and the bad, and though his taste may in some cases seem a little "loud" to the European connoisseur, he seldom buys anything which is absolutely worthless. He is recognized now in the European markets as one of the shrewdest, as well as one of the most liberal buyers. Throughout the world, whenever art treasures come under the hammer, the American will be found in competition with nobles, and even with crowned heads, and he is no mean competitor, for he carries a pocket full of dollars, and is not afraid to spend them where he is sure of getting his money's worth. Thus, during the past twenty years, there has been a constant flow of works of art to the United States. There is no city of importance in the country which has not its public gallery of painting and of sculpture, as well as many private collections in the houses of its citizens. These latter are often put on exhibition as loan collections, and exert a most beneficial influence in creating a taste for art.

Of course the United States can scarcely hope to form art collections comparable with those of the Old World, unless some unforeseen revolution should break up the great museums of some of its capital cities, when we might hope, and, indeed, expect, that many of their treasures would gravitate westward. But while the old masters are thus denied to us, we have some consolation in knowing that a large proportion of the best modern works are brought to this country. I have excellent authority for the assertion that the United States now possesses more and finer examples of the modern French and German schools of painting than are to be found in Europe. The modern Spanish and Italian schools are also well represented, the English school not so well, American taste gravitating rather to the realism of the French than to the romantic idealism of the British school.

It is useless for the critics to attempt to explain the extraordinary disproportion between the influx of British and French art into America by the assertion that the fine art dealers in the United States are mostly of French and German origin. Even if this were true, the dealers would not hesitate to import English pictures if there was a market for them. They purchase largely of English engravings, because there is a demand for them, and they can be had at a price whiich leaves a good margin for profit; they do not buy English paintings because they are held at prices much higher than in proportion to the talent displayed than are the works of French and German artists. This is sufficient in itself to account for the numerical preponderance of these two schools of art in the United States and for the gravitation of American taste in their direction. I would not draw any invidious comparison, but I am not sure—if I am called upon for a further explanation of the phenomenon—that the pre-

vailing fashion of buying French paintings may not have
a still more serious justification, for whatever the London critics may preach concerning the decadence of the
French school, the Salon is still, as it was under the Empire, the highest art tribunal in the world.

The foreign reader must not infer from what I have
said of the American predilection for the French school
of art that the Americans have no painters of their own.
They have good painters in all departments of art,
while in several branches they are able to compete with
any other country in the world. Their landscape school is
unexcelled and in marine painting they are fast approach-
ing the standard of the British school. In portraiture
they are equal to the English and French painters, and in
some respects they excel the latter, being free from the
academic tricks which detract from the dignity of Gallic
art. In genre they are not far behind the French and
German painters. In history and allegory they are as yet
weak, though several of the younger painters, now study-
ing under French and German influences, show signs of
phenomenal ability which may soon bring America to the
fore in these departments also. It may be urged with
some show of justice that these painters are Americans
in little more than birth and name, and that they ought
properly to be classed among the French and Germans,
under whose guidance they have been educated and have
won their laurels. But if so strict a rule of classification
were adopted we should have to give Poussin and Spag-
noletto to the Italians and, to take a more modern case,
send Alma-Tadema back to his home in the Netherlands.
Art is cosmopolitan and should have no country. Whatsoever land possesses the best schools and the best facilities for instruction through the possession of the master-
piece of the past, that land will attract students from
every other part of the world; and so long as the great

galleries of the Old World exist so long will American students cross the ocean to study what can never under any present possibility be found at home.

America has developed within the past half-century a school of sculpture which has won recognition both at home and abroad, though a visit to the national capital and to the public squares of some of the larger cities would scarcely induce such an opinion. Many of her sculptors have been educated under Italian influences, but have drawn their inspiration rather from the antique than the modern Italian school. Some who stand foremost at home to-day have not enjoyed the benefit of foreign instruction, and their works, consequently, possess more of the flavor of the soil, so to speak, than do those which have been executed in strict accordance with the academic rules transmitted from antiquity. It is possible that these may develop in time into a purely American school of sculpture which shall be recognized and take its place as such in the art history of the world.

In the sister art, architecture, though America's brief century of existence has not brought to light any transcendent genius like him who created the Taj Mahal or elevated the dome of St. Peter's, there has been sufficient advancement to meet the requirements of the country. American architecture in the past cannot be said to have had any individuality, but to have been rather the result of external influences, the reflection of the art developed in Europe through centuries of growth. Like all imitations, the imported style was generally exaggerated, and often applied to uses for which it was never intended. Thus, a half-century ago the Greek style was the prevailing fashion, and not only public buildings, like the custom-houses of New York, Philadelphia, and Boston, but also churches, town-halls, and even dwelling-houses were constructed in the semblance of classic temples. In the suburbs of any of the Eastern towns may still be seen white painted wooden dwellings, with pretentious porticoes of Ionic or Corinthian columns, combined with the absurdity of modern windows and green blinds.

The Greek style in time gave way to the Gothic, and the classic temple was superseded by a nondescript building modelled or supposed to be modelled after the mediæval cathedral. Some good churches were built in this style, the most successful one being Trinity Church in New York, erected in 1840–45; but, as the Greek style had been before, it was soon applied to uses utterly foreign to its purposes, and all kinds of buildings, including dwelling-houses, were decorated with Gothic gables, pinnacles, and battlements. This fashion in turn had its day, and in time the Gothic was restricted mostly to ecclesiastical edifices, while domestic architecture went through a variety of transformations involving all the styles known to the ages. In some of the larger cities, New York especially, the exigencies of space gave rise to narrow dwellings built in uniform blocks, generally of brick, faced with brown sand-stone, from which they were called "brown-stone fronts." Some of these long blocks of narrow dwellings, which caused the Grand Duke Alexis to remark that "the Americans live in bins," are really very handsome, especially in Fifth Avenue, New York, a street of city residences unequalled elsewhere in the world. During the past two decades a change has gradually been wrought in the style of city dwellings, and the uniform Italian brown-stone fronts have been superseded by a variety of styles, each building having a marked individuality which distinguishes it from its neighbors. Many of these new residences will bear favorable comparison, considered architecturally, with any in Europe, and in internal conveniences and modern appliances have not their equal anywhere. This is as true of the dwellings built of late years in other places as of those in New York, and the day is not far distant when every considerable town in the United States will have palatial residences rivalling those of the Old World.

The architecture of municipal and mercantile buildings in America is in a great degree, like domestic architecture, the reflection of foreign examples, modified of course to some extent by new requirements. Some of the more pretentious structures, though perhaps amenable to criticism as works of art, are notable examples of their kind and will bear comparison with similar buildings in Europe. The Capitol at Washington, though displeasing to Mr. Fergusson's critical eye, is yet a noble building and notwithstanding its shortcomings better adapted for legislative uses than the British Houses of Parliament; and the later public buildings at Washington, especially the French Renaissance structures for the use of the War and State Departments, are unexcelled. Many of the State capitols, notably those of New York, Connecticut, Ohio, and other Western States, are worthy of any country. In mercantile architecture the Americans are abreast of, if not in advance of the rest of the world. The stores or shops of all of the larger cities are equal to any in European capitals, and the magnificent structures erected by insurance, banking, and other corporations, are fit for the uses of even the merchant princes of Democracy. There is nothing elsewhere in the world to compare with these structures. Buildings equally fine are to be found in that great Western city, Chicago. One block there has thirteen stories, the highest hardly less elaborate in decoration or less perfect in its appointments than the lowest. Indeed, the rental of offices high up is greater than that of those nearer earth. Lifts shoot skyward with a swiftness that leads the unaccustomed aeronaut to think he

has left part of his anatomy on the ground floor, and
they drop down again with equal rapidity. The thirteenth
story is thus made as accessible as the third, while it possesses the advantages of purer air, and less noise.

"Music, heavenly maid," early visited America, but
finding no congenial abiding place among the sons of
toil who were battling with the wilderness, returned to
quieter scenes, to await the cessation of the struggle.
She has now taken up her permanent abode in the Republic; and finds herself at home even in the far West,
among the roughest scenes the continent can show.

The history of music in America is a record of spirited
enterprises and discouraging failures alternating with
almost rhythmic regularity. Artists of the first order, like
Malibran, made a temporary success even fifty years
ago; but it is only recently that a regular opera has been
established in any American city. Some of the most successful performances took place in New York half a century ago; yet at periods it was almost impossible to get
together half a dozen fiddles. A German who visited
New York in 1828 wrote:

"The orchestras are very bad indeed, as bad as it is possible to
imagine and incomplete. Sometimes they have two clarinets, which
is a great deal; sometimes there is only one first instrument. Of
bassoons, oboes, trumpets, and kettledrums one never sees a sight.
However, once in a while a first bassoon is employed. Only one
oboist exists in North America, and he is said to live in Baltimore.
In spite of all this incompleteness they play symphonies by Haydn
and grand overtures; and if a gap occurs, they think 'this is only
of passing importance,' provided it rattles away again afterwards.
. . . It is a self-understood custom that the leader, with his vio-
lin, takes part in every solo. Hence one never hears a solo played
alone by one person. This is probably done in order to get a fuller
sound."

This was three years after Garcia's Italian opera appeared in New York, and several amateur musical clubs had long been in existence. The practical and unromantic character of the English people long delayed acceptance of the opera in Britain. As Addison amusingly says:

"There is nothing that has more startled our English audience than the Italian recitative at its first entrance upon the stage. People were wonderfully surprised to hear generals singing the word of command, and ladies delivering messages in music. Our countrymen could not forbear laughing when they heard a lover chanting out a *billet-doux*, and even the superscription of a letter set to a tune. The famous blunder in an old play of 'Enter a king and two fiddlers solus' was no longer an absurdity, when it was impossible for a hero in a desert, or a princess in her closet, to speak anything unaccompanied with musical instruments."

In America the same cause continued to operate at a much later date. A native critic has written a passage about his countrymen similar to the above. Speaking of the opera-goers of fifty years ago, he says:

"If the inquisitive American looked in a critical way at the intellectual meaning of the Italian opera, he found little to satisfy his mind. On the contrary, he found it ridiculous—if he succeeded at getting at the plot of the fantastic libretto—to see an actor making such a fuss about killing himself or anybody else on account of some unsuccessful love affair, but who could not accomplish his bloody design on account of too much singing. He wondered why two lovers, having a secret to tell each other, should go about shouting it out in endless repetitions and endless cadenzas. He became impatient with a troop of soldiers, thundering ferocious threatening war-songs, but who, having so much to sing, could not move a step from their posts. All these things puzzled him, were a mystery to him, and annoyed and bewildered him. They on the whole appeared to him 'much ado about nothing.'"

Viewed in this matter-of-fact way, the opera does seem absurd; and we need not wonder that it long received scant recognition by our practical, long-headed people, who ask the why and wherefore of everything which claims their approval. At the present day, however, opera is flourishing like an indigenous plant, and New York supports two great opera houses, besides numerous theatres for opera comique, etc. Every important city has its opera house. Miss Nilsson found in a young Western town the best building for sound she had ever known. Jeffrey's "American Guide to Opera Houses and Theatres" contains particulars of nearly four thousand such buildings distributed all over the continent. Opening it at random, I find amongst hundreds of others the following:

"CENTRALIA: On Chicago, Kansas City & Denver Short Line of the C. & A. and W. St. L. & P. Railroads. Population, one thousand five hundred.

"Threlkeld's Opera Hall. Good stage and scenery. Terms reasonable.

"People's Theatre. First-class stage and scenery. Stage twenty-five feet by forty-eight feet. Piano. Rent, twenty dollars, etc."

Take Oshkosh, away out in Wisconsin, two hundred miles from Chicago, with a population of twenty-two thousand:

"New Opera House. Stage, forty-two by seventy feet; seats one thousand one hundred.

"Turner House. Stage thirty by fifty; seats eight hundred.

"Wacker Hall. Thirty by fifty-four; seats one thousand one hundred."

Here is Paris in Texas:

"Babcock Opera House. Seats one thousand.

"Paris Opera House. Seats four hundred and fifty."

Idaho was a wilderness a few years ago, as was Montana. Now I see Eagle Rock, Idaho, with a total population of only seven hundred, has

"Chamberlain Hall, with organ. Seats six hundred.
"Glen's Hall. Seats three hundred."

Butte City, Montana, has

"New Opera House. Seats eight hundred.
"Thomas' Amphitheatre. Seats one thousand five hundred.
"Grand Opera House. Seats one thousand."

But its population is ten thousand, so that it does not rival Eagle Rock, with its seven hundred population and Temples of the Muses to seat nine hundred.

The theatres and opera houses of the principal cities in America are, of course, much superior to those in Europe, because they were built recently and have improvements unthought of years ago; besides, the greater wealth of the country justifies greater expenditure upon everything. Musical societies are found in every Western town of importance. Milwaukee, with a history of only half a century, had its Musik Verein thirty-six years ago. In 1851 this enterprising club performed the "Creation," the "Seasons," parts of the "Messiah," and parts of Rossetti's "Jesus in Gethsemane." Every year since it has performed works of like character. The city has been a centre from which musical culture has radiated throughout the North-west. Cincinnati is another such centre. Situated midway between the Eastern cities and New Orleans, it has since early days been specially benefited as the calling-place of itinerant operatic and dramatic companies. St. Louis, Louisville, Chicago, Indianapolis, Detroit, Buffalo, Pittsburg, Denver, San Francisco, New Orleans, are all prominent examples of Western cities in which music is generally cultivated.

My experience in the two lands leads me unhesitatingly to accord the palm to the old home for vocal music. There is no society in the Republic to compare with those which delight the masses with vocal music in the monarchy. To hear one of the best choirs in Britain sing an oratorio is one of the greatest delights. Their voices seem smoother, and, above all, the enunciation is perfect. The American voice is thin to begin with—the effect of climate, I fear—and to this is added the abominable practice of slurring over or cutting off troublesome syllables. The American woman is the most intelligent, entertaining, and most agreeable in the world. If she had her English sister's voice and enunciation she would be perfect; but these she has not. There is a "snippiness" about her words which follows her even in oratorio. The men, of course, being more deliberate of speech are not such great sinners in this respect. America has still much to learn from the parent land in vocal music. I wish she would begin to take lessons soon. On the other hand, America leads Britain in instrumental music—probably owing to the large infusion of the German element with which it is blessed. I have heard several competent foreign musicians pronounce the Thomas orchestra superior to that of Richter in London, or to any other orchestra in Europe, and I have sufficient faith in this opinion to challenge the best London orchestra to a contest. Let us have an international orchestral trial, our performers going to London to play upon alternate nights with Richter's fine band, and theirs coming to New York next season for the return trial. To excel in instrumental music would be another feather in the cap of Democracy. Even to prove a worthy second to Richter's orchestra would not discredit us. The cause of music could not but be benefited by the friendly family match.

This year witnesses an ambitious attempt to found a

national Conservatory of Music which may rival the academy founded last year in Britain. The enterprise is in excellent hands and promises to give the Republic a new institution of which it may justly be proud. A school has already been started and pupils are being received. It is held that the time has passed when the gifted sons and daughters of the Republic should find it necessary to go abroad for the highest musical instruction. Even more daring is the attempt to produce American opera, which is now being made by these enthusiastics of the National School of Music. So far its success has surprised the public. The operas are, of course, the work of foreigners, but they are sung in English—or must we not begin to call it the American language? "Oh!" said a distinguished lady to another the other evening as she listened to the opera in her own language, "it's so queer to understand the language of opera, isn't it!" "I always did, dear!" was the response. Sooner or later, the new idea is bound to conquer. The Republic will produce not only a National School of Music, but in time develop a national music itself, for it is impossible that so numerous and so rich a people and one so unusually fond of music should long remain without an institution of the highest character for musical culture. We hail this present effort, therefore, with great pleasure and commend it to the support of the American people upon whom, and not upon any governmental aid, it must fortunately depend.

The material progress of the Republic is not the only progress made during the triumphant march of the Democracy. In art and in music the nation is advancing with a rapidity which belies the assertion that the tendency of Democracy is to materialize a people and give it over to sordid thoughts; that the unrestrained exercise of personal liberty ends only in the accumulation of dollars. Republicanism does not withhold from life the sweetness and light which mainly make it worth living. Hard, unremitting toil quickly seeks appropriate relaxation. The history of music and art in America is in miniature their history throughout the world. First came struggles with nature—hard-fought battles, with corresponding adaptation of temperament. Then with victory came leisure, and human nature was moulded into harmony with its milder conditions; and then as Dryden says:

> "At last divine Cecilia came,
>   Inventress of the vocal frame;
>   The sweet enthusiast, from her sacred store,
>   Enlarged the former narrow bounds,
>   And added length to solemn sounds,
>   With nature's mother-wit, and arts unknown before."

Unless the greatest and best of the race are wholly at fault in their estimate of the influence exerted upon men by art and music, we may accept the taste for these with which the Democracy can safely be credited, as an augury of promise. Life in the Republic is being rapidly refined—the race for wealth ceases to be so alluring. Ostentation in dress or living is "bad form." In due time fashion may decree that its devotees must be neither loud nor extravagant. Music and art create the taste for the most refined, not for the coarse expression of our surroundings. It is now certain that in love of art and music the Democracy even to-day is not behind the Monarchy, and evidence is not wanting that it is entering more and more into, and elevating, year after year, not only the few, but the great masses which make up the national life of the Republic.

Chapter XV
LITERATURE

"He hath never fed of the dainties that are bred in a book; he hath not eat paper, as it were; he hath not drunk ink; his intellect is not replenished; he is only an animal, only sensible in his duller parts."—SHAKESPEARE.

THIS was not written of the omnivorous American, for he has eaten paper, as it were, and drunk ink ever since he was born. These are his daily food. As far back as the year 1836, which brings us to the beginning of the fifty years under review, a writer in the Philadelphia *Public Ledger* for March 25, describing the extent of newspaper reading in America says:

"In the cities of New York and Brooklyn, containing together a population of three hundred thousand, the daily circulation of the penny papers is not less than seventy thousand. These papers are to be found in every street, lane, and alley; in every hotel, tavern, counting-house, shop, and store. Almost every porter and drayman, while not engaged in his occupation, may be seen with a penny paper in his hand."

This was the year when in England the newspaper tax was reduced from 4 pence (8 cents) to a penny (2 cents) per copy, when the usual price of London papers was 5 pence (10 cents) or 6 pence (12 cents). The great mass of the people, even if they could read, could only obtain a news-sheet by sharing among many the cost of the

luxury. The majority of the intelligent had to be content
with hearing articles read from papers to the company
in a hall or coffee-room. Several factors have conspired
to make the American people great newspaper readers.
The Puritan settlers were active political partisans.
Everything which concerned government was of deepest
interest to them; and it was among such as they that the
first manuscript news-letters had their largest circulation.
The descendants of these hardy pilgrims inherited that
jealous regard for the rights of the citizen which in
the sixteenth century manifested itself in political non-
conformity, and in the eighteenth century was the propelling force of the American Revolution. Every man,
woman, and child of New England at that trying time
habitually discussed politics and sought news with an
eagerness that we never feel, except under the stimulus
of a great political crisis. In 1800 the young Republic
had two hundred newspapers, of which several were
dailies. In 1810–11 disputes with England revived men's
interest in politics, an interest which became doubly keen
when war was declared, and every able-bodied man took
from its nail his trusty flint-lock in preparation for battle. Conceived in political tribulation, born amid the
throes of a severe political struggle, and nursed in the
midst of political excitements, the young American nation developed an aptitude for government which republican institutions have ever since tended to strengthen.
Where every man is a voter, every man is a politician;
and a nation of politicians is the journalist's favorite
field. A further cause is the education which during the
century has been so widely diffused. Teach a man how
to read and you at once invest him with the appetite
for reading. And what can be of greater interest than the
world's history read in contemporary lights? Again,
newspaper taxes have never existed in the United States.

As a consequence journalism attained maturity in America earlier than in Europe. These combined factors have made the American nation greater newspaper readers than any other people. The Republic has aptly been called the editor's Paradise; for certainly except in the "wild West," where revolvers are jocularly *said* to be as necessary to editors as ink-stands, journalists do have pretty much their own way.

In 1880 the number of periodicals of all classes published in the United States was eleven thousand three hundred and fourteen. Of these more than four-fifths are devoted to news, politics, and family reading. The remainder are technical publications, relating to trade, industry, the professions, science, etc. More than three-fourths of the whole are weekly publications, ten per cent. are monthlies; daily newspapers form rather less than ten per cent. Ten thousand five hundred and fifteen periodicals are published in the English language, and six hundred and one in German. The remaining percentage is contributed in the following languages, in this order: French, Scandinavian, Spanish, Dutch, Italian, Welsh, Bohemian, and Polish. There is, moreover, a Portuguese paper in New York, a Chinese paper in San Francisco, and a Cherokee one at Tahlequah, Indian Territory. In none of these languages does the proportion of periodicals reach one per cent. of the whole. The combined issue of the periodical press exceeds thirty-one millions. The copies printed aggregate, in a year, one billion three hundred and forty-four million, giving an average of two copies a week to every family.

The growth of American newspaper literature is no less astonishing than the growth of so many other things American. The first census of the press was taken in 1850, though Mulhall gives an estimate for 1840. The number of newspapers in 1850 was about eight hundred and thirty; ten years later it had increased to two thousand five hundred and twenty-six. In 1860 it reached four thousand and fifty-one; in 1870 five thousand eight hundred and seventy-one, while ten years later it had nearly doubled, reaching the number of eleven thousand three hundred and fourteen, or more than four times as many as in 1850. In circulation the increase has been even greater. In 1850 the average circulation per issue was five million one hundred and forty-two thousand one hundred and seventy-seven; it leaped to thirteen million six hundred and sixty-three thousand four hundred and nine in 1860; to twenty million eight hundred and twenty-four thousand four hundred and seventy-five in 1870, and in 1880 it reached the enormous number of thirty-one million seven hundred and seventy-nine thousand, six hundred and eighty-six. The morning newspapers of the principal cities consist of eight pages, like those of London, and are sold at the same price, 2 cents (1 penny).

The republican sheets are characterized by greater vivacity than the monarchical—more spicy news, and, above all, a much more attractive mode of displaying it. A leading English editor once remarked to me: "We have no 'editors' who rank with the American, but many writers who excel yours." This was a just criticism. We see, however, in nothing more strongly than the newspaper press of the two countries, the operation of that law of assimilation which tends to make their products alike. The American press is rapidly acquiring greater dignity, and the British press more sparkle. They will soon be as like as two peas, and the change toward each other will improve both. There are many things other than the press, in which a mixture of the old and new would be equally advantageous.

The falsest impressions of a country are created in the

minds of foreigners by its newspaper press, because people forget that the press deals in the uncommon, the abnormal. A column is given to some startling monstrosity, a three-headed calf, for instance, but it doesn't follow that American calves, as a rule, possess more than the usual number of head pieces seen in Europe. An unruly refugee with twenty aliases kills a Texan rowdy in a bar-room, farther away from New York than Cairo is from London, and the press on both sides of the water gives the fullest details. It isn't a corollary at all that human life is not respected in the Republic.

A defaulter absconds, and the world is filled with the news, not a word is said about the thousands of men in positions of trust who guard their charge to the last penny. My experience with newspapers upon both sides of the Atlantic has shown me how incorrect ideas are instilled of the one land in the other by the press. A New York sheet, referring to the meeting of a few hare-brained cranks in Hyde Park, a motley crowd, whose appearance made me feel as Falstaff did about his soldiers, "I'll not march with them through Coventry, that's flat," lays this episode before its readers headed in large type: "A GRAND REPUBLICAN RALLY." And many readers think the Prince of Wales has not the ghost of a chance.

I wish it were so indeed, and I honor these cranks very much—all real reformers are cranks in their day. Pym, Hampden, Cromwell were, and John Bright himself was a very pronounced one till he brought the nation up to his level; now he is a regulation statesman in "good form." But truth compels me to say that the republican rally in Hyde Park was not much of a rally; it was like the great ball which the Princess wished to give in Ottawa upon court lines of etiquette and could not. In Canada, society was all in vulgar trade. There was not enough left to make a ball at all. In like manner, a Socialists' procession marches through the streets in Chicago, probably not an American in the array—a parcel of foreign cranks whose Communistic ideas are the natural growth of the unjust laws of their native land, which deny these men the privileges of equal citizenship and hold them down as inferiors from their birth—and forthwith European papers alarm the timid and well-to-do masses of Europe by picturing this threatened assault upon property as the result of republicanism, the truth being that in no other country are the rights of property held so sacredly as in America. Legislation to fix values of anything here, as values of land are fixed in Ireland, for instance, would be decried from one end of the land to the other. The only true and abiding conservatism is that engendered by republican institutions—conservatism of what is just, what is good—for these no party seeks to destroy.

In like manner the books of travel written by visitors to any land must in their very nature be misleading. What strikes the stranger is not the thousand and one matters which are alike to those at home, nor the thousand occurrences which are common to him at home or abroad; it is the one exceptional matter, thing, or event which he notes down at once and says, "I can work that up—it is so strange." Very true, only it may be just as exceptional, just as strange to the native. The false impression is conveyed to the public, for whom he writes, by implying that it is the common and usual custom, or occurrence. Few travellers know how to arrive at the real every-day life of people, and yet from this alone is a just estimate of that people to be obtained. As the two divisions get to know each other better, they will understand that in the main, human life is very much the same on both sides of the Atlantic. It is after we cross the

Mississippi and come to the "great West"—that new
region which the hardy pioneer is rapidly bringing into
civilization—that life takes on different features. As
might be expected the difference in the press there gives
us the best idea of the chasm which still divides the settled State from the unsettled Territory.

When a party of prospectors have found a mineral
vein in the West, about the first thing they do after deciding to build a city, is to start a newspaper. With characteristic Western eccentricity this is named the *Lead-
gulch Screamer,* or the *Peek-a-Boo Avalanche.* Then a
press and type are brought in, the most literate of the
gang invests in a table, an arm-chair, and an inkstand,
and being already furnished with a revolver, he begins
to "run" the paper. As the town grows, competing editors come in, and soon the struggle for existence sets in
with an acerbity of feeling not excelled in those poetic

> "Dragons of the prime
> Who tore each other in their slime."

Specimens of "slime" are carefully collected by European bookmakers and quoted as representative of
American journalism. After the rough pioneering has
been done, the gentler evidences of white civilization
soon manifest themselves. Fine streets lined with handsome buildings and towering churches spring up on the
site of the wilderness; and literature takes upon itself
a milder form. Present editors in Western towns which
have originated and grown in this way, are men of culture, often graduates from Eastern universities; and
these are not the men who pen the articles so largely
quoted from by bookmakers. Dickens's amusing representation of the editorial combat in "Pickwick" will keep

in memory the fact that a few years ago British editors used inks of concentrated gall and venom.

In periodical literature the child land has for a few years excelled its mother. In *Harper's Magazine* and the *Century* the art of editing has joined the arts of printing and engraving and has surpassed anything before known in the history of periodical literature. These magazines, which for years have been educating the American people in principles of true art and instilling a love of pure literature, have done more than all the rest of the world's periodical publications to raise the artistic standard of printing. Not in America alone, but in England, has their influence been potent for good; and undisguised imitations of these magazines now appear even in Germany, which not many years ago seemed to have a monopoly of good engravers. It is in vain that any English or German magazine can hope to rival its Republican compeer; not because the necessary talent and skill do not exist, or at least, that it could not be created, but simply because it will not pay to employ it. The American publisher prints a quarter of a million of copies. This number has even been exceeded. The expense for art and matter, distributed among this huge edition, is a trifle per copy. What is the poor publisher to do who has not forty thousand subscribers? And this not one shilling magazine has in Britain or Germany. He yields the race perforce to the republican. *Harper's* and the *Century* actually sell more copies in Britain than any British monthly publication of equal price. Truly their venture in England is a strange and startling success. Let us note here that as population grows faster in the new than in the old land, more and more sure is it that the American publisher can afford to expend greater sums upon his magazine, which means that the native publications must encounter fiercer warfare than ever.

Periodicals of high order for the girls and boys of a nation are of vital consequence. The world has not anything comparable to the *St. Nicholas* or *Harper's Young People*. Every friend to whom I have sent them in Britain has substantially said: "We have nothing like these. Our children watch for their arrival as for a great treat. They are devoured."

It was all very well for the Democracy to supply the monarchies with pork and flour, cheese and provisions, the necessaries of life; a coarse, material triumph this, but what are we to say to this exportation of food for the mind? If Democracy is successfully to invade the higher province, and minister to the things of the spirit as well as to those of the body, before it is more than a century old, what is the Monarchy to set forth as that in which it excels? It is, at all events, to take the crumbs which fall from the republican magazine table. That much is settled, and it is with special pride we note the triumph of Democracy in these branches of art. The thanks of the Republic are due to *Harper's* and the *Century* for a successful and I hope a permanent and a profitable invasion of Great Britain. May their circulation never be less on either side of the Atlantic.

American journalists have become noted all over the world, as indeed have Americans generally, for enterprise and energy. American foreign correspondents have revolutionized their profession. Until Stanley was sent into equatorial Africa by the New York *Herald* to find Livingstone, such extraordinary missions were unknown; but English journals quickly followed, and O'Donovan, brave, bright, and young when he fell in the Soudan, was sent by the *Daily News* to Merv. The "Jeannette" expedition was a newspaper enterprise. The Bengal famine, the condition of Ireland, the Tunisian difficulty, the Burmah dispute, the exploration of Corea, all these and many other matters have come within the scope of the modern foreign correspondent.

It is interesting in this connection to see how the Anglo-Saxon race leads the world in journalism. Of twenty-three thousand newspapers in the world about half are American. Other papers published in English raise the total to more than thirteen thousand, leaving to the rest of the world—Germany, France, Italy, Spain, India, etc., only ten thousand to divide amongst themselves. The English language, gauged by those who speak it, is leaving the rest of the world even more hopelessly in the rear. At the beginning of the century our tongue was spoken by twenty million people and occupied only fifth place, coming behind even Spain and Russia. It now occupies first place, being spoken by more than a hundred million, while French and Spanish have not yet reached the fifties. Since 1801 the English language has advanced from twelve and nine-tenths to twenty-seven and one-tenth aliquot parts of all European languages. Of three hundred and sixty-eight million people now speaking the European languages, one hundred million speak English. Of course there is little question here as to the coming universal language. The world is to speak English, think English, and read English. The only question is, whether it will be aristocratic or democratic English, Queen's English or People's English, and there is not much question about that.

When we recollect the great amount of hard manual work which has been spent by the American people on the subjugation of their vast continent, it is a matter of surprise that literature and the gentle arts generally should also have attained such development. The hewing of wood, clearing of forests, the breaking of prairie-lands, railroad building, and canal digging are not conducive to development of the sort of brain which runs into brooks; and during the early years of the country, when brawn rather than brain was in demand, bookmaking received scant attention. The change consequent upon the cessation of the struggle with nature in New England was well described by Cullen Bryant at a publishers' celebration in 1855. He said:

"After his (Cotton Mather's) time, in the hundred and fifty years which followed, the procession of American authors was a straggling one; at present they are a crowd which fairly choke the way; illustrious historians, able and acute theologians, authors of books of travels, instructive or amusing, clever novelists, brilliant essayists, learned and patient lexicographers. Every bush, I had almost said every buttercup of the field, has its poet; poets start up like the soldiers of Roderick Dhu, from behind every rock and out of every bank of fern."

An idea of this increasing literary activity may be obtained from the fact that in the publication of original American books the year 1853 shows an advance of eight hundred per cent. in less than twenty years. In the twelve years ending 1842 there were published one thousand one hundred and fifteen works, six hundred and twenty-three of them being original. In the single year of 1853 seven hundred and thirty-three new books were published, four hundred and twenty of which were original American works. From these facts a well-known publisher of that period concluded that literature and the book trade had increased ten times as fast as the population. In 1884 more than four thousand books were published in the Republic.

To enumerate the tons of paper used for printing may be considered a curious way of estimating the literature of a nation. Still it has been done, and the result is interesting. About one hundred and seven thousand tons of paper are annually used in the United States, against ninety-five thousand tons in the United Kingdom, and seventy thousand tons in France. Canada, subject and dependent, contrasts unfavorably with the Republic in every way, but in none more than this. She uses but four thousand tons of paper a year—only about two-fifths of the Republic's ratio to population. The amount annually spent on books and newspapers by the Republic is $90,-000,000 (£18,000,000) against $80,000,000 (£16,000,-000) spent by Britain.

It is not fifty years since a British critic asked, sneeringly: "Who reads an American book?" To-day the same critic, if he be living and up with the times, will have to reverse his question, and ask: "Who does *not* read an American book?" A glance at the British trade catalogues will show how many American publications are reprinted in Great Britain, for the British publisher does not hesitate, in the absence of an international copyright law, to appropriate any successful American work, although he is apt to call his Yankee brother hard names for pursuing a similar policy in relation to British publications. The works of popular American historians, American poets, and American novelists are all reprinted in England, and are as well-known there as at home. Indeed, it has been said that Longfellow is more widely read in Britain than the lordly Poet Laureate himself. The very successful enterprise of Mr. Douglass, the Edinburgh publisher, is a case in point, the series of American stories which he republishes having had a wonderfully large sale. Two American lexicographers have contributed to the world two of the best English dictionaries, and the standard Greek lexicon, published by the University of Oxford, is printed from American plates, edited and made in New York.

Some idea of the American demand for books may be formed from a few illustrations. The ninth edition of the

"Encyclopædia Britannica," now in course of publication, has more than fifty thousand subscribers in the United States, probably more than five times as many as it has in its own home. Besides this, an unauthorized edition, a reprint, has had a large circulation. Let us pause here a moment and try to take in the full significance of such a fact as this. The "Britannica" is the one distinctively national work. One would think it was published surely for Britain; but no, it is not for the parent land, but for the Republic that this treasury of all knowledge is prepared. Its purchasers are not in Old but in New England —five to one. Thus at every point we stumble, as it were, upon startling proofs, that the dear old home is becoming the satellite of the republican giant whose mass is too great to be resisted. Its power of attraction begins to draw the smaller body out of its monarchical orbit into the great sweep of the republican idea—the equality of the citizen. The same firm which imports the "Encyclopædia Britannica" in the United States, Charles Scribner's Sons, of New York, are the publishers of the great "Statistical Atlas of the United States." Nearly eighty tons (one hundred and fifty-seven thousand five hundred pounds) of paper were used in printing the first edition of this work, which is one of the wonderful books of the century—wonderful even in America.

The "American Cyclopædia," published by D. Appleton & Co., New York, has also had an enormous circulation, more than a hundred and twenty thousand sets, of sixteen volumes each, having been sold by subscription, at the average price of a hundred dollars the set, making in the aggregate more than $12,000,000 (£2,400,000). The same firm have printed more than fifty million of "Webster's Spelling Book," and still print and sell a million copies every year. "Picturesque America," a costly work in two large volumes, has also had a phenomenal sale, more than a hundred thousand copies having been disposed of. Mr. Blaine's book, "Twenty Years in Congress," has more than two hundred thousand subscribers, and General Grant's "Personal Memoirs" more than three hundred thousand. The sums realized by each of these writers will exceed $250,000 (£50,000); the latter will probably double that amount, and I have seen an estimate which placed Mrs. Grant's prospective profits at $700,000 (£140,000). Milton was glad to get five pounds for "Paradise Lost." Even Macaulay's celebrated check for twenty thousand pounds, received for his "History," dwindles into insignificance compared with the princely compensation awarded to its favorites by the triumphant Democracy.

It is much the same with all standard British publications—all have a larger circulation in the Republic than in the Monarchy. Spencer, Tennyson, Smiles, Morley, the Arnolds (Matthew and Edwin) all have larger constituencies in New than in Old England; indeed, the first named, Herbert Spencer, was discovered and appreciated by American readers before he was recognized at home. And here let me, in passing, drop a tear over the one sad blot which disgraces the Republic. Her laws do not give protection to the foreign author. For this I have neither palliation nor excuse. It is, since slavery is gone, the one disgraceful thing of which, as a nation, she is guilty. It brings the blush of shame to my cheek as I think of it. There are now signs that the public conscience is awakening to the duty of removing the stain. A fair copyright act would probably have been passed by Congress at its last session but for the jealousies of publishers and the somewhat impracticable attitude—if they will permit one of their humble members to say so—of our Copyright League. Authors are not as a class distinguished, I think, for practical good sense in legislative matters.

Something must be conceded to publishers on this side, and something must be conceded by publishers on the other. It is asking too much, or, at least, more than is likely to be granted, for publishers abroad, who own a copyright on a popular author's works which they have enjoyed for many years and paid for only on the basis of the home market, to insist upon reaping a new harvest on such works in America. If the money would go to the author or his representatives the idea would not be so unpalatable.

In like manner publishers here insist that an author taking out an American copyright should publish his work in America as well as in his own land. It is a publishers' quarrel. Had the authors on both sides the power to adjust it the Republic would soon be relieved from the just reproach of stealing the work of men's brains—the most valuable work of all. Ere a new edition of "Triumphant Democracy" be called for, I hope to be able to record that a fair copyright act has been passed.

Libraries have multiplied very rapidly. Fifty years ago there were few large collections of books in America, except in the universities and collegiate institutions. Of other libraries prior to 1820 only ten are enumerated, and these were mostly of inferior grade. Since that period libraries have sprung into being in nearly every township or village. They dot the country almost as thickly as the public schools; while State libraries have been formed in every territorial division of the Union.

The spirit of local patriotism which characterizes equally the native American and the new settler, and which leads each to think that the particular spot of God's earth on which he lives is the best, is a spirit which prompts numerous great public works. The dwellers in a new settlement are animated by an amazing energy and spirit of self-sacrifice in matters concerning their "city."

Public works of all kinds are undertaken with feverish eagerness. Men subscribe money for the adornment and improvement of their town as readily as they would for their particular home. One is constantly surprised to find all the evidences of advanced civilization in cities of which the foundation was laid but as yesterday. Libraries, schools, club-houses, churches, theatres, court-houses, bridges, of the most elegant designs, are found in towns which had no existence a few years ago. Take St. Paul as an example. This young and enterprising city owns no less than three public libraries—the State library, with ten thousand volumes; the Historical Society's library and museum, with twenty-two thousand volumes; and the Free Circulating Library, with twelve thousand volumes, to which additions are being constantly made.

It is estimated that there are twenty-three thousand school libraries in America, containing forty-five million books—*twelve million more than all the public libraries of Europe combined.* Other educational establishments increased this number by two and a half million volumes; and thirty-eight State libraries contribute over a million more. The Congressional library, the Astor, the Boston City, the Philadelphia, the various mercantile libraries, the Watkinson Reference at Hartford, and many others will raise the grand total to much more than fifty million volumes, a book almost for every man, woman, and child in the United States. More than three hundred libraries contain ten thousand volumes each, twelve contain more than a hundred thousand volumes each, and two contain four hundred thousand volumes each. Even this statement but feebly shadows forth the truth as to the books and periodicals of the country as compared with those of other lands, for the American is not only a reader, but he is above all other men a buyer of books.

Circulating libraries are not so generally used as in Europe. It is when you enter the home of the American farmer or artisan that you are struck with the number of books and magazines you see—the two or three shelves and often far greater number filled with them—all of which are his own, except perhaps the few stray borrowed volumes which most collections contain, and which are conscientiously counted as belonging to another, to be returned some day, but somehow that some day never arrives. There must be a special punishment in store surely for such as do not return these treasures to their rightful owners. (This hint is not without a purpose.) The universal propensity of the American, young and old, for reading and writing, has sometimes seemed to me to lend countenance to Dogberry's dictum that while a good name was the gift of God "reading and writing came by Nature." These do seem to be part of the nature of the American.

Triumphant Democracy is triumphant in nothing more than in this, that her members are readers and buyers of books and reading matter beyond the members of any government of a class, but in this particular each system is only seen to be true to its nature. The monarchist boasts more bayonets, the republican more books. We know which weapon is the more effective in these days. "The paper bullet of the brain" is the moral dynamite of triumphant Democracy—the only dynamite which the peaceful and law-abiding republican ever has occasion or can be induced to use.

Chapter XVI
THE FEDERAL CONSTELLATION

"As far as I can see, the American Constitution is the most wonderful work ever struck off at one time by the brain and purpose of man."—GLADSTONE.

W<small>E HOLD</small> these truths to be self-evident that all men are created free and equal, and are endowed by their Creator with certain inalienable rights, among which are life, liberty, and the pursuit of happiness." Round this doctrine of the Declaration of Independence as its central sun the constellation of States revolves. The equality of the citizen is decreed by the fundamental law. All acts, all institutions, are based upon this idea. There is not one shred of privilege, hence no classes. The American people are a unit. Difference of position in the State, resulting from birth, would be held to insult the citizen. One and all they stand Brutus-like and

> "Would brook
> The eternal devil to keep his state
> As easily as a king."

Government of the people, for the people, and by the people is their political creed. The vote of an Emerson or a Lincoln weighs no more than that of the poorest negro. The President has not a privilege which is not the birthright of every other citizen. The people are not levelled down, but levelled up to the full dignity of equal citizenship beyond which no man can go.

The first voice of the people may not be always the voice of God. Indeed, sometimes it does seem to be very far from it; but the second voice of the people—their sober second thought—comes nearest to it of any tribunal, much nearer than the voice of any class, even that of the most highly educated, has ever come in any government under the sun. Hence there is no voice in all America which has the faintest authority when the ballot speaks.

It has often been objected to this republican theory of the State that under it a dead level of uniformity must exist. The informed traveller, who knows life in America, can be relied upon to dispel this delusion and to certify that nowhere in all the world is society more exclusive or more varied than in republican America. Certainly it is far less so in Britain. The difference is that while in monarchical countries birth and rank tend to override personal characteristics, republican society is necessarily founded upon real character and attainment. "Natural selection" has freer play. Congenial persons associate with each other, uninfluenced by birth or rank since neither exists. Nor has wealth of itself nearly so great an influence in society in America as in Britain. It is impossible, in the nature of things, that it should have, because it is much more easily acquired, and, what is much more telling, much more easily lost. The law of acquisition is indeed as free to act in the Republic as in the Monarchy, but then the law of dispersion is also allowed full force in the former, where primogeniture and entail are unknown and the transfer of land is easy. There are but three generations in America from shirt sleeves to shirt sleeves. Under such conditions an aristocracy of wealth is impossible. The "almighty dollar" is just like the restless pig which Paddy could not count, because it would not stand still long enough in one place to be counted. Wealth cannot remain permanently in any class if economic laws are allowed free play.

The Federal constellation is composed of thirty-eight stars, the States, and eleven nebulæ, the Territories, which are rapidly crystallizing into form. The galaxy upon the national flag has grown during the century from thirteen to thirty-eight stars, and "the cry is still they come." Every decade new stars are coming into view, and ere long the entire cluster of nebulæ will be added to the Federal constellation. They are to come forth as the new star in Andromeda came in the fullness of time. A new State sweeps into the Federal constellation every now and then like

> "A star new-born, that drops into its place,
> And which, once circling in its placid round,
> Not all the tumult of the earth can shake."

The question arises, "How is it possible to govern successfully under one head, not this nation, but this great continent of nations?" The answer is, "Through the federal or home rule system alone is it possible." Each of these thirty-eight States is sovereign within its own borders. Each has its own constitution, its own parliament consisting of House and Senate, its own president, courts and judges, militia, etc., etc. All the rights of a sovereign State belong to it, except such as it has expressly delegated in common with sister States to the central authority, the National Government at Washington.

One provision ensures solidity. Should a dispute arise between a State and the central government as to what powers are or are not delegated, the decision of the

Supreme Court of the nation is final and binding upon all. The theory is that all their internal affairs are matters for the States to deal with and determine, all external affairs are for the nation; all local matters are for the States, all general matters for the nation. The division is easily made and maintained. The Constitution defines it in a few clauses by stating what the National Government has charge of, as seen in section eight (appendix). Any powers not here expressly delegated to the nation remain in the States, to be exercised in any manner they choose.

The Supreme Court of the nation stands ready to inform States or nation of their respective powers. With the exception of the claim made in the interest of the slave-power, that a State had the right to secede from the Union, no serious question between State and nation has ever arisen. It is difficult to see how any can arise, since that has been definitely decided in the negative. The integrity of the nation having been assured, all other questions must be of trifling import and readily adjustable by the Supreme Court, which has proclaimed the nation to be "an indestructible Union of indestructible States."

The differentiations shown in the laws of the various States, which have resulted from the perfect freedom or home rule accorded them in their internal affairs, prove that the political institutions best suited to each community are thereby ensured, since they must necessarily be healthful growths of the body politic. Genuine outbirths of the people themselves, and therefore certain to receive their cordial and unwavering support. The number and extent of these differences in laws are surprising. The customs and habits of cold, cultured, old Massachusetts find expression in laws not best adapted for tropical, agricultural new Texas, just as the laws of England would be found less desirable for Scotland or Ireland than those which have been evolved by these communities, and which would be still more freely evolved by home rule, under their slightly different environments.

These stars, the American States, revolve each upon its own axis, within its own orbit, each according to its own laws, some faster, some slower, one at one angle and one at another, but around the central sun at Washington they tread the great national orbit under equal conditions, and constitute parts of one great whole. Here, then, we have the perfection of federal or home rule in its fullest and greatest development. The success of the American Union proves that the freest self-government of the parts produces the strongest government of the whole.

Let us proceed to note, in the order of their importance, the various branches of the National Government. We begin, of course, with the

SUPREME COURT OF THE NATION

Beyond and before, and higher than House, or Senate, or President, stands this final arbiter, sole umpire, judge of itself. More than once Lord Salisbury has said that he envied his transatlantic brethren their Supreme Court. Speaking at Edinburgh on November 23, 1882, he said: "I confess I do not often envy the United States, but there is one feature in their institutions which appears to me the subject of the greatest envy—their magnificent institution of a Supreme Court. In the United States, if Parliament passes any measure inconsistent with the Constitution of the country, there exists a court which will negative it at once, and that gives a stability to the institutions of the country which, under the system of vague and mysterious promises here, we look for in vain." He is right, and as he becomes more conversant with the results of political institutions founded upon the equality of the citizen, as I trust he may do, he will, in my opinion, find reason to envy many other of these more highly developed and in reality deeply conservative institutions, as much as that which now excites his admiration. The powers of the Supreme Court seem at first sight almost too vast to entrust to any small body of men; but it is to be noted that these powers are limited by the fact that it can neither make nor execute laws, nor originate anything. It only decides disputes as to existing laws, should such be properly brought before it, and its judgments are in all cases confined rigorously to the points submitted. It cannot interfere beforehand with any act of the government, nor with any act of the President, but can decide only whether such acts or orders are or are not constitutional, and the reasons for such decision must be publicly stated. Thus limited, its decision is final. Unless and until decided to be unconstitutional all acts of Congress or of the President are valid.

As may be inferred, the mere knowledge on the part of legislative bodies that their acts are subject to the decision of the Supreme Court, keeps them strictly within constitutional bounds. There is no use, even were there the disposition, to enact any law which is not reasonably certain to be sustained. Therefore the regulative power of the court upon great questions remains practically in abeyance. The power is there, which is all that is required. The questions bearing upon State relations, which it is called upon to decide, are few, and generally of minor importance. As, however, all causes which involve considerable sums between citizens of different States can be appealed to this court, it is kept busily engaged upon matters of large pecuniary interest, but of no political consequence.

The court consists of nine judges, who hold office during life, subject, however, to impeachment by Congress for misbehavior or removal for inability to serve. Vacancies are filled by nominations made by the President to the Senate for confirmation, no appointment being complete until confirmed by the Senate. The salary of the judges is $10,000 (£2,000) per annum, and the Chief Justice receives $500 (£100) more. They can retire at seventy years of age upon full pay during life. What pittances, I hear my monarchical friends exclaim. Perhaps so, but does any court in the world command greater respect than this Supreme Court? Are abler, purer lawyers, men clearer in their great office, to be found elsewhere? Certainly not. Even my Lord Salisbury regrets that there is not such a tribunal in Britain. When I see the quiet dignity of the Supreme Court Judges in Washington, their plain living, free from vulgar ostentation, their modest but refined homes, and think how far beyond pecuniary considerations their aspirations are, how foreign to their elevated natures are the coarser phases of position in modern society, I cannot but conclude that it would be most unfortunate if the emoluments of their positions should ever be made so great as in themselves to constitute a temptation, as they are in Britain. The American judge in the Supreme Court has no compeer. The pomp and parade which surround the entrance of a judge in Britain, the sordid pecuniary prize which he has secured by the appointment, his gilt coach, and all the tinsel of feudalistic times which is allowed still to survive under the idea that it adds to his dignity, but which borders upon the ridiculous in these days of general refinement—all this tinsel would seem most unfitting to the republican judge, detracting, not adding to, the inherent dignity of his great position.

The Supreme Court sits in Washington; but each of

the nine judges visits for a part of the year one of the nine circuits into which the country is divided, and assists the circuit judges. The circuits are again divided into districts, each of which has its own court and judge. These are all national courts, the judges of which are approved by the Senate upon the nomination of the President, and hold office during life or good behavior. The whole forms the national judiciary, to which every citizen has the right of appeal in any cause involving the citizens or corporations of another State. We come next to the

LEGISLATIVE DEPARTMENT

This consists of two Houses, a House of Representatives and a Senate, which meet at Washington twice a year upon fixed dates, March and December. The House is composed of three hundred and twenty-five Representatives. Every State sends members in exact proportion to its population as shown by each decadal census. The number of members is not regularly increased. The number of population to each Representative is raised; thus in 1870 every one hundred and thirty-eight thousand inhabitants returned a member; in 1880 it required one hundred and fifty-four thousand. After a census is taken the population is divided by number of members, the quota required to return a member being thus ascertained. Each State is then informed of the number due to it, and arranges its electoral districts accordingly. Thus every ten years electoral power is fairly, because equally, adjusted to the satisfaction of all. By so simple an automatic device the question of representation is removed from politics, and settled forever upon the rock of fair and equal representation. It never can be settled in a free State until equal electoral districts are reached. Educated man demands equality, nor can he rest until he has obtained it. This secured, he becomes quiet and contented. Representatives hold office for two years, their term expiring with each Congress on the fourth of March of every second year. As members are always eligible for re-election, and as the practice is to return men of ability from term to term, the new House is always under the guidance of experienced legislators. Members are paid $5,000 (£1,000) per year and travelling expenses.

The power of the purse is as tenaciously held by the House in Washington as in London; all money bills originate in it by express provision of the Constitution. Alike in this, the two Houses present an entirely different appearance; on entering the House at Washington the visitor is struck by the contrast. Instead of the uncomfortable benches at Westminster and the lack of all facilities for reading or writing, the newer House presents its members all sitting in good easy chairs, at separate desks, like so many good boys at school; they are busily at work with their correspondence, or consulting books of reference. Pages answer their call. They attend to their legislative duties when fresh during the day. When a division is called, instead of wasting twenty minutes, and requiring every member to get up and walk past tellers, the business is done in a few minutes without disturbance; the clerk calls the roll of names alphabetically, and each member nods or shakes his head, or calls out "aye" or "no." A record is kept, and result announced, and business proceeds. How simple. Business is not often obstructed in the House. When an orator exhausts its patience he is made to sit down by a call for the question, and unless he gets a majority in favor of hearing him further, he is ruled out. Yet neither party complains that this rule has worked serious injury; no party seeks to change it. It has not prevented full discussion, and it has enabled the House to transact business properly.

Next in order follows that one American institution which has received the unqualified approval of every man who has given an opinion upon the subject. I never heard even a British Tory utter a word in its disparagement. I cannot imagine what a man could say except in praise of the

UNITED STATES SENATE

Proud, indeed, may the man be who can style himself "Senator." To this august body each of the States sends two members, six years being the term of office. These are elected by the legislatures of the States, and hence reflect the popular desire. Senators are, of course, the adherents of one or other political party, as it obtains sway in the various States. As the terms of service are so arranged that only one-third of the Senators retire, unless re-elected, every two years, the tendency is for the Senate to respond somewhat less promptly than the Lower House to the changes of public opinion.

The Senate has large powers; all laws must be passed by it as well as by the House. No treaty with a foreign power is valid without its approval by a two-thirds vote; all ambassadors and agents to foreign powers must be approved by it. Much has been said about the patronage of the President; but he cannot appoint a postmaster unless the nominee is passed upon and confirmed by this august tribunal. It has been said by more than one political writer that the American Senate is the ideal second chamber of the world. Some assert that it is the only second chamber which possesses real power and is permanently fixed in the hearts of the masses. It is certainly regarded in America as a great promotion to be elevated from the House to the Senate, and it is none the less certain that the entire nation regards the Senate with pride and affection. All officials in America being paid, the salary of a Senator is the same as that of a Representative, $5,000 (£1,000) per year and travelling expenses.

Lord Salisbury will be envying this American institution as well as the Supreme Court ere long, mark you, for his own second chamber gives unmistakable evidence of decay, and in good time he may even come to see that an elected President is preferable to a hereditary ruler. We cannot despair of his reaching finally to the full measure of the political equality of the citizen since he begins so well with the chief American institution, the Supreme Court.

Here is indeed a lucky hit. Since these words were written a member of Parliament sends me confirmation of this prophecy. This hopeful student of republican institutions, my Lord Salisbury, has said in a recent speech:

"The Americans, as you know, have a Senate. I wish we could institute it in this country. Marvellous in efficiency and strength!"

So, another American institution envied! Truly this former Saturday Reviewer is a more promising pupil than Mr. Gladstone himself, and almost equal to Lord Rosebery. Nothing easier, my lord, than to get a copy of the American Senate. The secret of its marvellous strength and efficiency is an open one. You know it well. The Senate springs from and rests upon the suffrages of the people. There is not a trace of hereditary poison in its veins to steal away its power. In an elective assembly such as this, a man of real power like Lord Salisbury would be twice the man he is when leading a set of hereditary accidents.

Having already obtained Lord Salisbury's endorsement of the Supreme Court and the Senate, I am encouraged to go a step further and commend for his approval the institution he should next endorse, a Parliament of duly paid members elected by equal electoral districts for a fixed term of two years. Until this is secured the government of Britain must remain exposed to every passing gust of popular emotion, and hence exercise no steadying effect in periods of excitement. A British ministry does not govern, but bows to the clamor it should withstand. And upon my British readers let me once more impress the truth that in all the elements of true conservatism, in all that goes to make up a strong government, a power competent to maintain justice and to defeat attacks upon the rights or property of others, and when necessary, to keep the ship of state with its head against the wildest hurricane, the American system, as I must compliment Lord Salisbury upon being one of the first European statesman to discover, is infinitely beyond the monarchical. The man who knows both well, and has property in both lands, may be trusted to tell his inquirers that his republican title gives him much the less uneasiness. This is further demonstrated by the highest place being accorded by the world to the American national debt.

WAR AND TREATY-MAKING POWER

In two vital respects the powers of the executives of the old and new English lands differ. First, no treaty with a foreign power is binding until ratified by the Senate. Indeed, as we have seen, no Minister can be appointed to a foreign power until approved by this chamber. This vote of the Senate has several times kept the administration from entering into injudicious arrangements. Even General Grant and his cabinet committed themselves to the acquisition of San Domingo. Recently the late administration was led into a very questionable treaty with Spain. The temptation for a few men, and especially for one man, to characterize his administration by some brilliant stroke calculated to dazzle the populace at the moment, or to appeal to the national vanity, is a source of real danger in all popular governments. Not what is permanently valuable, but what is presently telling, is apt to be considered. Against this danger, for which the monarchical system has no provision whatever, the republican opposes the cool, deliberate decision of an impersonal judge, the Senate. No man's "glory" is brightened or dimmed by the decision. What is for the lasting good of the nation is thought of—not what will bring temporary popularity to a cabinet or save a ministry. It must surely be a prejudiced mind which does not feel that the advantage is here upon the side of the younger land.

The second vital difference is even of deeper import than that just recited. In the Republic, war can be declared only by the two Houses of Congress, approved by the President. Before the sword can be drawn both branches of the legislature must be wrought up to the pitch of this extreme and momentous act. The House, the Senate, and the Executive in the person of the President, must consider, discuss, and decide the question under surroundings of the deepest solemnity, and with the nation—the world—anxiously looking on. Every Representative of the people, and every Senator, may speak in his place and record his vote for or against. Public attention is thus fixed and concentrated upon the crisis, and public discussion enlightens the people. Time, precious time, which ever cools the passions of men and works for peace, is thus gained, and every official, every member of the legislature, publicly assumes the fearful responsibility of engaging in the slaughter of his fellow men. If ever war be proclaimed by the Republic, which God forbid, since all her paths are peace, it will not be the act of one branch or another of the government, but the solemn public act of all, legislative and executive. Contrast this with monarchical countries, in which a few excited partisans, sometimes only one or two real actors, who sit in a close cabinet chamber, commit the people to criminal war—sometimes to prolong their own tenure of office, or to promote some party end.

My American readers may not be aware of the fact that, while in Britain an act of Parliament is necessary before works for a supply of water or a mile of railway can be constructed, six or seven men can plunge the nation into war, or, what is perhaps equally disastrous, commit it to entangling alliances without consulting Parliament at all. This is the most pernicious, palpable effect flowing from the monarchical theory, for these men do this in "the king's name," who is in theory still a real monarch, although in reality only a convenient puppet, to be used by the cabinet at pleasure to suit their own ends. Next to the sapping of the roots of true manhood in the masses, by decreeing their inferiority to other men at birth, this is the most potent evil which exists to-day in the British Constitution, and it is chargeable solely to the monarchical system. It does not rank with the first evil, however, being mainly material, while the other is of the spirit, injury to which is the gravest misfortune which can befall a nation. But this vital truth not one of the so-called "practical" statesmen of Britain sees or will consider, or, perhaps what is nearer the truth, will venture to tell. Not one of them, apparently, has a soul above cheap corn, which is worshipped as the highest good. Indignities to the spirit of the masses, by which manhood is impaired, they seem to argue, may safely pass unnoted, so long as their bodies are fed. And yet better, far better, for a nation that its food for the body should be dear, and equal citizenship be the birthright of the soul. "We have many evils to remedy in our political system a million times greater than the Monarchy," once said to me a prominent statesman and possible prime minister. I looked pitifully upon him, his eyes blinded with the dust of conflict and his mind so absorbed with trifling party results that he could neither think nor see an inch before his face, much less study cause and effect. Could he do so, surely he would realize the truth that in the royal family, as in a nest, lie the origin of all the political evils which afflict his native land and which he deplores; all that this able, earnest, patriotic man is laboring to remove is only the legitimate spawn of this one royal family institution, and is never to be met with except where a royal family exists to breed it. Resolve that the head of the State shall be elected at intervals and thus found government upon the true idea—the political equality of the citizen—and all the political wrongs of the few against the many fall as if by magic. Were I in public life in Britain I should be ashamed to waste my energies against the House of Lords, Church and State, primogeniture and entail, and all the other branches of the monstrous system; I should strike boldly at the royal family, the root of the upas tree from which spring all these wrongs.

Surely the Democracies of Europe have no question to consider more vitally important than the war power. How many useless wars in the past would have been avoided had the republican method prevailed! How many in the future would be prevented by its prompt adoption. The masses are ever more pacific than their rulers, ever more kindly disposed to those of their clay in other nations than the rulers are to theirs. The people do not share the jealousies of their rulers. If the war power lay in the hands of the representatives of the people in Europe, as it does in America, there would be fewer wars.

The position of the Republic upon this question of war is still further advanced by the fact that both political parties, by special clauses in their declaration of principles, have pronounced in favor of peaceful arbitration of international differences. Thus, before America can have recourse to arms, no matter what party be in power, her adversary must first be offered arbitration and decline it. We envy not the nation which shocks the moral sense of mankind by refusing this olive branch of peace when presented.

Of all the desirable political changes which it seems to me possible for this generation to effect, I consider it by far the most important for the welfare of the race that every civilized nation should be pledged, as the Republic is, to offer peaceful arbitration to its opponent before the senseless, inhuman work of human slaughter begins; and for all the just and good measures by which the Republic has won my love, next to that by which she has made me her own citizen, and hence the peer of any man, kaiser, pope, or king, thus effacing from my brow the insult inflicted upon me by my native land at birth, which deemed me unworthy the privileges accorded to others—next to that, for which I will fight for her, if need be die for her, and must adore her forever—I thank the Republic for her position in regard to international murder, which still passes by the name of war.

THE EXECUTIVE POWER. THE PRESIDENT

The executive power is lodged in a President, who for four years, the term of his office, is the most powerful ruler in the world. He is not only first civil magistrate, but he is commander-in-chief of the army and navy, and of all the military forces of the nation, including the militia of the States whenever called upon by him. More soldiers would respond to his call than to that of any other ruler in the world. The number of men who in case of war might be enrolled in the militia approaches seven millions, almost every able man of whom would consider it his duty to shoulder his musket and march at the word of his commander-in-chief, the President. What are French, or German, or Russian hosts compared to this of the Democracy! Even man for man, as soldiers, they would not compare with the educated Republican. But this great army costs the States but little; it is always engaged in the pursuits of peace, and only to be called upon should emergency arise. The President's control over the forces is not merely nominal; it is real. When the most popular general in the army, during the Civil War, had fought his way to victory, and had the enemy at his feet, it was feared that unsatisfactory terms for his surrender might be made. The following telegram was therefore sent, which, though bearing the signature of the Secretary of War, was written without blot or erasure by President Lincoln himself. I have seen the telegram:

"WASHINGTON, *March* 3, 1865, 12 P.M.

"LIEUTENANT-GENERAL GRANT:

"The President directs me to say to you that he wishes you to have no conference with General Lee, unless it be for the capitulation of General Lee's army, or on some other minor and purely military matter. He instructs me to say that you are not to decide, discuss, or confer upon any political question. Such questions the President holds in his own hands, and will submit them to no military conferences or conventions. Meanwhile you are to press to the utmost your military advantages.

"EDWIN M. STANTON,
"*Secretary of War.*"

The General, of course, obeyed. Only a few days later General Sherman, just fresh from his "March to the Sea," entered into a convention with General Johnston which had political bearings. A telegram was promptly sent to General Grant instructing him to cancel General Sherman's agreement, and this was done. Suppose, if any one can suppose so lamentable an abdication of duty, that in a weak moment the American Government had sent a Gordon to arrange terms of peace, and that he disobeyed his instructions or had presumed to declare war upon his own account! In the President's opinion a simple order like the foregoing would scarcely have met the case. He would have had the insubordinate arrested, court-martialled, cashiered, and probably shot—no, not shot, but consigned for life to some lunatic asylum. President Lincoln could have court-martialled General Grant, or General Grant when President could have court-martialled General Sherman, or either President dismissed either general when at the height of that general's power, or arrested him, as Richelieu did his conspiring general, "at the head of his legions," without raising a murmur of popular dissent. The people would have reserved their judgment till the next election, and probably have enthusiastically approved, as indeed the British will approve if they ever see it—such a display of masterful power over all others by their elected Chief of the State.

No soldier has ever dreamed of questioning the supreme authority of the President, nor has the nation ever shown the slightest jealousy of its exercise. Why should it, since the President is not above its reach, but is only its own duly appointed agent for a specified term; when that expires he transfers his powers to his successor and seeks again the ranks of private citizenship. One returns to Congress as the representative of his district, another resumes the practice of law, a third becomes a farmer.

Neither sinecure, place, nor pension is bestowed upon an ex-President. He has been supremely honored by his fellow-citizens. He has in turn done his duty. The obligation is upon his side, and he remains profoundly grateful for the distinction conferred upon him. The State owes officials little; they owe the State much. Such is the Republican idea.

The salary of the President is now $50,000 per annum (£10,000). An official residence is provided for him at Washington, and a country house within a few miles of that city. At stated times for some hours each week the President receives such respectably dressed and well-ordered people as choose to call upon him. Being the servant of the people in a country where all citizens are equal, the humblest has the same right to call upon him and shake his hand as the most distinguished, he being as much the servant of the one as of the other. By many such significant customs the powerful President is reminded of what it would indeed be impossible for any one in the land to forget, that the sovereignty of the Republic resides not in the servants of the State but in the citizen, in every one of whom rests an equal share of it. The feelings and desires of the citizen it therefore behooves all officials to consider.

The President selects of his own will and without interference the members of his Cabinet, as the British Prime Minister does. They are removable at pleasure. The President being his own prime minister, the Cabinet officers are of equal rank. One difference between the two countries in regard to the Cabinet is that, while the British Cabinet sit in one or the other House and communicate orally with it, in America the members of the Cabinet do not appear in person before the legislature, but report to it in writing. This is, however, simply a matter of convenience; there is nothing but custom to prevent them from appearing and making their statements in person, although they could not take any part in the proceedings of the legislature. At first the President appeared and addressed Congress at the beginning of each session, but the plan of placing before it a written message as often as deemed necessary has been preferred. The people would not favor a change to the British practice, for the separation of the executive and legislative departments is held to be of much importance. Either House can call at all times upon the President for information upon any question connected with affairs, but as the call has to meet the approval of the House, the government is freed from the petty annoyances which it is in the power of any injudicious member to inflict under the British system of nightly questioning. The President, in like manner, has free access to Congress, and, indeed, it is his duty to report to it from time to time upon all matters of which, in his opinion, Congress should be advised. He is also invited to recommend measures for its acceptance.

The President represents the nation in its relations with foreign countries, and receives all ambassadors. It is he alone who has the power to pardon offences against the laws of the United States. He also has a veto power over the acts of Congress, which, however, is invalid should the measure vetoed be passed again by a two-thirds vote in both Houses. He is eligible for re-election, and several have been elected for two terms, or eight years in all, as Washington was, but he having declined re-election for a third term lest the office should seem too permanent, it has become the custom not to elect beyond two terms.

The Americans have indeed shown wonderful sagacity

in the selection of their Presidents. Considered as a body, it would be impossible to equal them in character, ability, education, or manners, by any body of men ever born, appointed, or elected to any other station. They furnish a striking contrast to the occupants or heirs of thrones in every particular. When Britain was disgraced by its George III, the Republic had Washington; and until Queen Victoria ascended the throne the comparison had certainly always been in favor of the Republic.

It is the fashion in all things to praise the past and claim that "there were giants in those days," but it is nevertheless true, in my opinion, that the Presidents of the Republic in our own times have been worthy successors even to Washington, Adams, and Jefferson of the past. Grant has a firm place in history among men possessed of great ability. Garfield's career from a poor school teacher to the Presidency is exceedingly difficult to parallel, while the political genius of Lincoln has never been surpassed. It is always well to remember that there are giants in our own day too.

The election of the President and Vice-President is not by a direct vote of the people but by a vote of the States in an electoral assembly in which each State has as many votes as it has Senators and Representatives in Congress, that is in proportion to its population. It has been claimed as an advantage of the Monarchy that, having a permanent head of the State, the excitement and expense of a general election every four years is avoided. But, it may be answered, the hereditary head of Britain is not a political head at all. An automaton would do just as well, for it could certainly be used as a model to set the fashions in clothes, and probably could be made to lay foundation-stones, or open fancy bazaars with little less careful coaching and attention than it is generally necessary to bestow upon the live figurehead;

besides it would be much less expensive. The real ruler of Britain is elected just as often as a President of the Republic is, for it is a curious fact that Parliaments last an average of four years, which is the Presidential term. Even as I now write, the appeal is being made to the British people, Gladstone or Salisbury, as clearly as in the late Presidential election it was Cleveland or Blaine. It is a fiction, therefore, that the Monarchy has any advantage, if it would be an advantage, which I dispute, over the Republic in this respect, for they are situated precisely alike; they each elect a ruler every four years. The excitement and the expense of a general election is far greater in the Monarchy than in the Republic, and in both equally the head is elected. Besides this, Members of Congress are elected by the States along with the Presidential ticket, just as Members of Parliament are elected when Gladstone or Salisbury is chosen. So that in one sense the election of the President costs nothing whatever, as State elections have to be held whether a President is to be elected or not, and voting for the electoral ticket when voting for Representatives involves no additional expense. Of course, more money is spent in Presidential years, but this is the personal contribution of zealous partisans and not a charge upon the State. It will surprise Britons to know that no sums comparable to what they spend on political contests are ever spent by the Americans. The total sum expended by the national committees of all the parties, even in the last exciting Presidential contest, did not exceed $600,000 (£120,-000).

The republican election, moreover, is conducted with far less riot and disturbance than unfortunately characterizes the appeal to the electorate in older England. An American is surprised and shocked at the rowdyism often shown at public meetings in Britain. He is accustomed to

have both sides granted a respectful hearing. I have
never seen any public meeting in America broken up by
gangs of the opposite side, nor a public man denied a
hearing. In this respect the example of the younger political community might well be followed by the elder. When
the people of Britain, however, obtain their full political
rights, there will be less exciting questions to discuss than
those which now press for solution, and political gather-
ings will then be more peaceably conducted. It must not
be forgotten that when a vital issue like slavery was
under discussion in America the right of free speech was
often violently assailed, as it still is in Britain.

When the surroundings of the President and the royal
ruler are contrasted, republican simplicity stands out in
strong relief. The President walks about as an ordinary
citizen, wholly unattended, and travels, as a rule, upon
ordinary trains; arrives in New York and registers at a
hotel without previous announcement. Beyond a brief
mention of the fact in the next morning's papers nothing is published about him. As I write he has gone to
Buffalo, the city of his former residence, in order to cast
his vote at the election for Governor of the State of New
York. It will weigh just as much as and no more than
that of the mechanics or laborers whom he will find surrounding the polling-booth. Although, go where he may,
he will be met with quiet evidences of universal and sincere deference as President, there will be no parade, no
cheers. The equipages of the President in Washington
have frequently been so common as not to rank with
those of the wealthy residents, and never in any instance
have they been the richest or best. All the Presidents
have been poor men. I have known three of them so well
as to state, of my own knowledge, that they left office
without means enough upon which to live respectably. Of
every American President it may be said as it was said of

Pitt: "Dispensing for years the favors of the State, he lived without ostentation and died poor." They have all left office poor and pure.

One turns from the dignified simple life of the republican ruler to that of the nominal head of Britain, feeling that there he meets a coarser and less finely developed civilization. The parade and vulgar ostentation which surrounds at every turn the nominal ruler of the parent land is indeed in striking contrast. The cost to the State is as ten thousand to six hundred thousand pounds. The entire family, mother and his "sisters and his cousins and his aunts," are supported, and bands of retainers who are supposed to dignify the throne. The state processions strike an American as grotesque masquerades, and the official coaches in which royalty moves about provoke the enquiry, "What circus has come to town?" One instinctively looks inside for the clown. This much for the crowned king. But the contrast is not all in favor of the Republic, for when the real ruler, the uncrowned king of Britain, is compared with his fellow-ruler here, then the palm for true dignity cannot be awarded to America. Nothing can exceed the simplicity of the surroundings of the prime minister of that great empire. His salary is only one-half that of the President. His official residence is a shabby, dingy, old brick house, instead of the noble Executive Mansion standing in its own park at Washington; it is simply No. 10 Downing Street, and is as shabbily furnished as a New York boarding-house. Mr. Gladstone lives and Mr. Disraeli lived as sensibly as our Presidents, and set just as healthful an example, which, however, counts for little in Britain, since the Prime Minister is not, like the President, the first personage in society. Indeed, when the Liberal Party is in power the Prime Minister can scarcely be said, in one sense, to be in society at all. He is proscribed, and has no influence upon it. But his day approaches; the Democracy will soon require that the man who has the people of England at his back shall no longer tolerate a king before his face. Wherever he appears in Britain, as in America, he will take precedence. "He shall stand BEFORE kings." The children of the Prince of Wales (the Prince himself, if he be unwise), and the children of all of the present dukes and lords of the empire are no longer to follow in the train of the pretender but in that of the only real, the elected king. It is so in the Republic, and what is here is to be yonder. What America does to-day, Britain reaches in the next generation. We must reverse the old proverb, "as the old cock crows the young one learns"; now-a-days, it is the young cock which leads the crowing. The old one does the learning. Room, then, and first place for the elected monarch of Triumphant Democracy in Britain!

We have now passed in review the three branches of government, judicial, legislative, and executive, for which the Constitution provides. The ease with which this instrument has not only done the work over the country for which it was originally designed, but with which it has without repeated change quietly enveloped in its operation a combination of forty-nine different political communities, occupying an area of three million square miles, and comprising most of the English-speaking race —this is not to be spoken of without wonder. With one exception—the dispute as to the right of a State to withdraw from the Union—a serious difficulty has never arisen. It seems as if there could be no limit to its powers of absorption. The whole world could to-day come into the American Union as equal States, and develop peacefully, each after its own fashion, no man being less a Briton, a Frenchman, a German, a Russian, or a China-

man, but all becoming possessed of a new title, proudest
of all, "citizen of the world." This wonderful Constitution stipulates for a republican form of government. All
the Democracy has to do is to discard hereditary rulers
as useless, dangerous, and therefore to be abolished. Sure
is it that they have deluged the world with wars, put man
against his fellow, and sought no end but their own aggrandizement. Not less sure, that they must ever stand
in the way of the brotherhood of the race which it is the
mission of Democracy to foster.

How easily within our grasp, fellow-citizens of the
world, seems the day when

> "The drum shall beat no longer,
> And the battle flags be furled,
> In the parliament of man,
> The federation of the world."

We may not look, however, for quite so wide and complete a Union. Oceans divide the races, and this fact will
keep them apart, for permanent political aggregations
must ever be conterminous; but as far as the continents
of the world are concerned there is no insuperable obstacle to their union each into one nation upon the federal
system. The American continent is evidently destined to
be so ruled. The European continent is slowly consolidat-
ing, for there are but five great powers to-day instead of
the hundreds of small ones which existed before the Na-
poleonic era. A league of peace to which each continent
will send delegates to decide international differences is
not quite so far in the future as may at first sight appear.
This would remove from the world its greatest stain—
war between man and man.

To all communities who are tending towards further

consolidations and to every man who can truthfully exclaim,

> "My benison with those
> Who would make good of ill and friends of foes,"

we commend a close study of that great work of triumphant Democracy, which Mr. Gladstone has pronounced "the most wonderful work ever struck off at one time by the brain and purpose of man"—the profoundly conservative and yet radically republican American Constitution.

Chapter XVII

FOREIGN AFFAIRS

"Peace, commerce, and honest friendship with all nations, entangling alliances with none."—JEFFERSON.

As WE have endeavored to point out, there is a great difference between the old and new lands in the management of their domestic concerns. This difference becomes radical in the domain of foreign affairs. Indeed, it is no longer a difference: it is a complete reversal. What the old land does the new land avoids; what the one land does not, the other does in dealing with other nations. The consequences of the two diverse policies are seen in diametrically different results. The huge debt, the constant war, or fear of war, and the international jealousies which surround the parent land contrast strangely with the freedom of the Republic from all these ills. The excuse made by British statesmen for the unfortunate contrast presented is that the Republic has no strong neighbors, and no colonies or dependencies far distant from its shores which it is bound to guard. I am persuaded that the cause of difference lies deeper than this. No nation is so temptingly placed as the Republic for becoming engaged in aggressive warfare. The materials lie around her upon every side. Had America been cursed by monarchical institutions, which ever breed strong military classes, to whom, as to the royal family and the

court, peaceful avocations are discreditable as compared
with military operations, there can be little question but
that the American monarchy would have involved itself
in endless disputes, treaties, and entangling alliances with
other powers, necessitating large standing armies and
fleets, from which would have come endless wars, or fear
of war. The Republic began early to pursue the paths of
peace. The messages of each succeeding President enforced the words of Jefferson, which we have placed at
the head of this chapter, and the sayings of American
statesmen abound with kindred sentiments. Washington,
in his farewell address, gave the key-note upon which all
subsequent changes have been rung. He says:

"The great rule of conduct for us in regard to foreign nations
is, in extending our commercial relations, to have with them as
little political connection as possible. * * * So far as we have
already formed engagements, let them be fulfilled with perfect
good faith. Here let us stop."

Madison's view of the Republic's mission was:

"To cherish peace and friendly intercourse with all nations
having correspondent dispositions; to maintain sincere neutrality
towards belligerent nations; to prefer, in all cases, amicable discussion and reasonable accommodation of differences to a decision
of them by an appeal to arms; to exclude foreign intrigues and
foreign partialities, so degrading to all countries, and so baneful
to free ones."

Adams speaks of

"The pestilence of foreign influence, which is the angel of destruction to elective governments."

Jefferson further lays down as "our first and fundamental maxim," "never to entangle ourselves in the broils

of Europe. Our second, never to suffer Europe to intermeddle with cis-atlantic affairs." And so was reached the great doctrine, bearing the name of Monroe, declaring to the powers of Europe that "we should consider any attempt on their part to extend their system to any portion of this hemisphere as dangerous to our peace and safety." "Our policy in regard to Europe," the Monroe message continued, "is not to interfere in the internal concerns of any of its powers; to consider the government *de facto* as the legitimate government for us; to cultivate friendly relations with it, and to preserve these relations by a frank, firm, and manly policy; meeting, in all instances, the just claims of every power, submitting to injuries from none."

This chapter could be filled with extracts from the Presidents' messages and from other sources, all preaching the same important lesson, that the Republic must be at peace with its neighbors and with the world. I need not, however, dwell upon the past. It is with the present we have to deal.

Let me give then a short statement of the course recently pursued by the Monarchy and by the Republic in the management of similar emergencies in their relations to other States. The one has a canal through Egypt to guard, and the other a railway across the Isthmus of Panama, that the traffic of the world may be unimpeded. A few months ago word was received in Washington that a disturbance had broken out at one end of the railway in the Republic of Columbia, and that there was grave danger that railway communication across the Isthmus would be interfered with. A force was at once despatched to the scene, and the admiral sailed under the following instructions, which were published in the newspapers that the nation and the world might see and understand all.

[TELEGRAM]

"NAVY DEPARTMENT, WASHINGTON, *April* 3, 1885.
"REAR-ADMIRAL JAMES E. JOUETT, U. S. S. "TENNESSEE,"
PENSACOLA, FLA.:

"In addition to the force under your command in the Steam-ships 'Tennessee,' 'Swatara,' 'Alliance' and 'Galena,' all of which should be at Aspinwall upon your arrival, you will be re-enforced by about two hundred marines, dispatched to-day from New York by the steamship 'City of Para' with tents and camp equipage. To provide for contingencies further supplies will be sent at once.

"The duty you are called upon to perform calls for the exercise of great discretion. The object of the expedition is the performance by the United States of their engagements to preserve the neutrality of and keep open the transit from Colon to Panama, and further to protect the lives and property of American citizens.

"The circumstances as understood, from which the necessity of the expedition has arisen, are in general, that a steamship belonging to Americans has been seized at Colon by an armed force and goods in transit taken from her, her officers and the American Consul imprisoned, and the transit across the Isthmus interrupted. With the consequences involved in these past acts you are not concerned. Your sole duty is confined to seeing that a free and uninterrupted transit across the Isthmus is restored and maintained and that the lives and property of American citizens are protected.

"If on your arrival at the Isthmus order shall have been restored and the Colombian authorities are adequate to the protection of life and property and the maintenance of the free transit, you will interfere in no respect with the constituted authorities, but report and await orders. You have no part to perform in the political or social disorders of Colombia, and it will be your duty to see that no irritation or unfriendliness shall arise from your presence at the Isthmus.

"The exercise of humanity towards American citizens in exigent distress must be left to your sound discretion.

"W. C. WHITNEY,
"Secretary of the Navy."

Note how careful that promising young statesman, Mr. Whitney, is to limit the operations of his admiral to the maintenance of the free and uninterrupted communication which his government had guaranteed! How solicitous that the authorities and people of Colombia should be so treated that no unfriendliness or irritation could possibly arise! The admiral found, upon arrival, that the disturbance was over, and soon returned. Not a shot was fired. Now the great point here is that not a voice was raised in all America suggesting that any part of Colombia should be held, or annexed, or that the people of that State should be in any way interfered with. Consequently no suspicions were aroused, no enemies created. American interests were not pleaded as a warrant for continued occupation. The great and powerful Republic was at Colon as the friend of its small and weak sister, but upon no account to interfere with her even for Colombia's own seeming good. Colombia might manage or, seemingly to America, mismanage her own affairs as to her seemed possible, or best. The admiral would no more have thought of interfering than he would had he been on the shores of Ireland and doomed to stand and see a poor tenant farmer evicted, or upon the shores of Scotland and had seen a poor crofter abused. If the quarrellers in Colombia had attempted to interrupt railway communication across the Isthmus he would have protected that, and in so doing would have received the thanks of all the good people of Colombia.

President Cleveland refers to this episode in his recent message to Congress. For the benefit of the unfortunate people of the Monarchy, and more especially for that of its statesmen, I quote the passage in full:

"Emergencies growing out of civil war in the United States of Colombia demanded of the government at the beginning of this

administration the employment of armed force to fulfil its guarantees under the thirty-fifth article of the treaty of 1816 in order to
keep the transit open across the Isthmus of Panama. Desirous of
exercising only the powers expressly reserved to us by the treaty,
and mindful of the rights of Colombia, the forces sent to the
Isthmus were instructed to confine their action to 'positively and
efficaciously' preventing the transit and its accessories from being
'interrupted or embarrassed.' The execution of this delicate and
responsible task necessarily involved police control where the local
authority was temporarily powerless, but always in aid of the sov-
ereignty of Colombia. The prompt and successful fulfilment of its
duty by this government was highly appreciated by the government of Colombia, and has been followed by expressions of its
satisfaction. High praise is due to the officers and men engaged in
this service. The restoration of peace on the Isthmus by the re-
establishment of the constituted government there being thus
accomplished, the forces of the United States were withdrawn."

Leaving for the present the Colombian difficulty as
peacefully settled without one trace of dissatisfaction
upon the part of the weaker power to plague the Republic hereafter, let us see how the Monarchy managed a
similar task imposed upon her.

England was apprised that a rebellion against the in-
famous ruler of Egypt had broken out and, being bound
with France to exercise dual control, she besought that
country to interfere jointly with her in suppressing this
righteous uprising of an oppressed people. The government of France was anxious to do so, but the people of
France unmistakably pronounced against this—a proof
that Democracy is beginning at last to show its legitimate fruit there. Instead of sending an expedition to
guard the canal, which, by the way, never was endangered, the government sent a large force to Egypt and
began an aggressive campaign to prevent the people of
Egypt from having such rulers as they desired. From

that unfortunate day to this Britain has gone deeper and deeper into trouble. Already $100,000,000 (£20,000,-000) and thousands of lives have been sacrificed; and for what? Absolutely nothing. The criminal side of the question has so shocked the moral sense of the best portion of the Liberal Party that Mr. Gladstone has deemed it necessary upon the eve of an appeal to the nation, to confess that the Soudan campaign was a mistake. It was worse than that, Mr. Gladstone; it was a crime, which would sully your fame forever were it not known that you had no part in it, but were overruled by the aristocratic element which you thought essential to keep in your Cabinet.

It may be argued that Britain was bound to interfere and support upon the throne a sovereign against the wishes of the Egyptian people, though this seems a strange position for so advanced a nation to occupy; or it may be said that Britain had neither right nor wish to interfere with the internal affairs of Egypt, but only wished to guard the canal. It matters not which position is assumed, the fact remains that the policy pursued has not produced the desired result upon either hypothesis, and the end arrived at is in lamentable contrast with the different policy pursued by the Republic. The strong Republic sees clearly from the start what end it has in view, and aims solely for that end. The weak Monarchy, ever subject to the popular breeze, the creature of circumstance, can have no decided policy. The British Constitution makes Britain the Micawber of nations, always looking for "something to turn up." The Republic has complied with its treaty obligations and retired from the scene, with the thanks of its weak neighbor. We are yet to learn what is to be the end of the management of the Monarchy. So far no contrast could be more striking than that between it and that of the Republic.

Let us pause here a moment to contrast the positions of the two admirals upon their respective stations at Colon and Alexandria. The republican official had every interest in maintaining peace. The responsibility of firing a shot was appalling. Behind him stood his superior, the Secretary of the Navy, every line of whose cautious but explicit instructions seems to regard hostilities with aversion. Behind the government, the admiral knew, stood the American people, loath to hurt the feelings of a weak neighbor and determined never to interfere with its internal affairs. No possible reward, no glory, would fall to this admiral from entangling his country in war. He would have been held to the strictest accountability for every drop of blood shed, and the verdict of public opinion at first would have been disposed to go decidedly against him. On the other hand, the surest mode of earning the thanks of Congress and of his country was so to conduct himself as to secure peace without firing a shot. So stood Admiral Jouett, the man of war converted into the messenger of peace. This is the attitude of the Democracy.

How was it with Admiral Seymour, the servant of a monarch? Let him refrain from bombarding from behind his iron walls the few miserable defences in Alexandria Bay, and never in his history perhaps would such an opportunity occur again to rescue his name from obscurity. If he decided to be patient and remain at peace, half-pay and oblivion would be his reward. He knew that if he began to bombard the Egyptian defences the ruling class, which alone could reward him, would applaud. Even the Queen, a woman, who should shudder at war and not publicly parade her interest in slaughter, would publicly congratulate him, and the Prince of Wales and all the aristocracy which move round the court, together with the military and naval classes who flourish only through war, would extol him to the skies. The government tempted the man to fire. All the forces behind him urged him on; while, as we have seen, all the forces behind the republican admiral held him to peace.

Admiral Seymour might have thus reasoned: "Negotiate this trouble peacefully, I remain poor and obscure. There is no danger; I am perfectly safe behind these iron walls; just open my guns and fame and honor and rank and wealth are mine." He yielded. Mr. Gladstone himself stood up in Parliament and advocated a peerage and a pension to the admiral who was bribed to begin the bombardment of Alexandria. Fortunately, not even Mr. Gladstone could force the Liberal party to grant the pension. Admiral Seymour received in cash his thirty pieces of silver.

Fellow-countrymen, what would you think of a judge upon the bench deciding his own cause, where a verdict for the defendant meant to the judge obscurity and half-pay, and a verdict for the plaintiff meant a peerage and twenty-five thousand pounds? Yet this was precisely the position of Admiral Seymour at Alexandria, and it is practically the position occupied by every British commander to whom is committed the issue of peace or war in the "exercise of his discretion." Need we marvel that while the Monarchy becomes involved in war after war, the Republic settles similar problems in peace and with the good will and cordial friendship of the power with which she has to deal!

Let us proceed just a step further and show the policy of the Democracy upon this subject of intervention or complications in the affairs of other States. The President's message from which I have just quoted refers to a treaty offered by Nicaragua, which proposed to give America the necessary land upon which to construct a canal of its own across the Isthmus—a tempting bait this to a Monarchy with imperial ambitions. But listen to the response of the republican President:

"Maintaining, as I do, the tenets of a line of precedents from Washington's day, which proscribe entangling alliances with foreign States, I do not favor a policy of acquisition of new and distant territory or the incorporation of remote interests with our own.

"The laws of progress are vital and organic, and we must be conscious of that irresistible tide of commercial expansion which, as the concomitant of our active civilization, day by day, is being urged onward by those increasing facilities of production, transportation, and communication to which steam and electricity have given birth; but our duty in the present instructs us to address ourselves mainly to the development of the vast resources of the great area committed to our charge, and to the cultivation of the arts of peace within our own borders, though jealously alert in preventing the American hemisphere from being involved in the political problems and complications of distant governments. Therefore, I am unable to recommend propositions involving paramount privileges of ownership or right outside of our own territory, when coupled with absolute and unlimited engagements to defend the territorial integrity of the State where such interests lie. While the general project of connecting the two oceans by means of a canal is to be encouraged, I am of opinion that any scheme to that end to be considered with favor should be free from the features alluded to."

Statesmanship in Britain would have required some life-long diplomat to negotiate for the privileges offered and the seed of many serious questions of the future would have been laid, the abused people of Britain being led to applaud the strong statesman who had promoted British interests and enlarged the bounds of the empire. A little common sense in the Democracy ensures the Republic a continuance of peace. But now and then the seeds of future trouble present themselves in more specious garbs. The Congo Basin attracts attention at present, and here is a paragraph bearing upon that subject, also in the same President's message which I have quoted.

"A conference of delegates of the principal commercial nations was held at Berlin last winter to discuss methods whereby the Congo Basin might be kept open to the world's trade. Delegates attended on behalf of the United States on the understanding that their part should be merely deliberative, without imparting to the results any binding character, so far as the United States were concerned. This reserve was due to the indisposition of this government to share in any disposal by an international congress of jurisdictional questions in remote foreign territories. The results of the conference were embodied in a formal act of the nature of an international convention, which laid down certain obligations purporting to be binding on the signatories subject to ratification within one year. Notwithstanding the reservation under which the delegates of the United States attended, their signatures were attached to the general act in the same manner as those of the plenipotentiaries of other governments, thus making the United States appear, without reserve or qualification, as signatories to a joint international engagement imposing on the signers the conservation of the territorial integrity of distant regions where we have no established interests or control.

"This government does not, however, regard its reservation of liberty of action in the premises as at all impaired; and holding that an engagement to share in the obligation of enforcing neutrality in the remote valley of the Congo would be an alliance whose responsibilities we are not in a position to ausme, I abstain from asking the sanction of the Senate to that general act."

The President does not even consider it worth while to submit the question to the Senate. It is so manifestly opposed to the traditions of the Democracy, whose business is to mind its own business and teach by example, not by interference. The sanction of the Senate not having

been obtained, of course the action of the mistaken delegates is of no effect, and the Republic lets the imperial
nations involve themselves in dangerous alliances upon
the Congo. We are soon to hear, no doubt, of disputes between these nations upon this very subject. When these
arise, the republican method can be once more referred
to with satisfaction.

I have mentioned three questions, all occurring in one
year, through any one of which future wars might have
arisen, had the Republic not known better than the Monarchy how to manage its foreign affairs. No, my readers,
it is not because America is so happily placed as to be
excluded from the necessity of interference, or that she
is not bound by guarantees and alliances with other powers, or freed from the necessity to engage in wars as
other nations do, but, as the instances just cited abundantly show, her envied position is the natural result of
resolute refusal to adopt the measures which must and
always do lead inevitably to wars. The Democracy does
not escape these terrible catastrophes by luck, but by
careful adherence from year to year, and in every emergency, to a sound policy. The American people are satisfied that the worst native government in the world is
better for its people than the best government which any
foreign power can supply; that governmental interference upon the part of a so-called civilized power, in the
affairs of the most barbarous tribe upon earth, is injurious to that tribe, and never under any circumstances
whatever can it prove beneficial, either for the undeveloped race or for the intruder. They are further satisfied
that, in the end, more speed is made in developing and
improving backward races by proving to them through
example the advantages of Democratic institutions than
is possible through violent interference. The man in
America who should preach that the nation should inter-

fere with distant races for their civilization, and for their good, would be voted either a fool or a hypocrite; such a classification need not be confined to this side of the Atlantic. There was nothing unkind in Mr. Leonard Courtney's policy of allowing the Egyptians "to stew in their own juice." This policy would have been permanently best for them. Mr. Courtney was the true statesman.

We ask careful readers to reflect upon what has been here shown, and consider whether the success achieved in the management of domestic questions is not admirably supplemented by the wonderful results attending the foreign relations of the Democracy. To the people of my native land I say, do not believe your statesmen when they attempt to excuse their failures and their follies by stating that the Republic escapes similar results because isolated from other nations while Britain is not. This is not true. The "silver streak" should act as an isolator more complete than any the Republic has; for the Republic has no such barrier either north or south. It is not further isolation which is required, but a government isolated from monarchical and aristocratical influences. When this is obtained there no difficulty will be found in the way of adopting the policy of the Triumphant Democracy, which avoids all entangling alliances, since the ally of one nation necessarily proclaims himself the enemy of others. Britain will then stand as the Republic stands, "The friend of all nations—the ally of none." The lesson which the Democracy teaches the Monarchy is that proper attention to its own affairs and freedom allowed to other nations to manage theirs in their own way, is the best and surest means to secure progress in political development throughout the world. Thus saith the Democracy. No nation can give to another any good which will compensate for the injury caused by interference with the sacred germ of self-government.

Chapter XVIII
THE GOVERNMENT'S NON-POLITICAL WORK

"Politically and socially the United States are a community living in a natural condition and conscious of doing so. And being in this healthy case and having this healthy consciousness, the community there uses its understanding with the soundness of health; it in general sees its political and social concerns straight, and sees them clear."—MATTHEW ARNOLD.

T HE man of ability in Britain is too often tempted into the political field. The rare talent for organization and administration of the American, on the other hand, usually finds a far more useful field in the management of affairs, much more important than politics, in a land which has finally settled all fundamental political problems and now rests at peace upon the rock of the political equality of the citizen, while the parent land is tossing about upon unruly seas, knowing no rest. I have often admired the various non-political bureaus at Washington as being strictly American—something which the Democracy has evolved far superior to any similar bureaus ever produced by monarchical forms of government. This is probably the ablest and purest service in the world. I had intended to visit Washington to examine the various branches of this work and write an account of them, but the time could never be spared. The happy idea occurred to me to send my secretary, Mr. Bridge, to perform the task, with a request to write up the subject and see what he could make of it. He has

done so well that I cannot do better than incorporate his
account, which is as follows:

One of Matthew Arnold's clear-thinking Yankees has
said, with epigrammatical brevity, that whenever three
Americans get together they organize: one becomes secretary, a second treasurer, and the other a standing committee of one to watch the executive. And, surely, this is
more than a saying. A people trained to govern itself,
even in the most minute affairs of local life, must of
necessity develop a great capacity for organization and
administration. Thus we find in America that groups of
men with allied interests invariably have an organization
to watch over the common weal. But for organization of
the completest and most comprehensive character it is
needful to see what the Federal Government is doing at
Washington. A visit to the numerous departments and
bureaus there is like a journey with "Alice in Wonder-
land." There in offices, some dingy, some magnificent,
one may see, lying on tables or on shelves, the charts
which indicate in every particular the nation's life and
health, its pulse-beats and respiration, its changing appetite and desires. Nay, the whole world, the universe itself
is told to "put out its wrist," that the experts may know
how it is doing. The present condition of crops in California or in Egypt; the degree of cloudiness in Dakota
or Maine; the number and condition of hogs in market
at Kansas City, or in transport to Chicago; the appearance of grasshoppers in Georgia; the wheat in store at
Duluth or New York; the number of bales of cotton at
Bombay or Mobile; the present position in mid-Atlantic
of a water-logged wreck, or a buoy adrift; a drought in
Arkansas; the southward flight of cranes in Dakota; the
change made yesterday in the revolving light in the bay
of Nagasaki, Japan; the coal at present available for
ships at St. Helena; the relative cloudiness of the planet

Mars—these and a thousand and one other matters, as diverse as can be imagined, are noted, docketed and labelled, every change being recorded almost as soon as it takes place.

Let me give an example. The Agricultural Department has in its service about ten thousand persons, dispersed all over the continent and a few throughout the world. Their service is mainly voluntary. From their reports is compiled a monthly record, which is exhibited in chambers of commerce and published in newspapers, giving the area and condition of crops throughout the world; cost of transportation to home and foreign markets; prices prevailing on farms and in principal cities; stocks on hand; requirements of consumption; sources of supply, etc. Thus the American farmer or merchant can always ascertain the amount of acreage in particular crops; the condition of the crops as regards growth, maturity, and probable yield; the number and local value of horses, cows, sheep, oxen or other cattle; the prices of labor in different localities; or any other data bearing on his work. Further, seeds are distributed and planted all over the vast continent, and the results of differing soils and conditions carefully noted, and deductions drawn as to the appropriate environment. Then the habits and life-history of insects and birds injurious to vegetation and the best means of destroying them are subjects occupying the attention of a separate division of the Department. In this work, specialists are at work in the field and laboratory; and the results of their labors, printed in special reports, are dispersed by the numerous local agricultural societies and institutions with which the Department is in intimate communion. In its own garden the Department cultivates new varieties of fruits and plants, for dissemination throughout the country. In this garden, Chinese sorghum or sugar-cane was first grown in

America, and the Chinese yam was introduced by the same means. The tea plant is another example, and the domestic product is largely consumed by the families who raise it. A Western orange planter writes to the Department:

"The Bahia orange sent to California ten years ago is conceded to be the best variety produced in this State. It is the largest size and finest flavor, and sells higher than any other kind. It is worth to California all that the Department of Agriculture has ever cost the country."

Amongst other work of the Department may be named the analyses of grains and fruits to determine their nutritive value, and analyses of soils and fertilizers; the microscopical study of plant diseases, especially fungi; the diffusion of knowledge concerning the uses of forest-trees in relation to agriculture; the investigation of specific diseases amongst cattle, and efforts to prevent or cure. In brief, everything that relates directly or even remotely to farming comes within the scope of the Agricultural Department. So complete is its supervision, that one examining its work is impelled to the belief that the American farmer has only to follow his instructions, and the government department will run his farm and see that it pays.

The United States Signal Service is another great organization, which, by its electric veins spread over a continent, receives crude material, assimilates it, and sends it back pulsating in a rich, life-giving stream. From Cape Breton Island to southern Oregon, and from San Diego, California, to Havana, an area three thousand miles long by two thousand miles wide, embracing one hundred and fifty intermediate stations, messages are simultaneously flashed over the wires to Washington twice a day, reporting all atmospheric phenomena. An

hour afterward the little room of the assistant signal officer in G Street, Washington, holds in its dingy precincts
a chart which indicates barometric pressure, direction and
velocity of wind, temperature, dew-point, rainfall, and
cloud areas of every part of the six million square miles
covered by its net-work of telegraphs. A stranger drop-
ping in at midnight of January 9, 1886, would have been
told that local snows were falling in the lake regions;
that the temperature had risen in the Gulf States; and
that the rivers had risen a foot at Cincinnati, Cairo, and
Memphis, and fallen five feet at Chattanooga; that cautionary off-shore signals were exhibited from Wilming-
ton to New York, and cautionary signals from New
Haven to Eastport. He would probably have been shown
the track of the storm which brought to Washington the
lowest barometric reading ever seen there; and the chart
being prepared under his eyes would show him the same
storm disappearing into Labrador. A few hours later the
finished chart, reproduced by telegraph, would be in the
office of every important newspaper, every postoffice,
thousands of railway stations and chambers of commerce
throughout the land from San Francisco to Boston, and
from Minneapolis to Key West in the Gulf Stream. The
people of New England would know on receiving the
morning paper that for the next thirty-two hours they
were to have cold, fair weather, with a rising barometer;
while those of Los Angeles, in lower California, and
Jacksonville, Florida, would be gladdened to know that
the cold wave was passing away. In Minnesota railway
officials would learn by the same report published in their
newspapers, or hanging in the ticket-office, that there
would be no immediate need of snow-ploughs, although
traffic would be slightly impeded by local snows. The
skipper who contemplated leaving New York and sailing

coastwise would hesitate on reading, at the breakfast
table, that cautionary signals were displayed; and influenced by the report of some army surgeon or amateur
meteorologist away in Dakota, he might possibly decide
to spenc' another day at home. All sorts and conditions
of men are affected by this chart. One postpones a journey; another, calculating on the arrival of grain in Eastern cities, sells before the market falls; emigrants decide to go West by the Southern Pacific route; physicians
relax their restraints as the improving weather admits
the invalid to the fresh air.

An amusing illustration of the extent to which the
warnings of the Weather Bureau are read and heeded
was lately afforded by a mistake made by a Western
observer in his report of local temperature. He reported
about forty degrees instead of four. The result was that
the officer who makes the predictions concluded from his
data that a warm wave was on its way east. Thirty millions of people living east of the Mississippi forthwith
left overcoats at home, and put on goloshes in preparation for a thaw, which never came. The unlucky weather
prophet at first excused the tardy arrival of the warm
wave by saying that Western railways were blocked with
snow, and arrivals of all kinds were delayed. But as the
days passed and no warm wave appeared, the newspapers launched forth an avalanche of ridicule—the American's mode of complaint—at the untruthful prophet;
and presently everybody in America was talking about
the young lieutenant in Washington, who, oblivious to
complainings and ridicule, went on drawing his isobars
and isotherms, and making his calculations and predictions. It implies great faith in this weather prophet, when
people complain that he ought to have corrected the
error made by the local observer in Colorado or Nevada.

It has come to this: that the weather prophet must not only predict correctly from his data, but even correct the data if these are wrong. Considering the haste with which the weather charts and predictions are prepared, it is surprising how few errors are made. Eighty-three per cent. of all the indications made last year for the Atlantic coast were justified; while on the Pacific the verifications averaged eighty-seven per cent. Of two thousand eight hundred and sixty-four cautionary signals displayed at ports, two thousand three hundred and one, or eighty per cent., were justified. Cold-wave signals were justified in about the same proportion, eight hundred and fifteen out of nine hundred and forty-six having been verified.

The Signal Service engages in much special work. It furnishes the *Farmer's Bulletin* with meteorological information that is of special interest to the agriculturist. This is an official publication, and the government has taken every available means to put it into the hands of the class for which it is intended. The rise and fall of rivers are watched, and timely warning given by telegraph of coming floods. The people of the Western plains receive similar warning of the approach of local storms, and the agriculturists, ranchmen, and others generally have twelve hours to prepare for the coming "Norther." The bureau has also undertaken the task of announcing the coming of locusts, grasshoppers, and other insect scourges. Frost-warnings for the benefit of the sugar industries of Louisiana and the orange growers of Florida have of late years made the Service popular in the South. The bureau has a very complete local service in the cotton belt which supplies information daily as to temperature and rainfall in every part of the district. Then once a month the Service publishes a review of meteorological observations made in every part of the world, including

Siberia, Greenland, Iceland, Borneo, Turkestan, Japan, China, and some places whose names are suggestive only of desolation and savagery.

An important extension of the Signal Service has been made to the sea-coast. Stations are placed at intervals along the coast, and connected by wire with each other, and with Washington. Her storm-flags and danger warnings are made visible to vessels moving off the coast. A ship sailing from the equator to New York as she passes Cape Henlopen may inquire by signals whether any hurricane is impending; and if so, whether she has time to reach Sandy Hook, or must take shelter behind the Delaware breakwater. Or a vessel bound south from New York may inquire at the capes of the Delaware whether any storm is likely to strike her before she can make Cape Hatteras, and receive full answer by telegraph from the chief signal officer at Washington, without interrupting his voyage. General Hazen, the chief signal officer, very properly thinks this division of his work of superlative importance. He says: "The time is not far distant when the possession of a coast not covered by sea-coast storm-signal and Signal Service stations, watching as sentinels each its own beat of sea and shore, and ready to summon aid by electric wires, will be held as much an evidence of semi-barbarism as is now among civilized nations the holding of any national coast without a system of lighthouse lights."

The achievements of the Signal Service are surprising even to those who know of its numerous observing stations spread over a land area nearly twice as great as that of Europe. But what shall we think of similar achievements on the ocean? If we are amazed at the extent of meteorological observations conducted on land, what will be our feelings on learning that similar work is being done on the sea, and predictions given for use of

mariners? I have before me a remarkable chart prepared
by Commander Bartlett, of the Navy.

And here mark the difference between a government
by the people and a government by a class: naval officers in America do not receive their highest rewards for
bombarding a defenceless Alexandria, or sacking a Ta-
matave. Their honors flow from life-saving services;
and shall it not be said that the Schleys and Bartletts of
America are greater than the Seymours and DeCourcys
of semi-civilized Europe whose "glory is to slay?" The
European method is to "make a solitude, and call it—
peace!" The American reverses the process, and by the
gentle arts of peace makes a teeming city of the solitude
and a garden of the wilderness.

To return to the chart, however. Here, at a glance, we
have the safe transatlantic route, carefully drawn to
avoid the ice, which in January hardly came further
south than latitude 53°. The sailing route to the equator,
calculated to give ships the benefit of the trade-winds, is
also as clear as careful drawing and good printing can
make it. The prevailing winds for the month are indicated, as well as the direction of ocean currents; while
special symbols mark the position of wrecks, buoys
adrift, water-spouts, and localities haunted by whales.
Directions for the use of oil in heavy seas are printed in
the corner of the chart. Derelicts drifting about in the
tracks of vessels are observed, and their changing position marked from month to month. Here, for example,
is a water-logged schooner, the "Twenty-one Friends,"
which, despite its name, has been more threatening than
twenty-one enemies. The vessel was abandoned off the
coast of Virginia on March 24. Being lumber laden she
continued to float; and by April 28 had drifted twelve
hundred miles. During the summer months she pursued
her solitary course across the Atlantic, ever followed by

watchful eyes in Washington. On September 20 she was apparently making for Queenstown, but suddenly headed off for Cape Finisterre, where she was seen early in December. She has probably ere this been towed into a Spanish port. Several other floating wrecks have been watched by anxious eyes in the hydrographic office, which, unable to send out and destroy such dangers in the track of commerce, could only give warning by indicating, as nearly as possible, their position. This wonderful chart is soon to give the positions of fogs in the north Atlantic. Thus the ferry between the old and new lands is ever being made safer. The weather predictions are, of course, only proximate, being largely based on the periodicity of meteorological changes in the north Atlantic. Here are examples of the weather indications given, copied from the chart for January, 1886:

"The storm area on the north Atlantic is at its maximum. Between the coast of the United States north of Cape Hatteras, and that of Europe, north of 47°, a gale of wind may be expected once in six days. These gales are most violent when the wind is between S. W. and N. W., but a large percentage do not develop a force of more than 10.

"Heavy northers may be expected along the Gulf coast of Mexico and Texas as often as once in ten days; some may extend as far east as Key West, and south over the Caribbean Sea to Aspinwall.

"There is little danger of ice in the routes of transatlantic steamers."

And then come recommendations in regard to passage off Cape Horn, which admirably show the deductive methods of modern weather prophets:

"In the summer season—that is, during the long days—there exists a barometric minimum over the vast plains of Patagonia; in consequence of the constant indrift due to this atmospheric condition the centres of depressions which travel from the Pacific to the Atlantic are deflected toward the north, causing violent storms in the region of Cape Horn and Tierra del Fuego. It is, therefore, desirable, after passing Staten Land, to stand to the southward as rapidly as possible to the 59th or 60th parallel, if the ice permits, where the influence of the navigable semicircle of the atmospheric whirl will be felt, in which relatively light north-east and south-east winds prevail and are favorable for making the passage into the Pacific."

"Here's fine revolution an' we had the trick to see 't." The Fuegians, who live in this inhospitable region, believe, as Fitzroy tells us, that storms are sent by evil spirits to punish the wicked; and here Captain Bartlett with unconscious iconoclasm says their cause is only a "barometric minimum" in Patagonia! These scientific experts are rapidly taking all romance out of life with their classifications and technical phraseology. If the Fuegians get a sight of Captain Bartlett's chart they will at once become a religionless race, for it is obviously vain to attempt to propitiate a barometric minimum.

The monthly publication of this encyclopædic chart is but a small part of the work of the Hydrographic Office. Branch offices are maintained at the principal ports to give information to mariners concerning routes, to adjust barometers and chronometers, to examine old charts, and point out their errors. Nearly eleven thousand persons received nautical information last year from the officers under the hydrographer; and nearly twelve thousand vessels were boarded and information collected from their log-books. Then every week notices to mariners are published and circulated all over the world, announcing changes in lights, buoys, and everything affecting navigation, whether at Kodono-Sima, in the Japanese inland sea, or in the Swash Channel at New York. The enormous work entailed by this may be gauged from the fact that there are about twenty thousand buoys in the world, and every change in color or position is immediately reported to the hydrographer, who at once announces the change to every American consul and to hundreds of mariners throughout the world. So, too, with the light-houses of the world, which are so numerous that a list of them fills six volumes of nearly three hundred pages each. This list, by the way, was compiled in the Hydrographic Office; and twenty days after receipt of the "copy," a three-hundred edition of this six-volume work returned from the government printers, ready for distribution in the navy. In this office the navy store of charts is kept; and every change referred to above is made on these charts by hand. The office likewise prints a great many charts itself; and of these the plates are regularly corrected to date. Altogether this Hydrographic Office is one of the wonders of Washington. If it were better known, it would probably be more subject to the invasion of sight-seers at the capital than the Washington monument. But it goes quietly along, working out its own salvation, and that of thousands of poor sailors who never heard of Captain Bartlett, the

> "Cherub that sits up aloft,
> To take care of the life of poor Jack."

In the same building is the Office of Naval Intelligence, where a chart is published, indicating from month to month the supply of coal at all the coaling stations of the world, and also the means of telegraphic communication accessible to mariners wherever they may find themselves.

In natural sequence should here come an account of the life-saving service, which, in America, is not an institution supported by voluntary contributions as in England, but is a department under the government. As a result of this difference, it is claimed that the American service is more efficient than that of Britain; that a discipline almost military in its severity is necessary to obtain the best results where groups of men are working under the conditions usual at wrecks. This is a healthful and worthy rivalry. Let this be the only form of contention between the mother and her child land. Details of this excellent organization are not called for here. Lord Salisbury's encomium is as applicable to the life-saving service as to the Senate—"marvellous in its efficiency and strength."

An important work done by the United States Army is the improvement of rivers and harbors. Here again, under republican institutions, the profession of arms has been turned to noble account. To do battle with shoals and snags would be considered poor work for the Burnabys and Hobarts of Britain; but in the Republic it has ever been held that to save life is a higher function than to destroy it. Great America's army, no larger than that of insignificant Roumania, is set to battle with nature, not with patriotic barbarians defending their own land. In the Signal Service, in the improvement of rivers and harbors, in the surveys of Western Territories, the Republic finds for her soldiers work which, while injuring no nation, brings them honor, and the country security and comfort. So extensive is the work done by the little army of the Republic, that in this division of rivers and harbors improvements alone, the year's report covers over three hundred pages. Upward of a hundred million dollars have been spent by the engineer corps on rivers and harbors since the beginning of the government; and the present annual appropriation for this purpose is still very large.

The light-house board, a division of the Treasury Department, has also done much important work in a like direction. It has control of nine hundred light-houses and light-ships, a thousand beacon lights on Western rivers, and more than four thousand buoys, fog signals, and other minor aids to navigation. It employs two thousand five hundred light-keepers, crews of light-ships, etc. Here again American ingenuity is conspicuous. Many dangerous reefs are marked by a whistling-buoy which can be heard more than fifteen miles. The rougher the sea the louder this automatic syren sends out its warning voice. This "Yankee notion" has been adopted by Europe.

Still tending to the facilitation of commerce is the Coast Survey, a division which has supplemented its regular function by much special scientific work. It has originated methods of determining longitude; explored the Gulf Stream; solved the problem of tides in the Gulf of Mexico, where only one tide occurs in twenty-four hours; studied the laws governing tidal currents, and the best methods of controlling them so as to aid navigation by deepening channels; and achieved many other valuable results.

The International Fisheries Exhibitions in London and Berlin have given a European renown to the work of the United States Fish Commission. At the closing of the London Exhibition, the Prince of Wales stated that "in many things pertaining to the fisheries, England is far behind the United States." And Professor Huxley has expressed his belief that no nation "has comprehended the question of dealing with fish in so thorough, excellent, and scientific a spirit as that of the United States." The Rev. W. S. Lach Szyrma, of Newlyn, England, has made a trite comparison. "At the Paris exhibition he considered Europe as a man in full vigor, Asia as a decrepit old man, America as a boy, Australia as a baby. In the present Fishery Exhibition the case was different. America was the gem of the exhibition." That these encomiums were justified is proved by the fact that at London the United States exhibit secured fifty gold medals, forty-seven of silver, thirty of bronze, and twenty-four diplomas. At the Berlin Exhibition America again headed the list, securing six gold medals out of ten. No wonder Europeans are astonished.

"If there be," wrote, in 1879, Sir Rose Price, author of "The Two Americas," "any race of people who exhibit more shrewdness than others in their ability to grasp and manipulate the apparently indistinct elements of what may lead to a commercial success, or be of ultimate benefit to their nation, those people are the Americans. No government throws away less money in useless expenditures, and no representative assembly more narrowly criticises waste; yet the Americans subsidize considerable sums of their national revenue for the purpose of restocking the rivers of the Eastern States by artificial culture, and with praiseworthy consideration their government supports several ably-conducted establishments from which fish ova are distributed gratis to all those who choose to apply. The very railroads assist this enterprise, and some by moderating their tariff, and others by generously conveying the ova free of charge, give every possible encouragement to what their common sense tells them must lead to so much national good. To expect an English Government to exhibit the same amount of foresight, or to practice a similar generosity, would be to credit them with virtues which have yet to be developed. The American example, however. should not be lost sight of."

The extent of the operations of the Fish Commission can only be barely indicated here. One fact alone shows the gigantic nature of its operations: it has planted German carp in *thirty thousand* separate bodies of water, distributed through all the States and Territories in the Union.

The American Navy adds to its numerous non-combatant functions the principal astronomical work done in the United States. It daily gives to every important city the correct time, and furnishes some data for the government publication, *The Nautical Almanac.* The naval observatory has acquired a just celebrity by its discovery of the satellites of Mars.

The Patent Office and museum is another important division of the government at Washington. Here are many thousand models of inventions of every possible kind. The list contains over four hundred different patents of a nut-lock. The policy of the Republic is to make the patent law the encouragement of inventors and not the means of revenue; with such good results that more than three hundred thousand patents have been issued since 1836. Last year the total patents issued exceeded twenty-four thousand—nearly eighty per cent. more than in 1880. Forty years ago the average number of patents issued annually did not exceed five or six hundred. If one wishes to realize the extent and versatility of the American inventor, it is needful to visit the enormous museum at the Patent Office. Miles of shelves and cases are filled with models, while acres of drawings and designs adorn the walls or lie hidden away in drawers. English visitors are usually greatly impressed with what they see there. Herbert Spencer could not withhold his admiration. He says:

"The enormous museum of patents which I saw in Washington is significant of the attention paid to inventors' claims; and the nation profits immensely from having, in this direction (though not in others), recognized property in mental products. Beyond question, in respect of mechanical appliances, the Americans are ahead of all nations."

One of the most important factors in the diffusion of knowledge among men is found in the system of international exchange carried on by the Smithsonian Institution. Originally intended for the distribution of its own publications, the Institution by degrees extended its privileges to learned societies of both hemispheres, and at present it forms a medium of scientific intercourse between about seven hundred home institutions and four thousand establishments distributed over all parts of the inhabited globe. The publications of any learned society in the world, whether in Japan, Norway, or California, if sent to Washington, will be distributed throughout the world, without cost to the sender. In 1885 about eighty thousand packages of books were thus sent from the Smithsonian Institution, containing in some cases its own publications, in others United States blue books, or the transactions of various learned societies, in America and elsewhere. Many railway and steamship lines carry these packages gratuitously. In this work the Smithsonian Institution stands alone. It is probably the most effective means of diffusing knowledge ever attempted, for it circulates to the ends of the world the knowledge which, put into volumes of transactions and blue books, has hitherto been relegated to the shelves of public libraries.

The official publications of the results of these bureaus are so numerous, that the United States Government is the largest printer and publisher in the world. In the book of estimates for the next fiscal year, just sent to Congress, $1,380,000 (£276,000) is asked for wages alone. There are on the pay-roll four hundred compositors. Fifty proof-readers are constantly employed, besides one hundred and fifteen press feeders and thirty-four ruling-machine feeders. The estimates call for one hundred thousand reams of printing paper, or forty-eight million sheets, equal to seven hundred and sixty-eight million pages. Of the annual report of the Commissioner of Agriculture, three hundred thousand copies are distributed. The reports of the Geological Survey, the Bureau of Ethnology, the reports of the Commission of Fish and Fisheries, the Bulletins of the National Museum, and hundreds of other documents and reports are sent free and postage paid almost to everybody or anybody. For the preparation of this chapter more than seventy separate government publications were obtained, the whole forming a perfect encyclopædia of governmental methods and results, of progress in art, science, and material resources; and this little library did not cost its collector a cent. Indeed, in some instances the books were sent free from Washington to New York. Such liberality is unparalleled. The Republic is clearly no niggard.

Much other extra governmental work is done either by the government or, as in the case of the Smithsonian Institution, under its direction; but further details are not called for here. However opinions may differ as to the propriety of a government engaging in every kind of non-governmental work, there can be no difference of opinion as to the excellent methods and important results of these bureaus in Washington. Most of them are models of equipment and method. Of the hundreds of thousands of packages sent out by Mr. Boehmer of the Smithsonian Institution not one has been lost. These offices are outside the influence of politics, and run on from year to year as freely and frictionless as if political parties were as distant as the satellites of Mars, or as deep down in the sea as the protoplasmal jelly fish about which these men of scientific light and leading write and print monologues at the public expense. Another fact elicited is that American progress is not limited to increasing crops or growing herds. In the higher domain of mind, in the alleviation of suffering, in the saving of life, in the facilitation of commerce, in the exploration of the world and the universe, in everything which tends to give life breadth as well as length, to make it more complete and more worth living, the Republic has contributed a very large quota.

This high estimate of the value of the government bureaus has often been concurred in by foreigners. More than one celebrated Englishman has lamented to me that his country should be so far behind in similar work. It is the cue of the ruling classes of Europe to misrepresent the government of the Democracy. They would have the people believe that it is weak, corrupt, and inefficient; but those who examine the subject carefully know it to be surprisingly strong, pure, efficient, and marvellously able. In none of the departments named in this chapter have politics the slightest influence. No politician could be found willing to apply any test but the suitability of the man for the work to be performed. These departments are generally under the control of permanent army and navy officers, who, I think my readers will not fail to note, are put by the Republic to much higher uses than the performance of their "professional" duties.

If we leave the general work performed under government control and consider what the people do for themselves, we are even more strongly impressed than ever by their extraordinary power of administration.

Take the city electrical service as an illustration. Police officers, fire-engine houses, hotels, cab stands, railway stations, banks, offices, and private houses are in direct electrical communication; and telephonic communication is rapidly becoming no less general.

The American fire department again is admittedly the best known. The horses are trained to rush out of their stalls into the shafts at the sound of the alarm, a single motion causes the harness to fall upon their backs. The men slide down posts from their bedrooms to the stable floor to economize time.

The ambulance corps is unknown beyond the Republic. Its headquarters are at the principal hospitals. Electric communication apprises the attendant of an accident, as in the case of the fire-engine; the ambulance with its soft bed, in charge of two surgeons, is instantly dashing through the streets, sounding its bell which notifies every vehicle to turn out of its path. In a short time the injured is lying upon a bed under charge of competent surgeons and is conveyed as rapidly as possible to the hospital. London physicians who see this American plan never fail to lament that even London has not yet attempted to produce any organization of like humane character.

This remarkable talent for organization which the American people possess probably was never more clearly displayed than in the Sanitary and Christian Commissions instituted by private citizens during the Civil War. The military rations of the government compared to those of any other government are to say the least exceedingly liberal—all well enough for professional soldiers, but for the patriotic volunteer who went forth from his home to defend the Union as a duty, that was quite another matter. Nothing was too good for him. The people demanded that as far as possible every luxury should be his; and to provide this committees were appointed in the cities and contributions solicited. The movement resulted in the two general organizations named above, which distributed more than $25,000,000 (£5,000,000) worth of extra supplies among the soldiers during the struggle.

The collection, transportation, and distribution of these supplies, which embraced everything from easy chairs for the wounded to delicacies for the sick, were admirably performed.

Bret Harte gives a poetic description of the enthusiastic reception accorded by the troops to the wagons of the Commission as they pushed to the front filled with the tender offerings of a grateful people.

"HOW ARE YOU, SANITARY?"

"Down the picket-guarded lane
  Rolled the comfort-laden wain,
  Cheered by shouts that shook the plain,
    Soldier-like and merry;
  Phrases such as camps may teach,
  Sabre-cuts of Saxon speech,
  Such as 'Bully!' 'Them's the peach!'
    'Wade in, Sanitary!'

"Right and left the caissons drew
  As the car went lumbering through,
  Quick succeeding in review
    Squadrons military;
  Sun-burnt men with beards like frieze,
  Smooth-faced boys, and cries like these,
  'U. S. San. Com.' 'That's the cheese!'
    'Pass in, Sanitary!'

"In such cheer it struggled on
  Till the battle front was won,
  Then the car, its journey done,
    Lo! was stationary;
  And where bullets whistling fly,
  Came the sadder, fainter cry,
  'Help us, brothers, ere we die,
    Save us, Sanitary!'

"Such the work. The phantom flies,
Wrapped in battle clouds that rise,
But the brave, whose dying eyes,
    Veiled and visionary,
See the jasper gates swung wide,
See the parted throng outside—
Hears the voice to those who ride:
    'Pass in, Sanitary!' "

But while these supplies were pushed forward to the front the attentions bestowed upon regiments passing to and from different fields of action were not less characteristic. I was then Superintendent of the Pennsylvania Railway at Pittsburg, through which, perhaps, more troops passed than through any other city. "Society" there determined that every regiment should be fed— banqueted would be nearer the correct word. No hungry volunteer should ever pass through that city without being made to feel that a grateful people wished to do him honor.

This being resolved upon, the young ladies, the daughters of the rich men, the millionaires, resolved that by no menials' hands should the defenders of their country be fed; they would organize and divide the duty among themselves, and with their own hands serve the men. The City Hall was placed at their disposal, tables and cooking arrangements provided, and the work began. Every night the list of ladies and gentlemen subject to call during that night was posted in the Hall. It mattered not at what hour a regiment or detachment of troops was to arrive, a telegram from my office apprised the City Hall, the men on duty went the rounds, one, two, three or four o'clock in the morning as the case might be, and one after another of the ladies were called and escorted through the darkness to the Hall.

One of the sights of my life—I can scarcely recall the scene without my eyes filling with tears even to-day—was to see a regiment of bronzed men (such splendid fellows, as unlike professional cutthroats as black is unlike white), to see them marched into the Hall, seated at tables loaded with the finest food, and then to witness their amazement as it dawned upon them, which, of course, it soon did, that the young women serving were not paid servants, but the darlings of society who had risen in the night and come forth to do them this honor.

The meal ended, the colonel rose and asked for three cheers for the Pittsburg Committee. Imagine how the boys in blue responded! But when, as was usually the case, there seemed something still lacking, some irrepressible longing which must find vent, and some one from the ranks called out, "Three cheers and a tiger for the young ladies of Pittsburg"—I hear their yell yet. I have seen enthusiastic crowds and heard ringing cheers, but of all the outbursts I ever heard, that of the bronzed veterans in honor of the young ladies of Pittsburg takes the palm; and mark you, men so treated went to the front determined to fight as they cheered. How could they fail, when the women of the land of their love came forth and said "Night or day, we are proud to be your servants." Six hundred and sixty-four thousand troops were fed in Pittsburg in the manner I have described. The funds were always forthcoming, and at one fair held in the city for the Sanitary Committee, $300,000 was netted (£60,000).

The age of miracles may be past. Matthew Arnold is authority for the statement that the case is closed against them, but to all those who extol the past and dwell upon its heroes and heroines, intimating that our own age is less heroic than some age which has preceded it, let us make answer, that for one true hero who existed in any age, a hundred surround us to-day; and as for heroines, the world has scarcely ever known what one was until the present age. Woman didn't know enough, as a rule, to be heroic until America educated her properly. There are a thousand heroines in the world to-day for every one any preceding age has produced. I thought twenty-odd years ago, and I am still of opinion, that there were more heroic young ladies in Pittsburg alone than the whole world could have produced not so very long ago, and Pittsburg was but one of many cities equally stirred to its depths. I have seen the American people, young, middle-aged and old, men and women, democrat and republican, touched upon the vital chord, and have heard and felt the response. Let no monarchical enemy of America—and all monarchists are her enemies—ever again flatter himself that the unity of the Republic does not command at all times the lives, the fortunes, and the sacred honor of the American people.

When the Americans determined to hold a Centennial Exhibition they went to work at it in the same business fashion; not a governmental official was called upon. They organized in Philadelphia, and the result was that not only was the display the best ever made in any country, according to the judgment of the foreign visitors, but the exhibition was visited by more people than ever before visited an exhibition. The facilities for transportation were such that the millions were moved on time and without accident. And, more marvellous than all else, the Centennial was so managed that it paid all expenses. An advance made by the government was repaid in full. The government had nothing to do with the management; it was exclusively an affair of the people and conducted throughout by them.

This universal self-dependence is manifest everywhere and in everything. I stood with Archibald Forbes on the

State Department steamer at Yorktown, Virginia, when the centennial anniversary of the surrender of Cornwallis was celebrated. We saw the disembarkation of some thirty thousand militia troops and a grand review. Mr. Forbes remarked, "What surprises me more than anything I have seen to-day, is the absence of a body of officials to take charge of the masses and assign them to places, etc. Every American seems to understand just where he is to go, what he is to do, and how best to do it, and then he quietly goes and does it, and all comes out successfully. There is nothing like this in Europe." Such is the universal testimony of competent foreign observers.

The cause of this self-governing capacity lies in the fact that from his earliest youth the republican feels himself a man. He is called upon to participate in the management of the local affairs of his township, county, or city, or in his relations with his fellows, in his church, trades-union, co-operative store, or reading-room, or even in his musical or dramatic society, base ball, cricket, or boating club. Everywhere he is ushered into a democratic system of government in which he stands upon an equal footing with his fellows, and in which he feels himself bound to exercise the rights of a citizen. Those with talent for management naturally rise to command in their small circles; and upon great public occasions, when thousands of such circles are massed, the orderly habits prevailing in each circle render possible the easy and proper management of the vast crowd.

We can confidently claim for the Democracy that it produces a people self-reliant beyond all others; a people who depend less upon governmental aid and more upon themselves in all the complex relations of society than any people hitherto known. At the same time their individual talent for organization and administration has been so concentrated as to produce through official channels various departments of universal benefit to the commonwealth, none of which have ever been equalled, and some of which have never even been attempted under monarchical government. We look in vain throughout the world for such beneficent organizations connected with the government of any country as those described in this chapter. So far, therefore, from the government of the people falling behind the government of a class in the art of government, we are amazed at the contrast presented between the old form and the new in favor of the new. The truth is that the monarchical form lacks the vigor and elasticity necessary to cope with the republican in any department of government whatever.

Chapter XIX
THE NATIONAL BALANCE SHEET

"A national debt is vicious in principle, deceitful in its effects upon the State which borrows, hurtful to posterity which must pay, and tending to lead rulers into useless wars and extravagant expenditure of public money."—THOMAS SPENCER.

NATIONAL debts grow troublesome. Year after year the burden they lay upon the productive energies of nations becomes harder and harder to bear. The twelve years between 1870 and 1882 have eclipsed all others in the amounts added to the already sorely burdened masses of Europe. Russia has saddled herself with $1,365,000,000 (£273,000,000) more debt in these short twelve years, an average increase of nearly $115,-000,000 (£23,000,000) per annum, a load fit to weigh an empire down. France's obligations have swollen to $2,215,000,000 (£443,000,000), and even Spain must be in the fashion and add $525,000,000 (£105,000,-000), and Italy, not to be behind in this mad race, has contracted $740,000,000 (£148,000,000) more, and even poor decaying Turkey has found credulous capitalists to lend her $90,000,000 (£18,000,000) during this period. The aggregate of these obligations in Europe has increased, since 1848, from $14,940,000,000 (£2,988,-000,000) to $20,935,000,000 (£4,187,000,000), and most of this increase has been consumed in wars which have left matters much as they were or would have been, if never waged. Such is the inevitable result of anti-democratic rule. Britain alone, let us record it to her credit, is the only power which has resolutely reduced her debt. It is less by $465,000,000 (£93,000,000) in 1884 than it was in 1857, while her wealth has enormously increased. It is easy to meet deficits by the proceeds of new loans, but it were well that nations should be of opinion with the Chinese laundryman of New York who refused to give a note bearing interest. "No notee," said our heathen Chinee, "notee walkee, walkee allee timee, walkee no sleepee." Nations forget this peculiarity of new issues; sleeping or waking the load of interest swells noiselessly on Saturdays and Sundays alike.

The Republic emulates her mother's example and cuts down her debt with unexampled rapidity. It is a curious fact that these, the two English-speaking nations, should be the only ones who resolutely set their faces strongly in the debt-discharging direction. The other races appear content to borrow as long as they can and let the future take care of itself. We are not without ominous signs that in some instances the strain upon their resources cannot be increased further without danger. Perhaps the Democracy is soon to awaken to the truth that these vast accumulations of debt have their real source in the rule of monarchs and courts, whose jealousies and dynastic ambitions, stimulated by the great military classes always created by them, produce the wars or continual preparation for wars which eat up the people's substance and add to their burdens year after year. A nation with a large standing army and navy is bound to make wars.

One great advantage which the Democracy has secured for itself in America is its comparative freedom from debt. The ratio of indebtedness to wealth is strikingly small. Including all debt, municipal, State, and national, it is but four and one-twentieth per cent., the national debt alone being less than three and a half per cent. as compared with eight and three-quarters per cent. in Britain; eleven and a third per cent. in France; twenty-two and a quarter per cent. in Italy; twenty-four and a half per cent. in Spain; and twenty-five and a half per cent. in Portugal. This was in 1880; since then the reduction of the national debt and the increase of wealth have been so great that it is close upon two per cent.—not one-fourth that of Britain, nor one-fifth that of France.

Contrary to the general impression, the debts of the various States which comprise the Union are trifling, being but six-tenths of one per cent. upon the valuation. Several States have no debt, others have revenues from public lands sufficient to pay the entire expenses of the State government. The municipal debts of the cities of America are likewise very small compared to those of Britain, being only one and two-tenths per cent. upon the valuation of city property.

Taking all the State and city debts of the Union and rating them according to valuation of property, both combined do not amount to one-fifth of the city debt of Manchester, nor to one-tenth the debt of Birmingham, while Liverpool owes in proportion to its wealth, £50 ($250) for every £1 ($5) owed by the cities of America taken as a whole. If we add to the municipal debts of America, the State, and also the national debt, Liverpool's municipal debt alone is still seven times greater than all of these combined. Even the city of Manchester, which does not rate high as a debtor, owes in its corporate capacity alone in proportion to its wealth two and a half times as much as the ratio of indebtedness of all American cities, all State debts, and all debts of the national government.

The cities of Great Britain owe $765,000,000 (£153,-

ooo,ooo) ; those of America, notwithstanding their greater number, population and wealth, only $575,000,-ooo (£115,000,000). If to the American municipal debt we add the debt of all the States we have only $865,-ooo,ooo (£173,000,000) for city and State debt as against $765,000,000 (£153,000,000) in Britain for city debt alone. The following are given by Mulhall:

Debt to Valuation		Debt to Valuation	
Liverpool,	. . . 32.5	Birmingham, .	. . 21.8
Manchester, .	. . 10.0	Leeds, . . .	. . . 15.8

London, which is in debt only three per cent., finds a worthy compeer in Philadelphia whose debt is even a fraction less. New York stands with Manchester at ten and four-tenths. America has no city so deeply involved as Liverpool, Birmingham, or Leeds. But in the case of Liverpool I am reminded of Artemus Ward who met in London a gentleman from that city who told him "there were some docks or something which he should have seen"; and in regard to Birmingham, no one who has been privileged to examine the work which that model of municipal life is doing will think the debt unwisely incurred. It is evident, however, that with all the push of the American, he is distanced by his illustrious ancestor in the race for debt in his corporate capacity.

The republican has so managed that the annual charge for all debt against him *per head* is not one-fourth of that which his brother in Britain has incurred. Every Briton owes of national debt, $110 (£22) ; every Frenchman, $120 (£24) ; every Italian, $90 (£18) ; while the American owes but $30 (£6). Every Canadian owes of public debt alone in *proportion to wealth,* $6.15 (£1 4s 6d) ; every Australian, $16.15 (£3 4s 6d), while,

as we have before seen, the American, with all his resources and rosy expectation, has burdened himself with
only $3.49 (14*s*), and is rapidly paying that off.

This is but one more added to the proofs that lie open
at all points to any one who will take the trouble to
examine and compare the facts that the masses made
equal politically under the sway of Democracy are not
prone to wild excesses. They have developed in the
United States into one of the most conservative communities in the world; conservative of their powerful government, of their Supreme Court and of their Senate,
and of all that makes for the security of civil and religious liberty, of the rights of property and the constitutional right of each individual citizen to the pursuit of
happiness in his own way, subject only to the limitations
that he interfere not with the enjoyment of the same
right by others. Let the student of American institutions
direct his attention to this fact, and see whether the Republic be not a very conservative Republic indeed. Nowhere is so well understood the difference between
liberty and license.

In 1835, just half a century ago, the Republic was not
only free from debt but had a surplus in the treasury.
How to dispose of this surplus was a matter of grave
concern. No wonder. For assuredly there existed no
precedent in the history of the world—and statesmen are
the slaves of precedent—to throw light upon the novel
question, not how a nation can wipe out its debt, that
would be hard enough, but how a nation is to get rid
of its surplus. Even as late as 1857, only twenty-eight
years ago, the debt was but $29,000,000, not £6,000,-
000. To-day the interest-bearing debt is about $1,500,-
000,000 (£300,000,000).

My readers may be ready to suggest that in no department has the Republic made greater progress than

in running into debt. Only twenty-eight years ago in debt thirty millions of dollars, and to-day fifty times that sum. It is quite as extraordinary an increase as is seen in her growth of wheat. Even the growth of the Bessemer steel industry does not much exceed it. And as we have had to award her the prize for rapid development in numerous branches over the mother land, let us hasten to credit the latter with setting an example to her precocious child, for the debt of Britain during the past thirty years has not only not increased, but has been reduced $310,000,-000 (£62,000,000).

The explanation of the increased debt of the Republic is, of course, found in the civil conflict between slavery and freedom. The two systems were antagonistic, and the irrepressible issue had to be met, sooner or later. Either the equality of the citizen was or was not the foundation of the State, there was no middle ground. It has been decided, but the cost was frightful. That part of it unpaid at the close of the struggle which could be represented by dollars, and that much the smaller part, amounted to $2,770,000,000 (£554,000,000). Unadjusted claims subsequently paid made the total debt more than $3,000,000,000 (£600,000,000). Thus stood the account in 1866, twenty years ago. The annual interest charge was no less than $146,000,000 (nearly £30,000,-000), being two millions sterling more than that of Britain. Many were the predictions throughout Europe that the masses who held full and unlimited sway would never take such a load upon their shoulders, and patiently endure the taxation necessary to carry it, much less pay it off. Much of the debt had been contracted at excessive rates of interest (six per cent.), and at periods when less than fifty per cent. in gold was obtained for the bonds issued. Universal suffrage could never be brought to pay back in gold the par value of such issues.

It would require a government of the educated and enlightened few, a monarchy for instance, to keep its financial honor untarnished. In Britain such ideas prevailed, especially among financiers. Mr. Gladstone gives them expression in "Kin Beyond the Sea:"

"In twelve years she (America) has reduced her debt by one hundred and fifty-eight million pounds, or at the rate of thirteen million pounds for each year.* In each twelve months she has done what we did in eight years; her self-command, self-denial, and wise forethought for the future have been, to say the least, eight-fold ours. These are facts which redounded greatly to her honor; and the historian will record with surprise that an enfranchised nation tolerated burdens which in this country a selected class, possessed of the representation, did not dare to face, and that the most unmitigated Democracy known to the annals of the world resolutely reduced at its own cost prospective liabilities of the State, which the aristocratic, and plutocratic, and monarchical Government of the United Kingdom had been contented ignobly to hand over to posterity."

The financiers of the Continent, and especially of Germany, knew the character of Democracy better, and profited accordingly. Many fortunes were made by investments in American bonds, which rapidly doubled in value. The most notable case in my own experience was that of an uncle in Scotland who had always, like John Bright, believed in the Republic, and had implicit faith in the American people in general, and perhaps in his nephew in particular. At the darkest hour of the conflict, when gold was worth nearly three times the value of currency, this staunch friend of the Republic remitted me a considerable sum of money, saying: "Invest this for me as you think best, but if you put it in United States bonds

*This rate of payment is little more than half the rate which has prevailed since 1880.

it will add to my pleasure, for then I can feel that in her hour of danger I have never lost faith in the Republic." Three times the value of his gold when remitted, and double the value of his patriotic investment since, has rewarded his faith in the triumph of Democracy.

Starting then twenty years ago, 1866, with $3,000,-000,000 (£600,000,000) as the national burden, with an annual interest charge of nearly $146,000,000 (£29,-200,000), what has the Democracy done up to January 1, 1885?

It has paid more than half of the huge sum and reduced it to less than $1,500,000,000 or £300,000,000. Here is the last monthly statement:

Debt, less cash in Treasury, January 1, 1886, $1,443,454,826
Debt, less cash in Treasury, December 1, 1885,   1,452,544,766
Decrease of Debt during the month, ...   9,089,940

The interest charge has fallen from $146,000,000 (£29,200,000) to $51,000,000 (£10,200,000). In two successive years of this period the reduction amounted to $270,000,000 (£54,000,000), but this rate being considered too rapid, taxes were repealed and large sums voted for increased pensions to the sailors and soldiers who crushed the rebellion.

The American has to continue for only twelve years more to reduce the national debt as he has for the past twenty years in order to wipe it out entirely. It may confidently be predicted that ere the close of this century, extraordinary events excepted, the last bond of the Republic will be publicly burned at Washington with imposing ceremonies, amidst the universal rejoicings of the people. The Democracy seems destined to set an example in many ways to the monarchies of the world, not the least important being that of a people resolutely pursuing the policy of reducing its debt until the last dollar is paid, that its resources may remain unimpaired to meet the emergencies which may arise to affect its position among the nations. Where is the monarchy which can vie with this Democracy in conservative finance or thoughtful care for its country's future? Mr. Gladstone says the parent land ignobly hands her debt over to posterity.

From a position so discredited that six per cent. bonds did not net more than half their par value in gold, the government of the people has risen in the estimation of the capitalists of the world to so high a point that its bonds bearing only three per cent. command a premium. What the world thinks of Democracy is this: that beyond the credit of any nation, even higher than that of Great Britain, stands the obligations of a government founded upon the equality of the citizen.

A leading Liberal Cabinet Minister (not Mr. Gladstone, nor Mr. Chamberlain, for they know America not much but still a little better), once asked me whether, in a contingency which then threatened to arise in the Republic, namely, a contested Presidential election (and which did indeed arise and passed away harmlessly), there would not be a revolution which would involve the stability of our institutions. My reply was, "Have you noticed to-day's quotations of American three per cents.?" "No," he said, "what are they?" "Higher than yours!" I said, and looked straight at him. That was all, but it was sufficient. Whenever a man, even a Liberal Cabinet Minister, begins to doubt the stability of a government of the people, for the people, and by the people, —and there are Liberal Ministers whose faith in the Democracy is as a grain of mustard seed—ask him why the credit of this new Democracy stands before that of the old Monarchy? Why would the world lend this Democracy more money and upon better terms than it would lend the best government of the few? Why does the world pay for American three per cents. more than it will pay for the British three per cents.? The answer is obvious. Because the reign of the whole of the people of a State is more secure than the reign of any class in a State can possibly be. A class may be upset, nay is sure to be sooner or later; the people are for ever and ever in power.

THE REVENUES OF THE GOVERNMENT

It was often said up to the breaking out of the slave-holders' rebellion in 1861, that the American did not know that he had a national government. Certainly as far as taxation was concerned he had little to remind him of the fact. In 1830 the total revenues collected were not quite $2 per head (8s); in 1840 they had fallen below $1.25 (5s), and even as late as 1860, twenty-five years ago, the American enjoyed all the blessings of government at a cost of $1.75 (7s) per annum. This was collected principally from customs and sales of public lands. There was no such thing known as an excise or internal tax, so that the citizen never was visited by a revenue officer of any kind. The American was born, lived, and died and was never asked to contribute a cent to his government. Unless he lived at a seaport and visited the custom-house he probably never saw a man whose duty it was to collect a national tax. In this blessed year of 1860, the total national revenue was only $56,000,000 (£11,200,000). In 1866 it reached its maximum or $558,000,000 (£111,600,000). After 1860 war taxes were necessary and the republican became aware of the fact, well known everywhere else, that it costs money to wage war. Internal and excise taxes were resorted to, and the citizen made the acquaintance of the revenue officer in full force. For the first time his revenues were made subject to an income tax, fairest of all taxes in theory, most odious of all in practice. It was, however, a graduated income tax which exempted the masses, but exacted five per cent. upon the largest incomes. During the six years from 1861 to 1867 enormous sums, from $400,000,000 to $500,000,000 (£80,000,000 to £100,-000,000), were raised by taxes by the general government. The republican might have fancied himself enjoying for a time the blessings of the British Monarchy, for the taxation was about equal, each nation drawing about $400,000,000 (£80,000,000) per annum from its people. With the collapse of the Rebellion the Republic began to set its finances in order. Taxes were rapidly reduced, and among the first to go was the income tax. Then followed the reduction or repeal of one internal tax after another till finally to-day, with the exception of the taxes on whiskey and tobacco, producing in the aggregate $145,000,000 (£29,000,000), but few of a trifling character remain. With these exceptions the republican knows nothing of internal taxation. His acquaintance with the revenue officer has almost ceased; once more he is free. He has neither income tax nor legacy duty.

We beg the careful attention of thoughtful moderate men to the fact that although the income tax was paid wholly by the few, yet the masses upon whom it had no direct bearing urged its repeal, because it was proved in practice that the honest were assessed while the dishonest escaped. Thus we get one more proof that the masses can always be trusted to act fairly and to correct injustice.

Since 1866, twenty years ago, when the national revenues from taxation amounted to a sum equal to $17 (£3 8s) drawn from each man, woman, and child in the country, they had fallen in 1880 to less than $7 (28s) and of this more than $1 (4*s*) per head went to reduce the debt.

The taxes are collected in America much as in Britain; about equally from foreign imports and from home products, although the recent rapid repeals and reduction of internal taxes in America have somewhat disturbed this division. In 1880 for instance the foreign products contributed more than the domestic, foreign giving $190,-000,000 (£38,000,000) and domestic $125,000,000 (£25,000,000). If it were not for the seemingly immovable determination of the people not to permit the manufacture of whiskey and tobacco to escape special taxation as articles, the free use of which should be discouraged, this difference between the production of taxation upon home and foreign products would soon be much greater; for to sweep away the entire department of internal revenue and thus reduce the number of government officials and free the citizen entirely from their supervision is a temptation hard to resist by the American people.

THE COST OF GOVERNMENT

We have seen that in 1880 the general government was in receipt of about $335,000,000 (say £67,000,-000), but notwithstanding great reductions made in taxes, both tariff and internal, the receipts of 1882 and 1883 reached $400,000,000 (£80,000,000). As the official figures for these years are obtainable, we shall use them instead of those for 1880. How, then, does the Republic get rid of her eighty millions sterling per annum, a revenue about equal to that collected by the British Government? Here is the record for 1883. First, of course, for interest upon the national debt; this required $50,000,000 (£10,000,000).

And what think you is the one greatest charge upon the State? For what does the Republic spend most money? Republics are proverbially ungrateful, you know, so says the monarchist. Well, this Republic certainly does not spend five millions of dollars per annum upon a single family and its appurtenances, nor lavish fortunes at one vote upon its high officials, or members of an aristocracy. Still it spends more money in pensions to the soldiers and sailors who served it in its hour of need than upon any branch of the service; more than upon army and navy combined, more than the interest upon its debt, more than upon anything else. To reward these men—not one man or a few high officers alone, as is the case in Britain and elsewhere in Europe, but every man, private as well as commander, in settled proportions as to rank—the Republic spent, in 1883, no less than $66,000,000 (£13,200,000). The Democracy may be trusted to insist, when they have the power, that the poor private who fought shall not be neglected when the State dispenses its rewards. I heard Mr. Cowen, the Radical —nay, the republican Member for Newcastle, in a speech in the House of Commons favoring the grant to Wolseley and Seymour, hold up to scorn the American Republic for the shabby manner in which it treated its servants. The difference here is just the difference between a monarchy and a republic, between the rule of the people and the rule of a class. In the monarchy the officers are unduly rewarded by their class, who are in power, whether called Liberal or Conservative, still their class, while the private, who has few or none of his class as legislators, is neglected. In a Republic the first care is for the masses in army or navy, the privates, and their widows and orphans; the officers come after, though both share liberally. So in all legislation, the good of the millions

first, the luxuries of the few afterward. This statement
is worth emphasizing. The Republic gives more each
year as rewards to the brave men, and their widows and
orphans, who defended the integrity of the nation when
assailed, than she thinks it worth while to expend in
maintaining all her military or naval forces. If republics
are, as a rule, ungrateful, at least we find a notable exception to the rule in the case of the greatest republic of
all. The truth is, that republics are only prudent in giving to the rich few, and prodigal to a fault in lavishing
upon the poorer masses. This is a failing which leans to
virtue's side. Time after time, since the close of the war,
the pension roll has been enlarged and the payments
increased. It seems as if the people could not lavish
enough upon, or sufficiently testify their gratitude to,
their soldiers and sailors who have been injured or have
become disabled in their service. Even as I am correct-
ing the proofs of this chapter the House of Representatives has passed by a vote of four to one an act to increase the pensions to soldiers' and sailors' widows
twenty-five per cent.—from $8 (£1 12s) to $10 (£2).

To the charge that republics are ungrateful, the reply
is that the one Republic gives more beyond their regular pay to its citizens who have served in army or navy
than all the other governments of the world combined.

Next in cost comes the War Department, which, although of ridiculously small dimensions compared with
that of other civilized nations, I regret to chronicle, cost
in 1883 no less than $49,000,000 (£9,800,000), which
was exceptionally great. The cost averages about $40,-
000,000 (£8,000,000). The Navy Department absorbed
$15,000,000 (£3,000,000).

As the army consists of but twenty-five thousand men,
we cannot look for any reduction there till the vast un-

occupied Territories are peopled. A strong-armed police force is required to keep the Indians in order, and the almost equally troublesome aggregate of restless spirits from all lands who naturally gravitate to the semi-civilized life which precedes the reign of law and order. In the States, as distinguished from the Territories, the American rarely sees a man in uniform, whose profession is the scientific killing of other men. The war expenditure, one is delighted to record, embraces the improvement of harbor and rivers, and upon this highly useful work many of the officers are constantly engaged. The engineer corps has rendered exceptionally valuable services in this department. An annual appropriation is made for improving rivers and harbors, $6,000,000 to $10,-000,000 (£1,200,000 to £2,000,000), and charged to the War Department, which sum should fairly be deducted from war expenditures, for this is not for destructive purposes, but emphatically in the interest of peace.

The American people annually spend upon the three hundred thousand Indians scattered over the land about $6,000,000, equal to $20 (£4) per Indian. They are as kindly treated as practicable. A commission of well-known philanthropic men of national reputation is appointed by the President to supervise all matters relating to these poor, unfortunate tribes. The success of the Indian policy may best be judged by the fact that out of the total number of three hundred and ten thousand no less than sixty-six thousand are reported civilized, the proof of civilization being that they pay taxes; and of all the proofs possible to adduce, we submit this is the most conclusive as to their civilization. The political economist, at least, will seek no further but rest satisfied. It is, indeed, surprising that one-fifth of all the Indians have abandoned their nomadic habits and embraced civilization. It is clear that the real live war-whooping Indian is being rapidly civilized off the face of the earth. We shall soon search as hopelessly over the prairies for the "noble redman" as we should do over Scotch moors and glens for the Rob Roy of Scott.

Under the head of miscellaneous come a thousand and one items of expenditure which embrace everything not under heads before given. The total is about $68,000,000 (about £13,600,000) in 1883. The principal items are for the agricultural, meteorological, and educational departments and the various bureaus which by their varied and useful functions cause such astonishment and admiration in foreign visitors to Washington.

As the Republic pays every official who renders service it may be interesting to compare the cost of this plan with that of the Monarchy which depends upon the gratuitous services of its legislators. Here is the account:

THE REPUBLIC

The President, ...	$ 50,000	£ 10,000
The Vice-President, ...	9,000	1,800
Seventy-four Senators ($5,000 or £1,000 each), ...	370,000	74,000
Three hundred and twenty-five Representatives ($5,000 or £1,000 each),	1,625,000	325,000
	$2,054,000	£410,800

THE MONARCHY

The Queen, ...	$3,100,000	£619,379
Prince and Princess of Wales, . . .	600,000	120,000
Other Members of the Royal Family .	600,000	121,000
	$4,300,000	£860,379

Members of the Cabinet are paid about the same in both countries.

I have known well-informed Britons who believed that the cost of government in America was greater than their own. The figures given prove that the amount paid by the Republic for the four hundred officers and legislators who form her governing body does not amount to half as much as the Monarchy squanders upon one family which has neither public duties nor official responsibility, and which sets an example of wasteful and showy living to the injury of the nation. One scarcely knows at which to wonder most, the fatuous folly of the people in permitting this great sum to go to one family, which is really one of the scandals of our age, or that any well educated family possessed of even ordinary sensibility can be found to take from a people, many of whom are sorely pressed for the necessaries of life, this enormous amount of their earnings and waste it upon their own mean and coarse extravagance. No fact more clearly proves the corrupting tendency of privilege or caste upon those unfortunately born under it. They must grow callous and unmindful of all but themselves.

It will puzzle my American readers to imagine how such enormous sums can possibly be spent upon one family. Sir Charles Dilke has charged that public funds, not embraced in the preceding figures, are squandered to the amount of £100,000 ($500,000) per annum upon yachts for Her Majesty's use, while, mark you, she has not been half a dozen times a year in a yacht during her entire reign. The sum spent by this model queen for useless pleasure-boats alone is greater than the American pays his President and Vice-President, the Cabinet officers, and all the Judges of the Supreme Court combined! One marvels, when such abuses are revealed, that any member of the royal family is safe in open day. We

should expect that public indignation would at least con-
centrate in one universal hiss. How long would Americans tolerate an abuse like this, think you? "Turn the
rascals out," would again be the cry, and the delinquents
would know better than to stay to be driven. The next
Cunarder would have them booked, under assumed
names, bound for happier climes. But the story does not
stop here. This family finds in every marriage of their
children a fresh plea for demanding more money, and
at every death they saddle the nation with the funeral expenses. The royal mother of her people cannot be
induced to support her own children during life, or even
to bury them decently at death, as long as the public can
be further bled. All this is no reflection upon the royal
family of England, for all other royal families do the
same. They are as good a royal family as anywhere to be
found. Certainly the queen is personally one of the best
women who ever occupied a throne. It is the fault of the
system that such callousness is bred in those who would
otherwise be good people. The system, not its victims,
is to blame. The royal family is only one of many evils
with which monarchical institutions infest a State. The
Financial Reform Almanac states that within the last
thirty-three years the dukes, earls, and marquises, with
their relatives, the inevitable brood of royalty, have
taken from the exchequer more than £66,000,000
($330,000,000), an average levy of two millions ster-
ling, being as great as the entire sum spent by the government for the education of the people. John Bright
told the people that the government was only a system
of outdoor relief for the aristocracy, and he was right,
as usual. It is well for the American people to get a
glimpse now and then of the blots of other lands, that
they may duly appreciate their own comparative purity.
Whenever an American is met abroad with the assertion

that government in the Republic is corrupt, he can safely say that for one ounce of corruption here, there is a full pound avoirdupois in Britain; for every "job" here, twenty yonder. Just look at some of the "jobs:" The Prince of Wales is colonel of this or that regiment, and draws salaries for duties he does not pretend to perform. He has many mean modes of drawing money from the public. He is made a field marshal; one brother gets a high command in India; the Duke of Edinburgh gets command of the Channel fleet; the Duke of Cambridge, although commander-in-chief, does not scorn to draw a salary as Ranger of Richmond Park, and royal favorites by the score monopolize sinecure positions. One nobleman gets £4,000 ($20,000) per year for walking backward before Her Majesty upon certain occasions, and so on through a chapter of "jobs," so long and irritating that no American could patiently read through it. When the Democracy gets firmly in the saddle we shall see a change in all this, a purifying of the Augean stables of Monarchy. The corruption then exposed will surprise the republican.

I do not believe that there could be found to-day a family whose head is in public life and honored by the Republic which would accept and use as the royal family accepts and uses the inordinate sums granted to them. The tendency of republicanism is to promote simplicity and a standard higher than that of showy living. President Cleveland in his inaugural message expresses the feelings of the people when he says:

"We should never be ashamed of the simplicity and prudential economies which are best suited to the operation of a republican form of government and most compatible with the mission of the American people. Those who are selected for a limited time to manage public affairs are still of the people, and may do much by their example to encourage, consistently with the dignity of their official functions, that plain way of life which among their fellow-citizens aids integrity and promotes thrift and prosperity."

The Monarchy thinks show grand; the Republic votes it vulgar.

To sum up all, the government of the people in eighteen years has reduced its debt at the average rate of $55,000,000 (£11,000,000) per annum and the interest charge of its debt in that period to one-third its cost.

It has abolished and reduced taxes from time to time, until there remains of internal taxation only the taxes upon whiskey and tobacco stamps, etc. The income tax has gone with the others. Such a record the world has not seen before.

The answer to doubters of the stability of Democracy, like Sir Henry Maine, is here: December, 1885,

Republican three per cents., ... $103\frac{1}{2}$
Monarchical three per cents., ... $99\frac{1}{2}$

Were the consols of America perpetual like those of Britain, and not redeemable at a fixed date, their value would be still higher. The triumph of Democracy is palpable in many departments. In education, in population, in wealth, in agriculture and in manufactures, in annual savings, as we have seen, it stands first, but to the conservative mind surely the last domain in which the Democracy could be expected to excel even Great Britain is that of credit. It has been the boast, one of the many proud boasts of the dear parent land, that her institutions were stable as the rock, as proved by her consols, which stood pre-eminent throughout the world. Now comes her republican child and plucks from her queenly head the golden round of public credit as hers of right and places it upon her own fair brow. It has been my privilege to claim many victories for Triumphant Democracy but surely the world will join me in saying none is more surprising than this, that its public credit stands before that of Great Britain and first in all the world.

Chapter XX
GENERAL REFLECTIONS

"The plain truth is, that educated Englishmen are slowly learning that the American Republic affords the best example of a conservative Democracy; and now that England is becoming democratic, respectable Englishmen are beginning to consider whether the Constitution of the United States may not afford means by which, under new democratic forms, may be preserved the political conservatism dear and habitual to the governing classes of England."—DICEY.

POLITICS are not the incessant theme in the Republic which they are in the Monarchy; this difference has its rise in two causes:

First. No party in America desires a change in any of the fundamental laws. If asked what important law I should change, I must perforce say none; the laws are perfect. These being settled as desired by all, it follows that a vital question can arise but seldom. The "outs" are left to insist that they could and would administer existing laws better or more purely than the "ins." A politician may safely be challenged to state wherein the Democratic and Republican parties of to-day differ. If one of the "outs" he will say that the "ins," having had control too long, have become corrupt, and that, as a new broom sweeps clean, a change is desirable. But ask him which if any of the national laws or forms he would change, and he is dumb.

Second. The nation having by universal suffrage and

equal districts committed to certain men the management
of affairs for a short term, public sentiment says, let them
have their innings and let us see how they succeed. We
shall soon judge them by their fruits. They cannot be
put out till their terms expire, therefore there is no
sense in our becoming excited over politics until the time
comes for an election. The party in opposition cannot
be stirred to action when it is impossible for it to obtain
power. Therefore the political excitement which always
exists in Britain, breaks out in the Republic only once
every four years. One hears more political discussion at
a dinner in London than during the whole season in New
York or Washington.

It is often charged that politics in the Republic are
generally in the hands of men of position and character
inferior to those of similar position in Britain. This is
quite true. Until the final form of her political institutions
is reached in Britain, the important work to be done will
attract able men. When the Civil War in America re-
vealed the need for able men, America's best came forward and met the need. A notable change took place in
the men who went to Washington. In the usual routine
of national life in America the only political work to be
done is such as young, briefless lawyers and unsuccessful
men of affairs can easily perform. They have to follow
public opinion, and are mere agents. When great issues
no longer divide the British people, the same result may
be expected. Able men not influenced by personal vanity
and desirous of leading lives of the greatest possible usefulness, will be unable to persuade themselves that attention to the administration of laws already fixed is the
highest field, and will leave it to those of inferior nature
or of less experience and ability. The highest ability and
purest character, though lost to politics, will not, however, be lost to the nation, but really constitute, in a

fuller sense, more vital parts of it, and enrich it more than they do now, when the final settlement of laws which is still to be made by the Democracy absorbs so much of their precious time.

The difference between the House of Commons and its offshoot in Washington, which is productive of the most far-reaching effects, but which has hitherto received but little public attention in Britain, is the payment of its members. This difference is fundamental. Pay members, and the people are then properly represented. Parliament is then the people's House. Refuse to pay members, and Parliament is primarily the House of the rich, and but imperfectly represents the masses. It is because this is the case that both Liberal and Conservative are found deprecating the payment of members, for it is still true that

> "Triumphing Tories and despairing Whigs
> Forget their feuds to save their wigs."

There are too many members of Parliament, both Liberal and Conservative, who owe their places to the fact that they can live without work to render any change easy. No other reason can be assigned against their payment, because members of the Cabinet and other great officers of State are paid as in America. Why should a Cabinet Minister receive a compensation and a Member none? It will hardly be contended that an ordinary Member of Parliament would be disgraced, or his tone lowered, by accepting remuneration for his services as do Mr. Gladstone and the Marquis of Salisbury. When the day arrives in which poor, but eminently capable, men can enter public life in Britain, there will be little left of aristocratic institutions. Until they can do so even the House of Commons is the house of the rich as the House of Lords is the house of the landlords. The people are represented by neither. In the Republic, as we have seen, every man serving the State is moderately compensated. But mark also this, no man is compelled to take it. Every one is free to serve the State gratuitously if he so desire.

The immense advantage resulting from the periodical election of officials is that they are less influenced by every passing wind of popular frenzy. They will more readily adopt a policy which their superior knowledge tells them will eventually produce good results, although at the moment excited popular opinion may be in opposition. They at least are firm and are able to steer steadily. They do not lose their official heads until their term of service ends. The Ministers and Members of Parliament in Great Britain are like so many agile performers on the tight rope; no one knows the moment they may fall, nor worst of all the cause which may throw them. The nation kept in a state of unhealthy suspense from day to day cannot unreservedly do its best work, because all eyes are turned to these performers. There is every morning the chance of a grand spill and no one wants to miss it. The fatal defect of the British Constitution, since the power of the Throne has gone, is a weak executive liable to be swept along by any gust of opinion. It cannot await the return of sober reason for the calm and settled conclusion of the people. It is the second and not the first will of the people which is the voice of God. As a consequence the members of the government do not hesitate to plead that they are not to be held responsible for such and such acts because public opinion demanded them; as if they had not been designated by the people expressly to withstand popular excitement and to do not what was popular but what was best, regardless of clamor. Such an excuse would be held in the Republic to disgrace a government.

The influence of this condition of affairs upon the politicians of Britain is bad in every respect. They are tempted to sacrifice so much in order to retain place, that instead of producing a body of men whose first and last thought is for principle, the tendency is to produce men who are pliable to a degree, and ready to adopt any measures necessary to maintain their own party in power. We lately saw the Conservative Party passing Liberal measures rather than resign office, and a short time ago we saw the Liberal Party adopting Tory policy in the Soudan simply because they were afraid that if they did not they might lose office. The most adroit, and must we say it, least scrupulous party managers and not the truest statesmen are the likeliest to receive and to retain power.

In these days when much is said against the dangers of Democracy, De Tocqueville's wise saying should be remembered: "Extreme democracy prevents the dangers of democracy." Not only is the Republic, with its fixed terms of office, its Supreme Court, and two chambers with real power a much more conservative form of government than the Monarchy, since the power passed from the aristocratic few into the masses, but the people themselves have become, under republican institutions, a much more conservative people in their political institutions than their progenitors—conservative in the sense that they desire no change. The national Constitution illustrates this. Since its adoption in 1787, it has only been twice amended, and for many years there has not been one word added or erased, and the recent amendments made have resulted solely from new questions created by the overthrow of slavery—on no other point has a word been changed. On the other hand, the British Constitution has been so tampered with from time to time as to become almost unrecognizable as its former self. Well may Tennyson write (I honor him by omitting "My Lord") :

"As to any 'vital' changes in our Constitution—I could wish that some of our prominent politicians, who look to America as their ideal, might borrow from her an equivalent to that conservatively restrictive provision under the Fifth Article of her Constitution. I believe that it would be a great safeguard to our own in these days of ignorant and reckless theorists."

Theories of the power of the people obtain in Britain which are unthought of in America. Such an Act as the recent Irish Land Bill, which took from the owners of property the right to let it in open market and enjoy the resulting revenues, would not find a party to advocate it, much less a House of Representatives to entertain it; and, even if passed by both Houses and approved by the President, the Supreme Court would be bound to make it void, for a change of the Constitution would be necessary to render such an act legitimate. Property! property! property! has been the cry of the owning and governing classes of the Monarchy, yet the sacred rights of property are to-day much more securely guarded by the Democracy of the Republic than they can possibly be in the Monarchy. The capitalist and property owner is more secure in the enjoyment of his property in the new than in the old country. In land, for instance, he has most citizens, sustaining him in his right, for the millions own the soil in small parcels. Property in land stands, and always has stood, upon the same footing as any other kind of property. Therefore land proprietorship has not been rendered odious by unfair advantages conferred upon it. Its sale is free; and it is taxed upon its value as other property is. It can be taken at a valuation for railways or other public purposes. There is neither primogeniture nor entail. The free play of the law of dispersion has been found quite sufficient to prevent the troubles which afflict Britain in its management of the soil. When land is free and subject only to the general laws regarding property, its owners will rest in peaceful possession, but never till then.

The cable informs us that in Mr. Gladstone's plan for home rule special means are to be taken to prevent unjust laws being enacted by the majority in Ireland against the landlords; and even so philosophic a man as my friend, Mr. Morley, is said to second the idea. With all due respect to these great men, I beg to point out that no surer means of making landlords more odious if possible than at present ever entered the human brain. It betrays a positive lack of knowledge of human nature. Give exceptional security or protection or privilege to any class, and it becomes at once a target for the bitter hostility of all other classes. Should unusual guarantees be provided, I venture to predict that instead of healing existing sores, these measures will become the seeds of graver ills to follow. Only what is equal rests in repose, and produces good fruit. There cannot be repose, *i. e.* equilibrium, without equality of the parts.

We see the question of a graduated income tax coming to the front in the Monarchy. The Republic had this when immense sums were required to meet the cost of the Civil War, but one of the first taxes abandoned at the close of the struggle was the income tax. It was not reduced or made uniform, it was abolished; nor has there ever been a movement to re-impose it. The masses favored its abolition although it was paid by the few, for all incomes below $2,000 (£400) per annum were exempt. I know of no temptation ever placed before a Democracy, to put the burden of the State upon the shoulders of the few rich citizens, as was contained in the suggestion not to inaugurate a new, but only to resist the repeal of this existing tax. They approved its repeal because it was shown that although theoretically the justest of all modes of taxation, in practice the honest citizen paid it and the dishonest escaped, and that to enforce its honest collection a thorough system of espionage and minute examination would be required not in harmony with the spirit of free institutions. The republican is jealous to a degree of the presence of a Government official armed with power to trouble him about anything.

Since the Republic adopted the Civil Service Reform, it can no longer be charged that at every change of administration the petty officials lose their places, which never was the case to the extent popularly believed in Britain, for the staff were necessarily retained. I know of no remaining charge against the Democracy except international copyright and the alleged corruption of local politics. As before explained, the "outs" must accuse the "ins" of corruption, since the policy of the one party is that of the other. There is rarely any other reason for a change to be alleged, but, as Matthew Arnold very justly observes, charges of personal corruption in America take the place of personal abuse in Britain, Salisbury being a "liar" and Gladstone a "madman" as these gentlemen are held to be respectively by their most violent opponents.

The question arises, if American officials—politicians, I should say, for the officers of the courts and the army and navy are beyond suspicion—if these be venal, where are those who have made fortunes by politics? I have known many hundreds of public men, but scarcely ever one who was not actually poor. When the tenure of office is short, and the chance is great that one of the opposite party will succeed and overhaul all accounts, malfeasance in office must be rare. So it is. Very few defalcations occur. In the case of legislators, who may be bribed to vote for measures, it is to be noted that but little private bill legislation is known. A general railway law in the States, and general laws by which questions are decided, leave but little room for personal aggrandizement. By this means legislation throughout the country is kept substantially pure. Comparing the National Legislature at Washington with the British Parliament, I am persuaded that at least as many votes are given from other considerations than those of honest conviction in the latter as in the former. True, the bribe is not the same in both cases; pecuniary considerations have less weight in the older land, but there is no radical difference whether members' votes are obtained by expected social rank or favor, or expected pecuniary gain. A longed-for title, even so poor a one as that of baronet, is not less a bribe than so many dollars. The nature reached by the dollar may be the lower man of the two, but he is at least not quite so silly. There is more sense in dollars than in titles—"patents of nobility"—at which the judicious laugh behind the wearer's back, whispering to each other: "Pity the weakness of a poor old man." Viewed thus broadly, there is as much corruption in politics in the mother as in the child land, only its form varies to suit the taste of its victims.

The trouble with the Liberal Party in Britain is that it *leaks at the top;* no sooner does a commoner do good work in Parliament and acquire a position as a Liberal member, than he gets a bee in his bonnet. He or his wife and family longs to leave the ranks of the people and receive a title. I know several worthy men who have deliberately sacrificed their proud position as English gentlemen, which is equal to any, to enter the ranks of aristocracy at the very lowest round of the ladder, some of them not even upon the ladder at all. By so doing they necessarily admit the idea of rank, and confess themselves the inferiors of all the other degrees of the class.

These men insult the people from which they sprung by leaving them for the aristocracy. By accepting rank the newly made baronet gives an implied pledge that his earnest Liberalism is at an end. He is simply bribed, and henceforth is a muzzled dog. If not, he is a traitor not only to his own class, but to the aristocracy he seeks to enter upon false pretences. By this sad aberration the Liberal Party is constantly denuded of its able men. A man born in the aristocracy may be respected, a commoner who accepts a new title rarely is, although he may be excused. The query of the old Duke, although not upon everybody's lips, is in everybody's thoughts: "How shall I treat these new men? They are not noblemen, and they have ceased to be gentlemen." Not until the Liberal is far too proud of his manhood to place himself beneath any order whatever, will the Liberal Party hold assured sway, or even very greatly deserve to do so.

The republican member could not be paid to change his name. The monarchist will generally pay largely in service for the ornamental appendage. The one is entirely free from all temptations to sacrifice conviction for social position, for this no government or official can influence in the slightest degree. The other must be possessed of rare independence indeed to escape the corrupting social influences which radiate from monarchical institutions.

If we compare the Senate with the House of Lords the most prejudiced mind must surely grant the palm to the republican assembly, for such a spectacle as a body constituting the land-holding class, so completely as to be justly called the House of Landlords, legislating upon land in its own interest, is not seen elsewhere. It is not a rare act for a member of the House in Washington to rise and beg to be excused from voting, because his personal interests are affected by a bill. Several presidents of national banks have done so when financial questions were being voted upon. We do not recall the name of any member of the Lords who has refrained from voting upon measures connected with the land. Even the bishops in that assembly may confidently be expected to vote against their coming expulsion instead of asking to be excused to act as public legislators to promote personal ends.

I have spoken strongly of the Supreme Court, and of the courts in general of the nation. The judiciary of the United States is pure and able, and possesses the confidence of the people to a degree equal to that justly reposed by the British people in their judiciary. Thirty years ago a few foreign-born citizens, known as the Tweed Ring, succeeded in casting such reproach upon two of the city judges of New York, as in the eyes of foreigners to envelop the entire judiciary of the country in a haze of suspicion, and at a later date, a disreputable railway owner, long since dead, corrupted another city judge. Even to this day, I find lingering traces of the bad effects of this in Britain. It is necessary to explain to them that New York City being then really controlled by the foreign-born vote, it was sometimes easy to elect as city judges very unsuitable material. These, however, it must be noted, were only city magistrates, their decisions being subject to appeal to higher courts. The discovery of this corrupt ring led to prompt corrections. The leader was required to surrender his property, imprisoned in the penitentiary and died there. Others fled abroad and lived in hiding. Had the people failed to rise and throw party considerations to the winds and sweep away the disgrace, we should indeed have reason to doubt the wisdom of popular institutions; on the contrary they rose *en masse,* and, incensed beyond measure, swept the rascals from place. Since then the city government has been comparatively pure.

Using the fact that three city magistrates in this foreign city of New York had become the tools of a corrupt ring as a foundation for general charges, I have heard people announce that in America the courts were not pure. This has no greater foundation than what I have stated. A moment's reflection will convince one that it would have been impossible for the commercial and manufacturing interests of the nation to develop so enormously were there not in every State pure and incorruptible tribunals to render justice between man and man. The truth is, that in settled parts of the Republic courts of justice are quite as pure as those in corresponding situations in Britain, and justice is much more cheaply and more expeditiously administered. In the semi-civilized Territories of the West, where society is beginning to crystallize, there are, of course, all kinds of courts, from the rude but generally strictly just vigilance committee to the improvised judge, who sits upon the plain pine board bench in his shirt sleeves, and has not the strictest ideas of either judicial dignity or integrity. It is of this kind of court that the story is told of the trial of a man charged with the most heinous of all crimes there—the stealing of a horse, the murder of a man in a street row being insignificant in comparison. The judge asked him if before sentence of death were pronounced he had anything to *offer* to the Court. "Wall, Judge," said he, "I haven't much, but if a hundred dollars would see me through, I think the boys" (looking appealingly around) "would raise it for me"; and they would have done so, no doubt, had the judge's words been meant as the prisoner construed them.

In due time all this will pass away, and the courts now in the wilds of Dakota or Montana will develop into tribunals as free from suspicion as those which elsewhere grace the settled districts. If a man, knowing both

countries well, had, unfortunately, to seek justice through
the courts, he would certainly elect to bring his action
upon this side of the Atlantic. The verdict would be much
more promptly rendered and the cost much less. In neither land, I make bold to say, would there arise in his
mind the faintest suspicion of the honor of the judges
who weighed and decided his cause according to the law
and the evidence, and this, I submit, is much to say for
both branches of the English-speaking race.

Throughout this book my readers will have noted how
frequently reference is made to the conservative nature
of the political institutions of the Republic, and to the
resulting trait of deep and abiding indisposition upon the
part of the people to enter upon novel measures or un-
tried fields of legislation. Lord Salisbury's sagacious
mind has evidently been struck with all this. The close
and critical study of the Constitution, and the various
branches of the American Government, which it has been
necessary for me to undertake in the preparation of this
book, has not shown me what I did not know before,
but I feel bound to say that, in a much fuller and clearer
light, the conservative character of these has been presented to me, and *per contra* that the essentially democratic structure of the British Constitution, with which I
have naturally compared the former in my progress, has
been shown to me in a remarkable degree. The political
power of the non-elective monarch being of the past,
although the social power is demoralizing upon the character of the people in every aspect of its operation, we
are face to face with a government without fixity of tenure, and consequently without power as against popular
tumult, exposed to every passion of the populace. As long
as the populace did not elect the Members of Parliament,
these were not compelled to give way to their temporary
moods, but now, when manhood suffrage practically

exists, these members are the servants of the masses, and will conform to their every whim. As a stanch republican with infinite confidence in the voice of the people, one who advocates the election of judges by universal suffrage, and who knows no civil rights which he is not perfectly willing to subject to the will of the majority, I warn the people of Britain that the masses are prone to be carried away temporarily by passion, and that it may be found necessary to interpose some shield between the sudden, fierce outburst of an excited population, and the officials subjected to the strain, not to thwart the sober judgment of the people, but to give it time to judge. This the Republic has in the fact that its executive and legislative officials are not subject to removal by the popular voice. They serve their appointed term, and they submit for approval or disapproval the results to their masters. With fixity of tenure in office, a Senate of which only one-third is changeable each two years, and a Supreme Court composed of judges approved by the Senate, and holding office for life, and retiring upon a pension, by whom all legislative acts are subject to be approved or rendered nugatory, our conservative friends will have no difficulty in reaching the conclusion that so far as security and sound government go, they have strangely missed the truth that the most democratic and ultra-republican community upon earth is much to be envied by the unfortunate supporters of an antiquated monarchical system which new conditions have robbed of all its virtues, leaving behind only forms bereft of power, to prevent liberty from degenerating into license, popular tumult from overthrowing governments, or to prevent the peaceful enjoyment of property from being ruthlessly disturbed. I speak thus earnestly because I was a sad witness from an advantageous stand-point of the supreme weakness of the government in regard to the late Egyptian War, and especially of its virtual abdication of authority in committing to a man wholly unsuited to perform delicate tasks, the issue of peace or war in the Soudan, not because he was, in the judgment of the Cabinet, the best agent, but because a whiff of manufactured popular opinion seemed for a moment to demand the appointment. In like manner responsibility for the Soudan has been disclaimed because the popular opinion demanded it. I speak thus, not of any one government or another, Liberal or Conservative. The evil is in the system. In the Republic no similar weakness is discernible. The government is secure and can consequently afford to do not what is popular at the moment, but that which will, from its good results, become popular by and by. Some of my Radical friends may esteem this strange doctrine for a republican to preach, but such are yet to learn that the equality of the citizen in a State is the surest antidote for violent revolutionary measures, and brings about, in many ways, deep and universal solicitude for calm, orderly administration. The privileges enjoyed by the masses are, in their estimation, far too precious to be disturbed. The Republic has seldom elected a popular orator, and never elected a public agitator as President. Believe me, the masses are only revolutionary when deprived of equality.

Here is the record of one century's harvest of Democracy:

1. The majority of the English-speaking race under one republican flag, at peace.

2. The nation which is pledged by act of both parties to offer amicable arbitration for the settlement of international disputes.

3. The nation which contains the smallest proportion of illiterates, the largest proportion of those who read and write.

4. The nation which spends least on war, and most

upon education; which has the smallest army and navy, in proportion to its population and wealth, of any maritime power in the world.

5. The nation which provides most generously during their lives for every soldier and sailor injured in its cause, and for their widows and orphans.

6. The nation in which the rights of the minority and of property are most secure.

7. The nation whose flag, wherever it floats over sea and land, is the symbol and guarantor of the equality of the citizen.

8. The nation in whose Constitution no man suggests improvement; whose laws as they stand are satisfactory to all citizens.

9. The nation which has the ideal Second Chamber, the most august assembly in the world—the American Senate.

10. The nation whose Supreme Court is the envy of the ex-Prime Minister of the parent land.

11. The nation whose Constitution is "the most perfect piece of work ever struck off at one time by the mind and purpose of man," according to the present Prime Minister of the parent land.

12. The nation most profoundly conservative of what is good, yet based upon the political equality of the citizen.

13. The wealthiest nation in the world.

14. The nation first in public credit, and in payment of debt.

15. The greatest agricultural nation in the world.

16. The greatest manufacturing nation in the world.

17. The greatest mining nation in the world.

Many of these laurels have hitherto adorned the brow of Britain, but her child has wrested them from her. The

precocious youth may be tempted to paraphrase Prince
Henry's boast to his father, and say to the world,

> "England is but my factor, good my lord,
>   To engross up glorious deeds on my behalf,
>   And I will call her to so strict account
>   That she shall render every glory up."

But please do not be so presumptuous, my triumphant
republican, I do not believe the *people* of Britain can be
beaten in the paths of peaceful triumphs even by their
precocious child. Just wait till you measure yourself with
them after they are equally well equipped. There are
signs that the masses are about to burst their bonds and
be free men. The British race, all equal citizens from
birth, will be a very different antagonist to the semi-serfs
you have so far easily excelled. Look about you and note
that transplanted here and enjoying for a few years similar conditions to yours the Briton does not fail to hold
his own and keep abreast of you in the race. Nor do his
children fail either to come to the front. Assuredly the
stuff is in these Island mastiffs. It is only improper training and lack of suitable stimulating nourishment to which
their statesmen have subjected them, that renders them
feeble. The strain is all right, and the training will soon
be all right too.

Much has been written upon the relations existing between Old England and New England. It is with deep
gratefulness that I can state that never in my day was the
regard, the reverence of the child land for the parent
land so warm, so sincere, so heartfelt. This was inevitable whenever the pangs of separation ceased to hurt, and
the more recent wounds excited by the unfortunate position taken by the Mother during the slave-holders' rebellion were duly healed. It was inevitable as soon as the

American mind became acquainted with the past history of the race from which he had sprung, and learned the total sum of that great debt which he owed to his progenitor. It is most gratifying to see that the admiration, the love of the American for Britain is in exact proportion to his knowledge and power. It is not the uncultivated man of the gulch who returns from a visit to the old home filled with pride of ancestry, and duly grateful to the pioneer land which in its bloody march toward civil and religious liberty

> "Through the long gorge to the far light hath won
> Its path upward and prevailed."

It is the Washington Irvings, the Nathaniel Hawthornes, the Russell Lowells, the Adamses, the Dudley Warners, the Wentworth Higginsons, the Edward Atkinsons—the men of whom we are proudest at home. Thus, in order that the republican may love Britain it is only necessary that he should know her. As this knowledge is yearly becoming more general, affection spreads and deepens.

So much for the younger land's share of the question.

And now, what are we to testify as to the feelings of the older land toward its forward child? My experience in this matter covers twenty years, in a few of which I have failed to visit my native land. I had a hard time of it for the first years, and often had occasion to say to myself, and not a few times to intimate to others, that "it was prodigious what these English did not know." I fought the cause of the Union year after year during the Rebellion. Only a few of the John Bright class among prominent men, ever and ever our staunchest friends, believed, what I often repeated, that "there was not enough of air on the North American continent to float two flags," and that the Democracy was firm and true. When the end came, and one flag was all the air did float, these doubters declared that the immense armies would never disband and retire to the peaceful avocations of life. How little these ignorant people knew of the men who fought for their country! They were soon surprised upon this point. I had to combat upon subsequent visits the general belief in financial circles that it was absurd to hope that a government of the masses would ever think of paying the national debt. It would be repudiated, of course. That danger passed, like the first. Then followed prophecies that the "greenback dodge" would be sanctioned by the people. That passed too. But well do I remember the difference with which I was received and listened to after these questions had been safely passed and the Republic had emerged from the struggle, a nation about to assume the front rank among those who had disparaged her.

I fear the governing classes at home never thoroughly respected the Republic, and hence could not respect its citizens, until it had shown not only its ability to overwhelm its own enemy, but to turn round upon France, and with a word drive the monarchical idea out of Mexico. And then it will be remembered that it called to account its own dear parent, who in her official capacity had acted abominably when her own child was in a death struggle with slavery, and asked her to please settle for the injury she had inflicted. This was for a time quite a staggering piece of presumption in the estimation of the haughty old monarchy, but, nevertheless, it was all settled by an act which marks an epoch in the history of the race, and gives to the two divisions of the Anglo-Saxon the proud position of having set the best example of the settlement of "international disputes by peaceful arbitration" which the world has yet seen. From this time forth it became extremely difficult for the privileged classes of Britain to hold up the Republic to the people as a mournful example of the folly of attempting to build up a State without privileged classes. Their hitherto broad charges now necessarily took on the phase of carping criticism.

America had not civil service; it turned out all its officials at the beginning of every administration. Well, America got civil service, and that subject was at an end. Then the best people did not enter into political life, and American politicians were corrupt; but the explanation of the first part of the charge, which is quite true as a general proposition, is, as I have shown, that where the laws of a country are perfect in the opinion of a people, and all is going on about to their liking, able and earnest men believe they can serve their fellow-men better in more useful fields than politics, which, after all, are but means to an end. "Oh, how dreadful, don't you know," said a young would-be swell to a young American lady —"how dreadful, you know, to be governed by people you would not visit, you know." "Probably," was the reply, "and how delightful, don't you know, to be governed by people who wouldn't visit you." All of the indictments against the Republic have about disappeared except one, and that will soon go as the cause is understood, for international copyright must soon be settled.

During the period covered by this sketch of my experience, Britons have begun to read and hear more and more about the Republic, and, I am happy to say, to run over and see for themselves what the main division of the race is about. The former visitor invariably made the mistake of taking the semi-English semi-foreign New York City for the country. He had seen most of what was to be seen if he had spent a week or two here. So he thought; but the really able Britons like Morley, Huxley, Froude, Freeman, Farrar, Irving, Rosebery, Bell, Richards, Pidgeon, Salt, Rogers, Seeley, Bryce, Spencer,

Arnold and others, who are all personages at home, and many of them personages anywhere, this class knows that until the Alleghany Mountains are crossed the real native is rarely to be met with. And certainly not unless the visitor has access to the homes of those who figure little or none in political life, can he see the best people of the land, or understand the foundation of personal worth upon which the State mainly rests. All this, these good friends of ours know quite well, and, upon the whole, I think the Americans may be quite satisfied with the impression they have made upon this class of British visitors. Their reports about America—as far as I have heard them, direct or from those to whom they have been spoken—have ever been flattering, so that to-day I believe the affection with which the republican regards the old land is in a fair way to be reciprocated.

When the example of a nation is quoted by the leading men of another in grave crises as the best means of rousing their own people to creditable action, we may safely infer that its position in their esteem is at least secure. The instances in which the Republic is now-a-days called upon to serve as the inspirer of the old land are too numerous to mention, but only last evening I read a speech, made by Mr. Chamberlain, who is certainly nearer to the Premiership of Britain than any one except Mr. Gladstone, from which I extract the following:

"To preserve the Union the Northern States of America poured out their blood and treasure like water, and fought and won the contest of our time; and if Englishmen still possess the courage and stubborn determination which were so lately the ancient characteristics of the race, and which were so conspicuous in the great American contest, we shall allow no temptation and no threat to check our resolution to maintain unimpaired the effective union of the three kingdoms that owe allegiance to the present sovereign."

Note the IF, my fellow-citizens. "If Englishmen still possess the courage and stubborn determination which were so conspicuous in the great American contest!" Americans have been praised for their energy, their devotion to education, and to religion, their inventiveness, their resolute payment of debt, and for other qualities, but who could have believed that a leading statesman of Britain would cite their high courage and stubbornness to the old bull-dog race of Britons. Mr. Chamberlain, however, in my opinion, does the original race injustice. Men decreed by the laws of a State unworthy at birth to be equal citizens thereof, have no reason to fight very hard and sacrifice much for its maintenance. Give them the rights of the American, my dear Mr. Chamberlain, and you will then see in Britain what patriotism means. There is not yet in Britain a government *of* the people but a government *and* a people. Government is always thought of by the masses as something not of, but apart and above, themselves. Americans may not be able to understand this, but it is quite natural in a country where government is based upon the idea that its head springs from a higher source than the voice of the people and is beyond their control, descending from parent to child by right of birth. Yet so advanced a man as Mr. Chamberlain, it will be observed, speaks of the three kingdoms which owe allegiance to the sovereign. He does not seem to realize that just as long as the people owe allegiance to anybody but themselves, so long will he look in vain to his countrymen for the love and devotion to their country which is found in the breasts of Americans for theirs. They have not equal reason to love the land which gave them birth. The Republic honors her children at birth with equality; the Monarchy stamps hers with the brand of inferiority.

The following from the most powerful Liberal organ in Britain, the *Spectator* (December 26, 1885), also invokes the action of the Republic as an example for the original race.

"Democracy ought to be strongest of all in its insistency that properly represented parts of the body corporate shall not set the body corporate at defiance and set up for themselves. It was found equal to this strength of purpose in the United States, and we trust that it will be found equal to it in the United Kingdom. The trial was severe, and the conflict was long; but the tenacity of the Democracy triumphed at last. We believe that it will be so with us. If we show indecision, if we show weakness, if we show that the spirit of determination to put down the Secessionist tendencies of the day is not high within us, we shall undoubtedly be giving the first serious signal of national decay. We do not believe that it will be so. We believe that Great Britain, directly the situation comes out clearly before her, will nerve herself to *as strenuous* a policy as that which secured the integrity of the American nation in the great crisis of 1861."

Democracy was found equal in the United States and *we trust* it will be found equal in the United Kingdom! The Democracy triumphed and *we believe* it will be so with us; we BELIEVE that Great Britain will "nerve herself to *as strenuous* a policy as that which secured the integrity of the American nation in the great crisis of 1861!"

If the old land, you see, only comes up to the standard set by the new, it is all that is even hoped for, but under monarchical institutions it is impossible they can ever reach the standard.

Monarchical institutions emasculate even educated men, and the ignorant masses in greater degree. There is probably not a man of the rank of Cabinet Minister in Britain, no not one, but would have bowed, and that

low and repeatedly, if desired, to Gesler's cap, and smiled
to think he had done himself no injury by so doing, since
it was not a "practical question." Of course men can kiss
the hand of the Queen, as one is proud to kiss the hand
of any good woman, but how will it be when the Prince
of Wales holds out his hand, and Messrs. Chamberlain
and Morley, Collings and Illingworth, Trevelyan and
Fowler, and others are required to kiss *that!* I am not
sure but that even these Radicals may find it no stain
upon their manhood to incur this degradation, but the
first man who feels as he ought to feel, will either smile
when the hand is extended at the suggestion that he could
so demean himself, and give it a good hearty shake, or
knock his Royal Highness down. I have heard of ladies
of high rank who say they never would kiss the Prince's
hand, but they need not trouble themselves upon this
score, for the Prince will make himself immensely popular by reversing the process and kissing their hands instead. He is a gallant gentleman. It is not the man we
declaim against but the effect of the customs, fit only for
serfs, by which monarchy is surrounded, and which tend
to keep men—even Radicals—subservient.

The masses of Britain always have been, and are now
with the Republic to the core. Their warmest sympathies and intensest admiration are bestowed upon the
Republic. This sentiment has already reached the educated Liberals; the more pronounced the liberalism, the
more affectionately is the freer land regarded. The position of the country and its recent amazing strides, the
peace and content which everywhere prevail, and, beyond all, the regard for law and order and for the rights
of property, the unmistakable conservatism of the American people upon which I have dwelt, are fast making a
decided impression upon the hitherto timid and misbe-

lieving but educated people of the Conservative party. They cannot quite account for it, and are not yet open to the truth that political institutions, which make all citizens equal, necessarily produce the virtues which I have recounted; but as no other explanation is seemingly possible, we may soon expect them to advance to its admission. Tory Democracy may not, then, be an apparent misnomer, after all.

I should like Americans to observe how rapidly the thinkers of Europe are discovering the merits of their institutions and example. Several of Britain's foremost men have recently visited the country. The historian Freeman came first. Listen to what he says:

"Your Constitution above all has gone through the most frightful of trials, and it has stood the test. I remember twenty years ago how shallow people were crying out that the principle of a federal system was proved to be worthless because certain members of a particular confederation wished to separate from it. I can only suppose that they fancied that no revolts, no separations, no dismemberments, had ever taken place in lands governed by kings. The retort is so obvious that I need hardly point out that the recent experience of Greece, of Belgium, of Poland, of Lombardy, of Sicily, of half-a-dozen European lands, proved at least as much against monarchy as the secession of the Southern States proved against federalism. At all events, they did not stop to think that, after all, they were only bucking up one federal commonwealth against another. They must have shut their eyes to the fact that the Southern Confederacy, in its short-lived constitution, re-enacted all the essential features of the Constitution of the United States. The fact is one which I should turn about in another way. I can conceive no more speaking tribute to the wisdom of any political system than the fact that the men who were most dissatisfied with its actual administration, the men who were most anxious to escape from its actual fellowship, of set purpose re-enacted its chief provisions for their own separate use."

Mr. Freeman was followed by their foremost literary man, Mr. Matthew Arnold. Here is his conclusion:

"As one watches the play of their [the Americans'] institutions, the image suggests itself to one's mind of a man in a suit of clothes which fits him to perfection, leaving all his movements unimpeded and easy. It is loose where it ought to be loose, and it sits close where its sitting close is an advantage. The central Government of the United States keeps in its own hands those functions which, if the nation is to have real unity, ought to be kept there; those functions it takes to itself and no others. The State governments and the municipal governments provide people with the fullest liberty of managing their own affairs, and afford, besides, a constant and invaluable school of practical experience. This wonderful suit of clothes, again (to recur to our image), is found also to adapt itself naturally to the wearer's growth and to admit of all enlargements as they successively arise."

The third of the trio is the historian Mr. Froude, and here is his verdict:

"The problem of how to combine a number of self-governed communities into a single commonwealth, which now lies before Englishmen who desire to see a federation of the empire, has been solved, and solved completely, in the American Union. The bond which, at the Declaration of Independence, was looser than that which now connects Australia and England, became strengthened by time and custom. The attempt to break it was successfully resisted by the sword, and the American Republic is, and is to continue so far as reasonable foresight can anticipate, one and henceforth indissoluble.

"Each State is free to manage its own private affairs, to legislate for itself, subject to the fundamental laws of the Union, and to administer its own internal government, with this reservation only—that separation is not to be thought of. The right to separate was settled once for all by a civil war which startled the world by its magnitude, but which, terrible though it might be, was not disproportioned to the issues which were involved. Had the South succeeded in winning independence, the cloth once rent would have been rent again. There would not have been one America, but many Americas. The New World would have trodden over again in the tracks of the old. There would have been rival communities with rival constitutions, democracies passing into military despotisms, standing armies, intrigues and quarrels, and wars upon wars. The completeness with which the issue has been accepted shows that the Americans understood the alternative that lay before them. That the wound so easily healed was a proof that they had looked the alternative in the face, and were satisfied with the verdict which had been pronounced.

"And well may they be satisfied. The dimensions and value of any single man depend on the body of which he is a member. As an individual, with his horizon bounded by his personal interests, he remains, however high his gifts, but a mean creature. His thoughts are small, his aims narrow; he has no common concerns or common convictions which bind him to his fellows. He lives, he works, he wins a share—small or great—of the necessaries or luxuries which circumstances throw within his reach, and then he dies and there is an end of him. A man, on the other hand, who is more than himself, who is part of an institution, who has devoted himself to a cause—or is a citizen of an imperial power—expands to the scope and fullness of the larger organism; and the grander the organization, the larger and more important the unit that knows that he belongs to it. His thoughts are wider, his interests less selfish, his ambitions ampler and nobler. As a granite block is to the atoms of which it is composed when disintegrated, so are men in organic combination to the same men only aggregated together. Each particle contracts new qualities which are created by the intimacy of union. Individual Jesuits are no more than other mortals. The Jesuits as a society are not mortal at all, and rule the Catholic world. Behind each American citizen America is standing, and he knows it, and is the man that he is because he knows it. The Anglo-Americans divided might have fared no better than the Spanish colonies. The Anglo-Americans united command the respectful fear of all mankind; and, as Pericles said of the Athenians, each unit of them acts as if the fortunes of his country depended only on himself. A great nation makes great men; a small nation makes little men."

We have also as recent witness the English writer Mackenzie, author of a remarkable history of the nineteenth century, and an excellent work on America. Here is the last paragraph of his work:

"America has still something to learn from the riper experience and more patient thinking of England. But it has been her privilege to teach to England and the world one of the grandest of lessons. She has asserted the political rights of the masses. She has proved to us that it is safe and wise to trust the people. She has taught that the government of the people should be 'by the people and for the people.' Let our last word here be a thankful acknowledgment of the inestimable service which she has thus rendered to mankind."

And, finally, we have Sir Henry Maine's "Popular Government," a work at which we must often smile, for Sir Henry is sorely afraid of Democracy, and charges popular government with all the ups and downs of the Spanish republics of South America and the French republic, and never, seemingly, stops to ask himself how these communities have gone on, or how they would go on were the rule of a class again tried by them—how France did under the monarchy or the empire for instance. Nevertheless, when he comes to the American Constitution he gives us pages of favorable comment, and closes his book with these remarkable words:

"The powers and disabilities attached to the United States and to the several States by the Federal Constitution, and placed under the protection of the deliberately contrived securities we have described, have determined the whole course of American history. That history began, as all its records abundantly show, in a condition of society produced by war and revolution, which might have condemned the great Northern Republic to a fate not unlike that of her disorderly sisters in South America. But the provisions of the Constitution have acted on her like those dams and dykes which strike the eye of the traveller along the Rhine, controlling the course of a mighty river which begins amid mountain torrents, and turning it into one of the most equable waterways in the world.

"When the American Constitution was framed there was no such sacredness to be expected for it as before 1789 was supposed to attach to all parts of the British Constitution. There was every prospect of political mobility, if not of political disorder. The signal success of the Constitution of the United States in stemming these tendencies is, no doubt, owing in part to the great portion of the British institutions which were preserved in it; but it is also attributable to the sagacity with which the American statesmen filled up the interstices left by the inapplicability of certain of the then existing British institutions to the emancipated colonies. This sagacity stands out in every part of the 'Federalist,' and it may be tracked in every page of subsequent American history. It may well fill the Englishmen who live *in fæce Romuli* with wonder and envy."

So, my fellow Republicans, the world is coming rapidly to your feet, the American Constitution is being more and more generally regarded as the model for all new nations to adopt and for all old nations to strive for.

As I have said in a previous chapter, Americans need not expect the aristocracy ever to regard with other than prejudiced mind and vindictive hate a State which flaunts in their faces the truth that their existence is a positive injury to the nation upon which they feed like parasites. How can a peer of Britain who is not more of a man than a peer, which few of them are—how can he have the slightest wish for the prosperity of a nation which would not tolerate his existence as a peer within its bounds?

If any man believe that Queen Victoria, or the Prince of Wales, or Kaiser William, or any member of a royal family could receive more welcome news than that of the downfall of the Republic which proves every hour to the parent lands that these royal people are only ex- crescences upon the State, the setters of bad example, and the very core round which the worst vices of Eng- lish life gather and fester—if any one can believe this, his estimate of human nature differs from mine. There is not a crowned head in the world, nor a member of a royal family who could refrain from secretly rejoicing at any disaster which befell a republic, and the joy would be in proportion to the magnitude of the disaster. This is not at all to be wondered at. Indeed it is obviously in- evitable, and I must confess that when I hear of the downfall of any hereditary privilege I croon to myself, and am happy. No message so sweet. I have my revenge. The overthrow of a monarchy and the birth of a repub- lic, as in the case of France, is a perfect well-spring of joy to my heart. I fancy there are few Americans who are not equally delighted. Then let them know and un- derstand that with a bitter hate is the Republic hated by the royal families and aristocrats, no matter how well they may dissemble and appear to wish it well for policy's sake. Let but the Republic be in danger and it will soon see how ready they are to stab it from behind. Fortu- nately their power to injure grows less and less, and even to-day is quite impotent to arrest the constantly increas- ing volume of genuine admiration and affection with which this country is regarded by all but this small nox- ious class which is rapidly fading away.

The assimilation of the political institutions of the two countries proceeds apace, by the action of the older in the direction of the newer land. Year after year some difference is obliterated. Yesterday it was an extension of the suffrage, to-day it is universal and compulsory edu- cation, to-morrow the joining of law and equity, and the next day it will be the abolition of primogeniture and entail; a few years more and all that remains of feudal-istic times will have disappeared and the political insti-tutions of the two divisions will be practically the same, with only such slight variations of structure as adapt them to the slightly varying conditions by which they are surrounded. It has been and is my chief ambition to do what little I can, if anything, to hasten this process, that the two divisions may thereby be brought more closely into unison; that the bonds between my dear native land and my beloved adopted land may be strengthened, and drawn more tightly together. For sure am I, who am in part the child of both, and whose love for the one and the other is as the love of man for mother and wife, sure am I that the better these grand divisions of the British race know each other, the stronger will grow the attach-ment between them, and just as sure am I that in their genuine affection and indissoluble alliance lie the best hopes for the elevation of the human race. God grant, therefore, that the future of my native and adopted lands may fulfill the hope of the staunchest, ablest, and most powerful friend of this land and the Great Commoner of his own, that "although they may be two nations, they may be but one people." Thus spake John Bright, and echoing once more that fond hope, I lay down my pen and bid my readers on both sides of the Atlantic—Fare-well.

THE END

INDEX

Academy of Design, National, 259.

Adams, John, 124, 147, 170.

Affairs, foreign, 317.

Agriculture, 144; capital invested in, 163; capital invested in farms, 145; comparative table of progress, 147; crops, 152; farm system, 150; fifty years ago, 91; improved implements in, 51; in 1880, 91; live stock, 158; Mulhall's table, 152; ratio of females employed in, 101; statistics in 1880, 146.

Agriculturists, American statesmen as, 147; number of, 100.

Allegheny City, 53, 194.

Ambulance corps, an American institution, 349.

American hive, the, 100.

Americans, fifty-five years ago, 68; of to-day, 72.

Animals, live, export of, 165, 215.

Appleton, D., & Co., 285.

Antimony, 205.

Architecture in United States, 263.

Arfedson, 53, 66, 228.

Army, 5, 306.

Arnold, Edwin, 286; Matthew, 20, 23, 273, 286, 330, 352, 384, 402.

Arsenic, 205.

Art, Americans as patrons of, 316.

Art and music, 254.

Art Union, American, 259.

Athenæum, Boston, 259.

Atkinson, Edward, 31, 219, 220.

Atlas, Statistical, of United States, 285.

Australia, 88.

Authorities quoted: Adams, John, 124; Addison, 267; Arfedson, 53, 66, 228; Arnold, Matthew, 330, 402; Atkinson, Edward, 31, 219, 220; Bell, Lowthian, 94; Berkeley, Sir William, 106; Bishop, Mr., 170; *Blackwood's Magazine*, 1824, 253; Boston Records, 106; Bright, John, 407; Bryant, William Cullen, 283; Burke, Edmund, 131; Caird, Mr., 166; Carpenter, Philo, Mr., 230; Chamberlain, Mr., 397; Channing, 168; Cleveland, President, 223, 321, 326, 327, 374; Cobbett, William, 37, 61; Confucius, 102; Cowen, Mr., 368; Cowper, 11; Cutter, Rev. Manasseh, 247; D'Argenson, Marquis, 226; *De Bow's Commercial Magazine*, 132; *De Bow's Review*, 61; De Tocqueville, 36, 381; Dicey, Mr., 377; Dryden, 272; Du Boy's "History of Criminal Law," 143; Eigenrac, 58; *Financial Reform Almanac*, 373, 374; Fisher, Dr. Swainson, 39; Fiske, John, "American Political Ideas," 82; Forbes, Archibald, 353; Fraser, Rev. Mr., 114; Freeman, Edward A., 401; Froude, James Anthony, 106, 402; Giffen, Mr., 166; Gladstone, Mr., 290, 316, 323, 362; Guizot, 253; Hall, Capt. Basil, 53; Harte, Bret, 350; Hazen, General, 337; Hinton, "Topography of United States," 90; Holmes, O. W., 213; Huxley,

neapolis, 46; in New York, 40; in Philadelphia, 40, 53; in Pittsburgh, 53; in Rochester, 53; in San Francisco, 43; in Scranton, 53; in St. Paul, 46; in Toledo, 53; in Minnesota, 46; in Iowa in 1830 and 1880, 37; in the United States, 1; in Wisconsin, 39; in the fifty largest cities, 41; proportion of colored to white, 34; white between Lake Michigan and Pacific, in 1835, 39; yearly increase of, 39.

Postal system, 62.

President, extracts from message of, 321, 326, 327; power of, 305, 309; and Prime Minister of Britain compared, 313.

Produce, dairy, 159; statistics of the National Butter, Cheese, and Egg Association, Chicago, 160.

Products, agricultural and pastoral, 144, 145; value of agricultural in 1884, 158.

Pullman, George, 239, 240.

Quicksilver, 205.

Railway system, 13, 72, 233.
Railways and waterways, 226.
Reflections, general, 378.
Religion, 121.
Representatives, House of, compared with House of Commons, 298.
Republic, The, 1; and Monarchy, in recent emergencies, 319.
Revenues of the government, 365; in 1935, 9.
Richards, Windsor, Mr., 191.
Rivers and Harbors, 342.
Rochester, 53.
Rosebery, Lord, 88, 300.

Salisbury, Marquis of, 294, 300, 342.
Sandstone, 205.
San Francisco, 43.

Salt, 205.
Savings of America, 1880, 4.
Scott, Thomas A., 238.
Scranton, 53.
School system, common, 15, 79; law of Massachusetts, 1642, 105; libraries, 288; tax, 113.
Schools, in Connecticut, 106; cost of public, 1880, 117; in Massachusetts, 106; of music, 271; normal, 108; number of, 114; of painting, 262; private, 113; public, support of, 113; in New England in 1834, 108; Virginia, Sir William Berkeley on, 106; for women, 116.
Scribner's Sons, Charles, 285.
Sculpture, 263.
Sects, religious, 124, 126.
Self-dependence, American, 354.
Senate, American, 299 and House of Lords compared, 386; Lord Salisbury on the, 300.
Seward, Wm. H., 17, 48.
Seymour, Admiral, 324.
Sherman, General, 307.
Shipping, tonnage of, in United States, 219, American, 4.
Signal Service, 334, 339.
Silver, 201; mines of United States compared with Spanish America, 208.
Slavery, 14, 32,
Smiles, Samuel, 286.
Smithsonian Institution, 346.
Society, Historical, New York, 260.
Spencer, Herbert, 11, 13, 18, 74, 286, 345.
Stanley, Henry M., 281.
Stanton, Edwin, 48, 306.
States, Northern, 33, 35; relative size of American and European countries, 31, 226; Southern, 33, 35.
Stead, Isaac, Mr., 94.
Steamboat, Fulton's, 243; first in Mississippi Valley, 243; on

COSIMO is an innovative publisher of books and publications that inspire, inform and engage readers worldwide. Our titles are drawn from a range of subjects including health, business, philosophy, history, science and sacred texts. We specialize in using print-on-demand technology (POD), making it possible to publish books for both general and specialized audiences and to keep books in print indefinitely. With POD technology new titles can reach their audiences faster and more efficiently than with traditional publishing.

> **Permanent Availability:** Our books & publications never go out-of-print.

> **Global Availability:** Our books are always available online at popular retailers and can be ordered from your favorite local bookstore.

COSIMO CLASSICS brings to life unique, rare, out-of-print classics representing subjects as diverse as *Alternative Health, Business and Economics, Eastern Philosophy, Personal Growth, Mythology, Philosophy, Sacred Texts, Science, Spirituality* and much more!

COSIMO-on-DEMAND publishes your books, publications and reports. If you are an Author, part of an Organization, or a Benefactor with a publishing project and would like to bring books back into print, publish new books fast and effectively, would like your publications, books, training guides, and conference reports to be made available to your members and wider audiences around the world, we can assist you with your publishing needs.

Visit our website at www.cosimobooks.com to learn more about Cosimo, browse our catalog, take part in surveys or campaigns, and sign-up for our newsletter.

And if you wish please drop us a line at info@cosimobooks.com. We look forward to hearing from you.

CPSIA information can be obtained at www.ICGtesting.com
Printed in the USA
BVOW05s0952081014

370011BV00001B/3/P